# The Geography of Settlement

**Second edition**

**Peter Daniel** M.A.
Head of School of Humanities, Bedford College of Higher Education

**Michael Hopkinson** M.A., M.Sc., Ph.D.
Senior Lecturer in Geography, Bedford College of Higher Education

Maps and diagrams drawn by Tim Smith

# Oliver & Boyd

**Acknowledgements**
The authors and publishers wish to thank all those who gave their permission to reproduce copyright material in this book. Information regarding sources is given in the captions.

**Oliver & Boyd**
Longman House
Burnt Mill
Harlow
Essex CM20 2JE
*An imprint of Longman Group UK Ltd*

ISBN 0 05 004286 6

First published 1979
Second edition published 1989
Fifth impression 1993

Set in 10/12pt Linotron Times Roman

Produced by Longman Singapore Publishers Pte Ltd
Printed in Singapore

The publisher's policy is to use paper manufactured from sustainable forests.

# Contents

# Editor's Note

An encouraging feature in geographical education in recent years has been the convergence taking place of curriculum thinking and thinking at the academic frontiers of the subject. In both, stress has been laid on the necessity for conceptual approaches and the use of information as a means to an end rather than as an end in itself.

The central purpose of this series is to bear witness to this convergence. In each text the *key ideas* are identified, chapter by chapter. These ideas are in the form of propositions which, with their component concepts and the inter-relations between them, make up the conceptual frameworks of the subject. The key ideas provide criteria for selecting content for the teacher, and in cognitive terms help the student to retain what is important in each unit. Most of the key ideas are linked with assignments, designed to elicit evidence of achievement of basic understanding and ability to apply this understanding in new circumstances through engaging in problem-solving exercises.

While the series is not specifically geared to any particular 'A' level examination syllabus, indeed it is intended for use in geography courses in universities, polytechnics and in colleges of higher education as well as in the sixth form, it is intended to go some way towards meeting the needs of those students preparing for the more radical advanced geography syllabuses.

It is hoped that the texts contain the academic rigour to stretch the most able of such candidates, but at the same time provide a clear enough exposition of the basic ideas to provide intellectual stimulus and social and/or cultural relevance for those who will not be going on to study geography in higher education. To this end, a larger selection of assignments and readings is provided than perhaps could be used profitably by all students. The teacher is the best person to choose those which most nearly meet his or her students' needs.

W. E. Marsden
University of Liverpool

# Preface to the Second Edition

In the decade since we wrote the original text of this book a number of changes have taken place both in the world it describes and the methods of geographical study employed in schools and colleges. For example, the period of post-war expansion which permitted a fairly optimistic assessment of urban development has given way to economic stagnation in many countries and lately to a much more cautious allocation of central government funds to urban renewal and industrial decentralisation. On the other hand, while Britain, along with much of Europe, has become increasingly polarised politically and economically, there have been major attempts at environmental improvement and urban conservation. In geographical education, enthusiasm for quantitative techniques with their assumptions of logical positivism has faded to become just one of the many methodologies from which students can draw. *Relevance* has succeeded *realism* and *theory* as the touchstone for inclusion in the syllabus (Beddis, 1982). Despite these changes and the lack of coherence which some critics find in the subject, we can still assert that 'geography matters' in Massey & Allen's phrase (1984) and we hope that readers will find we have taken account of new emphases and concerns in this edition while not discarding too much of the previous version. Our thanks are again due to our colleagues, students and families for their criticism and support, and to Enid Desert for miracles of typographic transformation.

# Preface to the First Edition

In this book we have tried to do three things. Firstly we have traced the development of the towns and villages of England and Wales in a chronological order to give an idea of how the present landscape of settlement came into being. Then we have analysed the theoretical structures which geographers erect to give order to the distributions and interactions within the landscape and have applied them and illustrated them within the context of recent urban growth. Thirdly we have tried to draw out the perceptions that people living in settlements have about their environment and to show how these ideas shape the urban fabric. To try to unite these three geographical worlds of objective reality, idealised models and contemporary perceptions we have relied upon a conceptual framework in which each aspect of the geography of settlement is pegged to a geographical idea that can be expressed relatively simply but developed to levels of complexity appropriate to the reader's interest. Often we have included examples from outside Britain, and some sections of the book are concerned with chronology whilst others are concerned with exemplifying static concepts. We hope, however, that the overall pattern is one of comprehensible, if not comprehensive, explanation of settlement location, functioning and interaction.

We are grateful for the help of many people in producing this book; not least to the urban geographers, historians and sociologists on whose work we have drawn for our material. In addition we owe a considerable debt to Bill Marsden for his guidance on the style and format of the text; and for his meticulous editing and the many helpful suggestions that we have incorporated.

We should also like to thank John Bale, author of a companion volume, for his judicious comments, and Enid Desert for transforming our manuscript into legible form.

Finally, without the patience and support of our wives and families, the book could not have been written.

Peter Daniel     Michael Hopkinson

# 1 Introduction

## A. Changing Geographical Method

Settlements may be defined as places which are inhabited on a permanent basis, as distinct, for example, from camps or fairs. Although they may be categorised according to their size, status and range of facilities provided, so that hamlets may be distinguished from villages, villages from towns and so on, it is important to bear in mind that, in reality, there exists a *settlement continuum* and each category merges gradually into the next.

Settlement provides a focus for interdisciplinary study. The economist, sociologist, historian, psychologist and geographer are all able to examine a settlement from a clearly defined disciplinary base. Geography acts as an integrator, borrowing from the other disciplines but, at the same time, making its own distinctive contribution, particularly with respect to spatial organisation. Looking for patterning both within and among settlements provides some insight into how things are organised spatially.

## 1. Descriptive approaches

Traditionally, the geographer was content to describe these relationships while at the same time examining cause and effect in a rather subjective and unscientific manner (Pattison, 1973). Frequently, cause was related to the physical environment. For example, the location of a town might have been explained in relation to its position at the lowest bridging point and head of navigation on a river, or as a springline settlement established at an assured supply of fresh water. Geography was also concerned with the unique. The distinctiveness of a town was stressed; the nature of its site, its development through time, its employment structure, major industries and so on. This in turn led to the classification of settlements according to the characteristics of their site (such as hill top, scarp foot, meander core) and their functions (such as market town, mining town, resort, centre of heavy industry).

## 2. Quantitative approaches

The search for common characteristics was gradually extended to include a search for order in both the spacing of settlements and their internal organisation. At first this was based on careful observations or empirical research, from which generalisations were made and broad principles identified which seemed to have some universal application. These concepts and principles were embodied in models which acted as simplifications of reality, enabling a general statement to be made about how things are organised spatially (Chorley & Haggett, 1967). Many of the classical models which throw light on spatial organisation within and between settlements are discussed in the ensuing chapters. For example, in Chapter 5, you will study the internal structure of towns and discover how a number of models have been developed which purport to give some insight into how different activities or functional zones are arranged within towns and cities. The application of statistical techniques allied to the increasing use of computers (which enable vast volumes of data to be handled) have meant that the generalisations can be tested against the real world, and the models refined and reformulated where necessary. The 'quantitative revolution', as it became known, meant that scientific method was adopted by the geographer in the search for a greater understanding of spatial organisation. Hypotheses were formulated and tested to try to discover geographical concepts relating to location, patterning, and spacing of settlement, functional zoning within settlements, rural–urban interaction and so on.

Underlying the quantitative revolution was the belief that problem-solving was a rational process, relying upon logical thought and accurate information for its success. An example of this in geographic terms is Allan Pred's (1967) model of the choice of profitable sites. Given that there is a 'best' site for an industry, a shop or a settlement, indeed for almost any sort of human activity, he argues, individual choice will depend upon the accuracy of information available and the wisdom of the decision maker in evaluating that information. True, there may be factors which distract from a logical choice but, by and large, rational 'economic people' will make a predictable wise decision.

## 3. Behavioural, humanistic and radical approaches

While reliance upon economic theory, mathematically analysed data and a logical approach is attractive and appears eminently reasonable, many geographers have grown dissatisfied with the effectiveness and relevance of such methods when applied to real world problems. They are aware that not all decisions are the result of rational economic forces but that other factors need to be considered. For example, it may well be that the structure of a town can be understood only when attention is paid to subjective factors. One aspect of this relates to the environment as it is perceived by its population at local levels and through the filters of different cultural traditions. In Chapter 6, you will learn how the pioneering work of Walter Firey (1945) in Boston is extremely important in this respect. Firey recognised that certain parts of Boston have acquired symbolic and cultural connotations and this has prevented them from being overtaken by economic forces and developed in a predictable way. In another important pioneering work, Anne Buttimer (1969) argues that space has social as well as purely physical attributes and that these will exert a strong influence on the way in which a settlement develops. Goodey (1971) suggests that people's perception of the environment is arrived at through the interaction of primary and secondary sources of information. Primary sources involve direct personal contact with the environment through work, leisure, shopping trips and so on, and secondary sources are the descriptions of places obtained from the media or in talking with friends and acquaintances. The behavioural approach therefore argues that human decisions cannot be explained in purely rational terms because human actions are greatly influenced by the perceptions people have of their environment.

Considerations of spatial inequalities, and the social problems that they represent, have led geographers to diverge in their response. Some have argued that there are underlying causes of such problems as unemployment, poor housing, educational disadvantage and poor health facilities in our inner cities. They see the problems as a sign of the inadequate social structures which a capitalist or 'free market' society creates, because wealth inevitably becomes concentrated in the hands of an elite minority and the peripheral members of society (and peripheral regions of the world) are starved of resources and investment. These structuralist geographers see individuals as largely powerless to improve their economic or social condition unless the structure of society is changed, and many advocate more or less radical political action to achieve such changes.

Other geographers, especially in North America, have argued that the attempt to apply general theories to the landscape is too deterministic. They seek a return to the French and German traditions of regional geography, stressing that landscapes of particular places are unique, the product of history as well as contemporary forces and that environmental quality and local character are worthy of study. Some are concerned with urban and rural conservation and others with the insights that art, music and literature can give to our understanding and appreciation of the environment in which we live. They are generally hostile to forces they see as threatening the individual's sense of place and are thus often allied politically with 'green' movements in their respective countries. Both 'humanistic' and 'radical' geographers have had significant influence on the recent study of rural and urban communities, and we have included reference to them in this text (Meinig, 1979; Lemon, 1978). Again, their tradition of concern for the environment which they study has respectable antecedents in both Europe

9

and North America (Jacobs, 1961; Harvey 1969) and is related to the long history of utopian thought which sees environmental quality as an important constraint on human achievement (Goodwin & Taylor, 1982).

## 4. The relevance of settlement geography

Each successive development within the study of geography has enriched it. One approach does not supersede another, but rather each new development builds on what has gone before. There is still a need for the student of geography to have a sound factual basis: to know where places are situated, to have some conception of the relative size of settlements, and so on. But it is equally important to have some sort of historical perspective, to have some insight into the way in which settlements have evolved through time and the historical forces which have helped to shape them. At the same time, there should be some grasp of spatial organisation both within and between settlements. Students should be able to apply scientific method to gain greater understanding, while remaining aware of the importance of cultural/behavioural considerations. We would hope that after studying the settlement component of an 'A' level geography course, you would know how to begin to structure an investigation of a town which is unfamiliar to you.

Geography is an exciting and dynamic subject, concerned with issues which affect us all no matter where we live. We are all to a greater or lesser extent concerned with environmental quality and social well-being: urban transport policies, the plight of the inner city, patterns of retailing and related topics are relevant to us all. Increasingly, through greater public participation in the planning process, we are all being given the opportunity to contribute to the formulating of decisions which will affect the way in which settlements will develop in the future. It is one of our objectives in writing this book that you will be better equipped to contribute to such discussion and be able to make judgements based on knowledge rather than prejudice.

Clearly, however, one must be aware of the values and prejudices of those writing about urban geography from particular viewpoints. Both conservative (logical-positivist) and radical (structuralist) traditions have strong political assumptions in their methodologies. We have tried to present both stances, believing that in a mixed economy such as that prevalent in most of the Western world, there is room for a range of interpretations and values. Students intending to pursue their study of geography beyond the sixth form will find a wide selection of literature on the philosophies and ideologies which have contributed to the development of the discipline (Holt-Jensen, 1980; Johnston 1983).

10

## B. The Structure of this Book

In examining the geography of settlement, the book attempts to synthesise the approaches outlined above. The early chapters are historical in treatment. Chapter 2 examines the sequence of occupation in rural areas from prehistoric times. Chapter 3 continues the sequential development of the town from the medieval period through to the twentieth century and the effect of early attempts at urban planning is discussed. Particular attention is given to post-war urban growth and the factors regulating the British housing market. Chapter 4 traces the evolution of town planning, from its inter-war origins and examines the development of housing policies. In Chapter 5 theories of urban morphology are considered and interpreted, and a new model of the European experience of urban zoning is proposed. Chapter 6 focuses on change in the inner city, examining the nature of the problems and range of policy options which have been developed in attempts at urban regeneration. Chapter 7 focuses on the central business district and includes sections on its structure, delimitation and future. In Chapter 8 we examine the basis and application of central place theory, and test its relevance for the real world. The final chapter continues the exploration of urban hierarchies by considering the interconnected systems which together build up the pattern of rural–urban linkages which we term the urban field.

In each chapter we have tried to identify key ideas which are exemplified in the text. These are summarised at the end of the chapter. Each chapter is subdivided into sections which are followed by individual assignments: pieces of work which the student is asked to do to reinforce a grasp of the immediately preceding material. There are also additional activities at the end of each chapter, which are designed to relate to the chapter as a whole. The assignments and activities vary widely in type and are designed to give a range of experiences to the student. It is important to stress that the summaries of key ideas and assignments are intended to be integral rather than supplementary to this introduction to modern settlement geography.

We would also like to emphasise that the sequence of chapters is, in general, progressive rather than arbitrary. We feel that the reader should be careful to ensure, by reference to preceding chapters, that he or she is aware of the ideas which are being built upon and which might be missed if later sections were read in isolation. Throughout the text there is an attempt to balance the chronological study of settlement development with the application of current methods of urban analysis and measurement. The two elements are seen as complementary in explaining the present settlement landscape. Restrictions on the length of the text have made it necessary to concentrate on British and, to a lesser extent, other 'first world' case studies. Students wishing to learn more about urbanisation and its effects in third world societies will find the topic considered in a companion volume

(Barke & O'Hare, 1983). As over three-quarters of the population of the 'Western' developed world, 70% of the population of Latin America, two-thirds of that of the Soviet Union and about a third of that of Asia and Africa lives in towns, it is inevitable that any text on settlement will concentrate on *urban* settlements. Discussion of contemporary *rural* communities can be found in our companion volume (Bull, Daniel & Hopkinson, 1985).

## Key Ideas

*A. Changing Geographical Method*

1. It is recognised that all subjects have characteristic organising concepts or key ideas. Those of geography are markedly spatial in kind.
2. The traditional approaches of geography as a study of landscape relied heavily on describing man/land relationships, examining cause and effect in a rather subjective and unscientific manner.
3. These were challenged in the 1960s by a more mathematically oriented methodology, based upon data collection and hypothesis testing.
4. The role of individual and group behaviour and perception has increasingly replaced a logical and mathematical approach to geographical study in the last decade.
5. All geographical perceptions of society are influenced by the philosophical and political stance of their authors. Care is needed in distinguishing the assumptions of geographers when considering social issues, which commonly arise in the study of settlements.

## Additional Activities

1. Read Chapter 5 in Holt-Jensen's (1980) book or the article by Richard Lawton (1978, pp. 2–9). What main developments in geographical method have occurred since the early 1960s?
2. Read Firey's (1945) and Buttimer's (1969) articles. How is it possible for space to acquire social characteristics?
3. Should an academic subject have one main investigative method? Does it matter that geography seems not to have such a distinctive *paradigm* at present?

# 2 Settlement Origins and Growth

In the introduction we define a settlement as a place which people inhabit and where they carry on a variety of activities: trade, manufacturing, defence and so forth. This study of settlement will touch upon almost all aspects of human social and economic activity: so that the study of settlement geography provides an introduction to the study of social geography in general.

## A. Geographical Concepts of Settlement Location and Morphology

### 1. The choice of location

In the past, geographers have argued that the physical conditions in an area – rock type, climate, slope and so on – actively determined the pattern and organisation of settlement, land tenure and usage as well as the type of crops that could be grown to support the population and the minerals that might be exploited. Today this concept of 'physical determinism' has been superseded by the realisation that social factors are also important in the location and developing character of any settlement. Geographers recognise that while almost any kind of settlement form is possible in a given landscape, the probability is that certain locations will be chosen in preference to others, and how they are used will depend upon the levels of skill and technology available to the people living there. In this chapter we shall examine some basic concepts about rural settlements, and how they are exemplified in the British landscape.

The boundaries of English parishes represent the limits of the area which a village utilised and controlled. These areas vary in size, often as a result of local characteristics of terrain and organisation. The air photographs (Plates 2.1, 2.2) illustrate the variety of parish shapes and sizes in different parts of England. An important consideration by early settlers in a new area was the choice of *site*: the actual location upon which to erect their dwellings, stockade and workshops. The size of this original location often became too

Plate 2.1   Austwick, North Yorkshire. A village in upland Britain. Note the small, stone-walled fields near the village for livestock grazing, the open moorland and the evidence of the effect of relief on land use. There are many individual farms, but no manor house visible. (Photograph: Aerofilms)

small and inconvenient as population grew, but the nature of the initial site often continues to exert control over the present plan of the settlement.

If physical conditions provide a range of options from which to choose, we can get some idea of what sort of site would seem a suitable one to a group of colonisers if we know the following:

(a) what conditions are needed (in their experience) for an ideal site;
(b) what degree of choice is open to them; how much they must compromise their ideal version of a site in the face of real constraints;
(c) why, how and by whom decisions in the particular society were made.

We will rarely know all these factors, but comparison of a number of settlement locations together with a knowledge of local physical conditions can often lead us to a fair perception of how earlier settlers viewed an area.

Plate 2.2 Husbands Bosworth, Leicestershire. A lowland parish. Note the compact site, the absence of farm houses in the fields (a sign of late enclosure) and the fine church showing the former prosperity of farming in this area. Field boundaries are hedgerows, rarely designed to be stock-proof in this arable area, and in the foreground evidence of former cultivation (ridge and furrow) can be seen. The local 'great house' in its park is on the left of the picture. (Photograph: Cambridge University Collection)

Obviously *site factors* will change in their relative importance over time. With new methods of transport, improvements in techniques of cultivation, and the simple increase in population, some sites will become obsolete and others will appear more attractive. However, we may assume that for early settlers in an area such as lowland Britain, the site requirements would be

15

fairly simple. It has been suggested by Michael Chisholm (1966) that the basic requirements of a group of Saxon settlers would be: defence, water, fuel, building materials, land for crops (arable) and livestock (grazing). The degree of importance which they attached to these would be conditioned by the frequency with which they would need to use them, and their choice among settlement sites, though subjective, would reflect their evaluation of these needs.

If we can start to view the landscapes through the eyes of the early settlers we may be able to determine what would constitute good choices of sites for them, bearing in mind that their knowledge of a new district would be imperfect.

## 2. Identifying settlement form

The use to which land around a settlement was put often influenced building patterns: whether all the farmsteads could be grouped together for defence and sociability, or whether individual houses were built out in the fields, giving the village a more fragmented appearance. The former types are collectively referred to as 'nucleated', indicating a grouping around a central nucleus, and the latter as 'dispersed' settlements. If we consider the whole of England and Wales, we can find a general pattern of settlements which are predominantly of one type or the other. We should note, however, that a similarity of arrangement or *morphology* does not necessarily imply a similarity of origin or rationale behind this pattern on the ground.

### (a) Nucleated villages

Villages of the nucleated type are of common traditional pattern, often related to the way in which land has been owned and worked. The following factors may encourage nucleation:
(i)    joint and co-operative working of land (the open field system);
(ii)   defence (hilltop location, sites within a meander);
(iii)  shortage of water (spring line);
(iv)   swampy conditions and a shortage of 'dry point' sites;
(v)    lack of suitable building materials.
For example, Anglo-Saxon settlers who were allocated strips of land in 'open fields' and who farmed their lands on a rotation system tended to have a nuclear village in the midst of their land. A rare survivor of this type is Laxton (Plate 2.3).

### (b) Dispersed settlement

When the open fields were enclosed, from 1500 onwards, it became more logical to build farmhouses out in the fields of the newly established

Plate 2.3 Laxton, Nottinghamshire. Three great fields with the village at the centre can still be discerned although some encroachment has taken place. The houses line the street boundaries between the fields with long strips of land running away behind them. There are remains of a common at the top of the street, and of a glebe area around the church, which was originally for the priest's use. (Photograph: Aerofilms)

farmsteads, and a dispersed pattern often resulted. Dispersed patterns are also associated with:

(i)   livestock farming (e.g. Scotland and north-west Lancashire);
(ii)  agricultural specialisation (e.g. market gardening in areas of very fertile soils). Such specialisation and improvement of crops was not possible if land use was frequently and arbitrarily changed by a decision of all the villagers;
(iii) very low densities of population (e.g. upland regions, and the crofting settlements in coastal areas where farming is a part-time occupation);

17

(iv) dissolution of very large estates (e.g. the break-up of monastic lands at the Reformation).

The entire process may be summarised in the following way. High land, poor soils and much available water help to create dispersed settlement, while lower areas, better soils and shortage of water seem generally to be associated with nucleated settlement. This summary could be qualified, but these environmental factors seem the most important in nearly all areas.

The pattern of settlement and land use was established when land was under common ownership, but during the agricultural revolution of the eighteenth century in Britain, growing migration from rural areas to new towns reduced the numbers of people who were obtaining a living from the soil. Landowners were therefore encouraged to press for the *enclosure* of their lands so that agricultural experiments and increased productivity could be pursued. This process had been going on in earlier days but the rapid spread of 'Parliamentary Enclosures', as they were called, led to the setting up of field boundaries and the evolution of the 'English' style of farmsteads that today we regard as traditional.

The process of enclosure was so called because landlords built enclosing fences around the common grazing land in the villages, and divided up the great fields which had formerly been farmed by the inhabitants as a group. New land holdings were leased out in the form of separate farmsteads, and this often meant that new farmhouses were built at a distance from the old village. Such investment in new agricultural 'plant' became especially worthwhile in the nineteenth century because of the improved yields and profits made possible by the agricultural revolution.

*(c) Effects on the landscape*

Nucleated villages tend to have survived in arable and mixed farming areas, where land had been worked under open field systems. Equal shares of land of varying quality were ensured by the system of allocation of strips in large fields. Although this pattern was retained in Laxton, Nottinghamshire (Plate 2.3), the practice of communal cultivation is rare in Europe today. However, the retention of farm buildings in village streets, and a pattern of field boundaries based upon the old strip system, is still common. Isolated examples of strip holdings do persist in some remote areas where terrain is difficult, although even here the regrouping of land holdings into larger and more economic units in the interests of efficiency is likely to have taken place.

The consolidated farm provides more opportunity to plan land use rationally and independently, and reduces the number of journeys for the individual, but it is commonly the case that the farm buildings are retained in their nuclear form, unless the new farm is too far away for easy access. A compromise which allows the farmhouse to remain in the village centre, is for land holders to 'farm out' from the centre, so that each holder still retains a 'toe-hold' in the community. This is often true of areas of late enclosure when travelling distance was less of a problem. Such patterns are sometimes referred to as *evolved*, whereas those deliberately reformed at the time of field enclosure are more obviously *planned*. Often the two exist side by side, for reorganisation was on a parish basis at the whim of local landowners until the later Parliamentary Enclosures.

Enclosure of land is not the only factor which disturbed the evolution of village pattern from a three-field rotation system to an owner–occupier system. When dairying became profitable, serving the needs of growing market towns as communications improved, some land was enclosed to form individual units. Another example is where landowners took a rather rough hold of the economy of farming. Consider this account of the clearance of part of the Scottish Highlands in the summer of 1807 by the notorious Patrick Sellar, to enable the Earl of Sutherland to graze sheep:

> *Our family was very reluctant to leave, and stayed for some time, but the burning party came round and set fire to our house at both ends, reducing to ashes whatever remained within the walls. The people had to escape for their lives, some of them losing all their clothes except what they had on their backs ... The people were driven away like dogs ...* (**Lively, 1976**).

Although there were cases of extreme hardship where eviction was ruthlessly carried out, in most of the rest of Britain the process of land enclosure was slower and more orderly. It might be resisted by some tenant farmers and the poorer villagers, but often the opportunities it provided for improved husbandry were felt to outweigh the disadvantages. The extracts below describe the parish of Oakley in Bedfordshire before and after the greater part of the land was purchased by a large landowner and subsequently enclosed. They are taken from work done by students at Bedford as part of their course on village studies.

> *Like most of Bedfordshire's parishes, Oakley was an open field village before the coming of the Agricultural Revolution in the late eighteenth century. This meant that the land was divided into four great fields with farmers working scattered strips within each field.*

> *It is interesting to note that in 1737 there were 36 owners of land in Oakley but by 1799 this number had fallen to 24. This was mainly due to the activities of the Dukes of Bedford, who, after the 4th Duke purchased Oakley House in 1737, gradually extended their interests in the parish and soon came to dominate it.*

> *The attitude of the farmers towards enclosure varied; some were pleased to take on new leases, but others left their farms rather than*

*carry out instructions as to the crops they should produce and the methods of farming they should employ, which were written into their leases. The farm houses and buildings were kept in repair by the Duke as landlord.*

*With the exception of the freeholders, all the villagers would have been dependent on the estate, in some way, for their livelihood. Most of them would have been employed as agricultural labourers with a smaller group fulfilling the roles of craftsmen and domestic servants.*

*According to the 1801 census, 265 people were resident in Oakley. The unemployment situation was particularly bad during the years 1812–13 and 1819–20 when the poor relief rose to its peaks.*

Although nucleation and dispersal are useful concepts to apply to the pattern of settlement, the internal structure of villages (their *morphology*) is more complex. It has been suggested (Roberts, 1986) that a classification based upon shape, degree of regularity, and the presence or absence of a green, together with a consideration of overall size, may provide us with a way of distinguishing the main types of village form to be found in Britain. Roberts' classification is shown in Figure 2.1, and forms the basis of one of the assignments for this section. He argues that the explanation of a particular village form lies in a combination of site constraints, population change, and 'the presence or absence of lordly power'. We shall return to this important idea of 'lordly power' in the consideration of social relations within the village in a later section. Ultimately, of course, each individual settlement is only explicable in terms of its own history; the researching of which can be a lengthy though fascinating task.

ASSIGNMENTS

1. *Choose two O.S. maps at 1 : 50 000 scale, of contrasting areas of Britain and, using tracing paper, map the parish boundaries and location of villages. In each of the areas studied calculate the average size of parishes and the sizes of the largest and smallest parishes. Parish size may be calculated by superimposing the map over squared paper on a light-table and counting the number of whole and part squares contained within the parish boundary. Secondly, calculate the ratio between the longest and shortest distances across the parish. This ratio may be expressed by the formula r=l/L, where l is the longest distance across the parish and L the shortest.*

Figure 2.1   Village forms: principles of classification. Distinctive associations of plan elements identify groups of plan families, and the classificatory framework provided by the grid allows particular plans to be placed within a broader context. (Source: Roberts, 1986)   ▶

# VILLAGE FORMS: PRINCIPLES OF CLASSIFICATION

You need to answer five questions:

(a) Is the village **nucleated\*** or **dispersed?**
(\*less than 150 m between farmsteads)

< 150 m

< 150 m

(b) Is the plan based on **rows** or **agglomerations** of buildings?

plan based on rows

Wasdale Head 1862

plan based on agglomerations

Braithwaite 1866

(c) Are the elements in the plan arranged in a **regular** or an **irregular** way?

| rows | agglomerations | | |
|---|---|---|---|
| — regular row plan | # regular grid plan | ✳ regular radial plan | The symbols which show various elements may be used as a short-hand for mapping the plan types |
| − − − irregular row plan | irregular grid plan | ● irregular agglomerated plan | |

(d) Is a **green** present or absent?

green present
Middridge c. 1844

green absent    Appleton-le-Moors 1895

(e) Has the village a simple or a **composite (polyfocal)** plan?

Grewelthorpe 1890    composite/polyfocal plans    Fenny Compton 1886

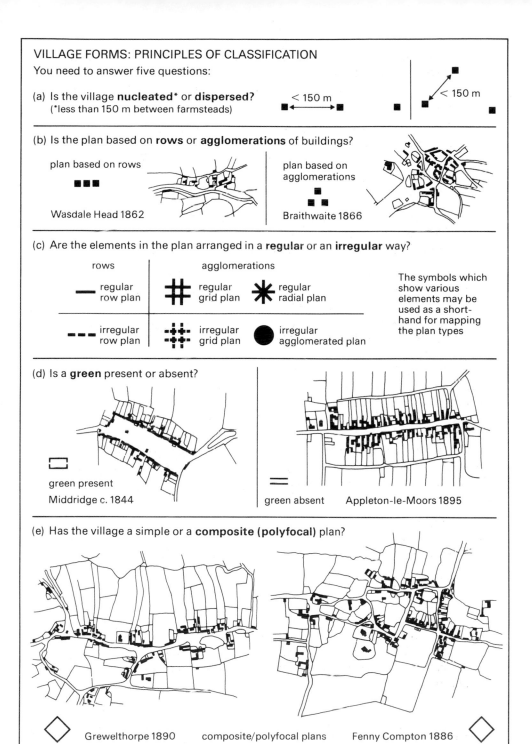

21

Add the principal streams and rivers and the major contours to your map to gain a general impression of the relief of the area. Geology could also be added if you have access to an O.S. Geological Survey map. Can you explain the differences in parish size and shape?

2. *Work in groups. From the accompanying map (Figure 2.2) determine three suitable sites for settlement, on the basis of the factors listed by Chisholm (see page 16). Do the sites vary in attractiveness if the importance attached to the factors is changed? Do all members of your group agree upon the locations of the sites? If you 'entered' the map area from the south-west corner which site would you encounter first? Would this have any bearing on your settlement decision?*

3. *The date is 1800. Assume that you are either a large landowner, or a small tenant farmer, and justify the case for or against enclosure of your local parish to a village meeting. Useful background information and ideas may be obtained from the books by Ashton (1968), Hoskins (1977), and Orwin (1954) listed in the References.*

   *Questions that you may wish to ask might include:*

   *(a) What effect will enclosing the land have upon farm labourers?*

   *(b) Will there have to be new building, or realignment of roads?*

   *(c) How will the land be apportioned?*

   *(d) Will the village support as many people in future?*

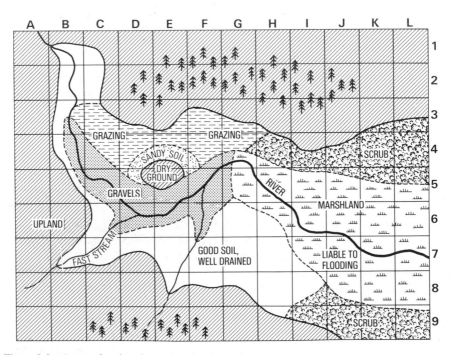

Figure 2.2   A map showing alternative sites for settlement.

(e) *What effect will there be upon community life: the church, inn, local tradespeople?*

4. *Using 1 : 25 000 O.S. maps for two different areas of Britain attempt to classify the village forms they show on the basis of Roberts' method. Does any pattern emerge, and is it explicable by reference to physical features, routeways or other landscape evidence? You may wish to compare the pattern with that provided by place name evidence, using a place name dictionary or practical geography book as a guide (Ekwall, 1974; Guest, 1974).*

*If your school has copies of the Old Series '6 inch' maps of local villages (produced between 1908 and 1946) these are very valuable for such an exercise as they will not contain details of recent housing development, which may spoil the underlying historical pattern.*

## B. Settlement Evolution in England and Wales

Having considered the morphology of rural settlement in Britain we may now turn to consider its distribution and how this changed over time. You will see how some areas experienced waves of immigration which have left evidence in place names of predominantly one language or period. The effects of farming requirements on the character of rural settlement at different periods have just been mentioned. Let us now try to distinguish the residual or relic features in the present rural landscape and the systems which operated at the period of their establishment.

There is evidence of human occupation in Britain from about 4300 B.C., although actual settlements are later in date. All over Britain and Europe many examples of earthworks and burial mounds survive from before 2000 B.C., but there are few remains of the buildings which Neolithic people must have occupied.

## 1. Pre-Roman settlements

Early Bronze Age dwellings form the first examples of recognisable houses, though the earliest dates of settlement in a particular area may range from around 1500 B.C. to 500 B.C. (see Figure 2.3). Examples of the former can be found on Dartmoor, which may imply that it was in the more exposed upland areas of Southern Britain that these communities developed. Admittedly the subsequent cultivation of lowland south-east England may have destroyed evidence of early settlements there, but the hill forts were probably more realistically defensible (see Plate 2.4), and although cultivation in Britain dates from about 700 B.C., it is likely that only when specialist mould-board ploughs had been developed could the heavier lowland clays be tilled. Village and hamlet growth required a stable surplus of food so that settled agriculture could be possible. An early Iron Age

23

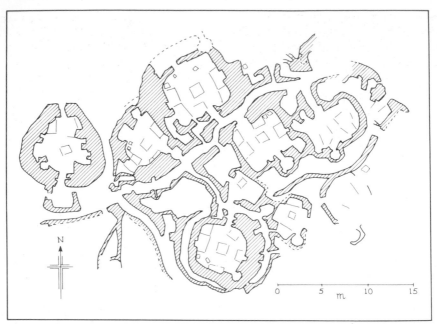

Figure 2.3  An early Celtic site. Skara Brae, in the Orkneys, may be the oldest domestic site in Europe. Consisting of eight circular huts, of diameters between 4 and 6 metres, it was preserved by drifting sand dunes until being rediscovered in 1850. Originally believed typical of Bronze Age or early Iron Age settlements, it is now thought to date from 2500 B.C., and may have been occupied by an elite group of priests or elders, as no evidence of farming has been uncovered. Early sites, often undefended, are particularly common in Scotland, Wales and the west country and are generally classed as ceremonial (e.g. Stonehenge) or burial sites. The ordinary homes of the people have often perished, being constructed of timber. Some have been preserved in peat bogs in Ireland. (Source: Mackie, 1975)

Plate 2.5   Chysauster, Cornwall. In the west country, remains of pre-Roman settlements, with stone walls and comprising groups of semi-circular huts, are to be found. These Iron Age hamlets were supported by the growth of vegetables and tin smelting. In lowland Britain the 'Celtic fields' of terraced cultivation in chalk areas are contemporary. Both represent the larger scale that agriculture reached when Iron Age replaced Bronze Age techniques of cultivation around 300 B.C. (Photograph: Crown Copyright. Reproduced with the permission of the Controller of Her Majesty's Stationery Office)

example is Chysauster in W. Cornwall (Plate 2.5) where eight or more houses, each of several rooms around an open court, line a cobbled street. Each house appears to have possessed garden plots and the hamlet was surrounded by arable fields. This settlement dates from about 200 B.C. and appears to have been continuously occupied until Roman times. These isolated hamlets and farmsteads are mostly identified in the south-west peninsula, although as the Celts retreated westward their settlement names may have been superseded by invaders. In the west country the physical features of hills and rivers have retained the names most successfully (e.g.

Plate 2.4   Maiden Castle, Dorset. The vast extent of this fortification can be seen by the scale of the road running past and the buildings nearby. The height of the earthworks and the depth of the trenches has been greatly levelled over time but the maze like entrances are still visible. (Photograph: Cambridge University Collection)

Axe, Esk, Usk (*isca*: water), Case (*us*: water)) although in parts of the Pennines similar words (including Dove, *dube*: black) also persist.

Iron Age huts were commonly located in defensive circles at relatively inaccessible sites. The Holyhead Mountain circles discovered in 1865 on Anglesey are an example of this. In areas where there was no suitable natural eminence to ensure safety, the early inhabitants followed the pattern of the terpen dwellers of the Low Countries and built lake villages. There is evidence of one such village at Glastonbury, Somerset.

## 2. Roman settlement (50 B.C. to A.D. 400)

During the four centuries of Roman occupation the total population of Britain rose to something approaching half a million, and a dualistic economy developed. The Romans as administrators and military lived in villas side by side with indigenous Celtic villagers. In the first phase of the settlement, the new conquerors concentrated on opening up harbours and communications in a manner emulated by all subsequent imperialists. Burke describes the process:

> *During the first forty years they constructed some 6000 miles [approx. 9700 km] of highways with six routes radiating from London, which was already recognized as the country's natural gateway. Comparison of the Ordnance Survey Map of Roman Britain with a modern map reveals how closely the routes selected by Roman surveyors for main radiating highways correspond with those chosen by nineteenth-century railway engineers for main-line routes (**Burke, 1976**).*

The foci of these routeways were the Roman towns, some based upon Celtic settlements and forts, others new (see Figure 2.4). Derived from Italian models with formal plans and walks, they existed as defensive and administrative centres and hence relied upon a subservient rural landscape for food. They established the pattern of a city-region, though their size was limited by the technology available to cultivate and transport food. Even London could aspire to a population of no more than 30 000. Though smaller than cities located by the Romans in more productive agricultural terrains, these towns still represented a vast increase in complexity, area and scale over anything previously seen in England. It has been suggested that larger settlements such as London covered some 120 hectares, and it is noteworthy that until late in the medieval period London had not expanded far outside its northern and eastern boundaries, although building along the Strand to the administrative centre at Westminster had transformed the western edge. Even smaller cities such as Caerwent covered about 20 hectares and must have seemed infinitely superior in technology to the indigenous population compared with their own structures.

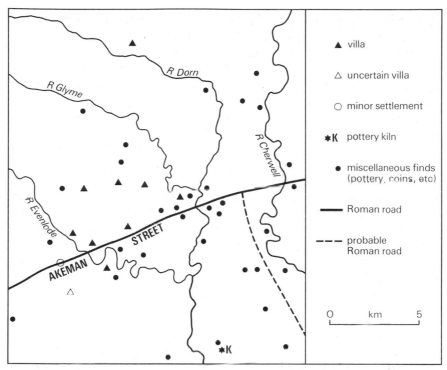

Figure 2.4  Romano–British settlements in part of Oxfordshire. The concentration of Roman settlements along the Cotswold escarpment is clearly shown in this map. There was a great concentration of settlement where ancient sheep-droving routes along the valleys met the newer Roman Akerman Street along the scarp. The importance of obtaining water in this oolitic limestone area was also a locating factor. (Source: Hoskins, 1977)

In the later years of the occupation, a local Romano-British upper middle class developed villas, clearing large areas of natural vegetation and building self-contained estates on new sites, especially on the chalks, oolites and gravels of south-eastern England. As prosperity and security increased, dependence upon the *castra*-camps lessened, and over 500 of these villas have been located. From them, agricultural districts were administrated with a community of workers including the *villacus* or overseer, the *coloni* or freemen, and slaves, all of whom lived in the central complex of buildings. Important villas include Chedworth (Gloucestershire), Bignor (Sussex), North Leigh (Oxfordshire) and Rochbourne (Hampshire). Many of these villas are extensive – Rochbourne has over 60 rooms – and some later became centres for industry including metal work, pottery, or cloth fulling as at Chedworth. (See Plate 2.6 and Figure 2.5.)

The distribution of villas was often separate from that of the villages of the indigenous population. The two systems appear to have existed side by side in the less densely settled areas, whereas in more populous areas such

Plate 2.6   Chedworth Villa. One of the large villas of the Cotswolds, with well-preserved foundations and hypocausts. The house in the centre is a nineteenth-century museum and the roofs in the lower part of the picture are modern to cover excavated mosaics, but the layout is essentially as the Romans left it. Such villas housed both farm workers and their lord so extensive storage and communal facilities were needed. (Photograph: Cambridge University Collection)

as North Oxfordshire there was much more intermingling and contact. In the remoter districts, the effects of Roman culture might have been confined to the use of the pottery and coinage of the new overlords in the old settlements of circular huts and pits surrounded by fenced fields. It is

28

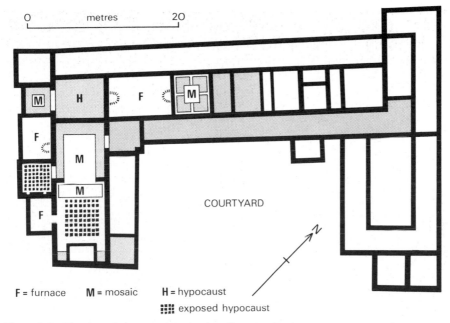

Figure 2.5   The plan of a house at Verulamium (St Albans) c. A.D. 160. Many Romano–British houses and villas were built around an open courtyard, facing in a southerly direction to catch the sun, with separate quarters for family and servants. Heating for the apartments and baths was effected by a system of underground air ways (hypocausts) heated by furnaces. The floors of bath houses and public rooms were normally covered in mosaic tiles, many of which have survived. The open layout shows that defence was of little importance for the occupying aristocracy; and the whole plan prefigures later 'ranch type' complexes in Imperial estates (e.g. plantations in India, farms in South Africa) where workers co-resided with employers in self-sufficient units.

probable that the villas and their estates decayed gradually during the decline of Roman power and were difficult for the Romano-British to maintain after the Imperial withdrawal. The network of roads serving cities with agricultural produce from the estates and in turn providing highways for defence and administration also broke down and the towns were looted for building materials. Whereas the complex and large-scale fabric of urban life was difficult to sustain, village life may have been more durable. There is evidence that these sites continued as local centres in the more isolated and localised agricultural systems which persisted after the fourth century A.D. One example is that of Ashmore in Dorset, and there are others in Hertfordshire and Gloucestershire: regions of relatively dense population and intense land use, inland from the more vulnerable areas which were disrupted by Germanic raiders.

## 3. Anglo-Saxon settlement (A.D. 450–1066)

The Saxon invasions of the fifth and sixth centuries were preceded by raids which penetrated the old Roman colony to test its resistance and, discovering

29

it weak, led to more prolonged settlement. 'The Britons fled from the English like fire' (*Anglo-Saxon Chronicle*, A.D. 571). Most Anglo-Saxon villages occupied new sites, often along river valleys in the southern and

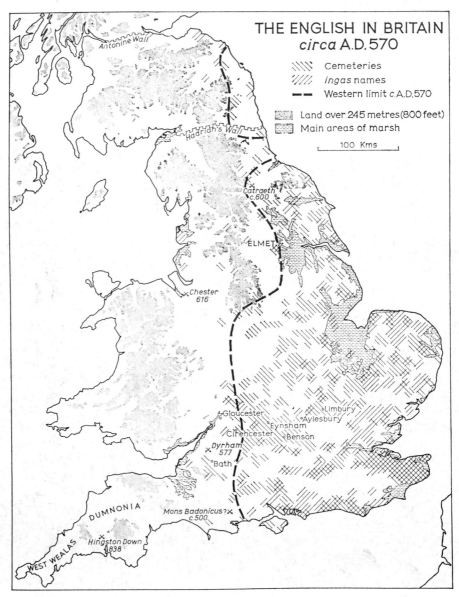

Figure 2.6   The main areas with identifiable English names are shown together with burial sites. The gradual extension west and north into Celtic areas can be discerned, but as yet there has been no threat from the continent, so that eastern areas are the most popular, being warmer and more easily farmed. (Source: Darby, 1976)

eastern areas of the country, ignoring the Celtic and Roman settlements (see Figure 2.6). The newcomers cleared much more woodland with axes and the use of fire, and often this practice is recalled in the names of their new settlements; for example

| | |
|---|---|
| Swithland (Leicestershire) | 'The land cleared by burning' |
| Barnet, Brentwood (Essex) | 'Burntwood' |
| Brindley (Cheshire) | 'Burnt clearing' |

Timber was valuable for building and for fuel and, once removed, the activities of grazing animals destroyed seedlings and prevented regeneration. It is to the Saxons that we owe the characteristic *green village* of lowland Britain, although examples occur westward as far as Devon (see Plate 2.7). In the north-east a similar but distinctive form is found in County Durham

Plate 2.7   Finchingfield, Essex. One of the most famous 'green villages' with the buildings grouped around the green which is also the area of the pond. The pond is artificially formed in the gully of a tributary of the River Pant, and on the far side of the gully the Norman church can be seen on slightly higher ground. (Photograph: Aerofilms)

with two rows of dwellings facing across a rectangular or linear green with long narrow plots of intensively cultivated land behind (tofts).

Around most green villages were grouped the fields with their characteristic strips. Of these Hoskins (1977) writes:

> *In its simplest form it probably consisted of two large fields – one on each side of the village, and often called the East Field and the West Field, or the North Field and the South Field. Each field covered perhaps a few score acres to begin with, but every decade and generation added to their area by clearing the woodland and other wild ground around their circumference.*

Three-field or four-field rotations were later developments. In contrast, the linear *street villages* are somewhat later, some having been developed along busy main roads in medieval times. Others are older, one was described in a life of St Cuthbert in the seventh century, and several pre-date the Norman invasion. In less densely settled areas it may have been easier to expand along the line of the clearing rather than to hack out new areas in the forest behind the habitations. Both green and street villages presupposed the 'hierarchical democracy' of Saxon local government, where elders determined farming policy at village *moots* and elected leaders to represent them at Shire moots and *wittans*. The movement of people that this involved helped to produce a new network of routes across the landscape. Where leaders were not found, or if individual squatting took place, fragmented (loose) villages of no discernible pattern tended to grow up, for example Middle Barton, Oxfordshire.

Although urban life seems generally to have collapsed after the withdrawal of the Romans in the middle of the fifth century, 300 years later it was becoming re-established, as in the Saxon kingdoms of Wessex and Mercia, where a new system of law and order was imposed upon the landscape. In some cases, such as Reading, Lambourn and Bloxham, the Saxon towns were based upon royal manors which collected and marketed livestock and crops obtained in taxation from lesser landlords. Others were revitalised Roman fortresses, now the seats of bishops, such as Dorchester, Winchester and Lincoln. A third group were fortified *burghs*, erected to combat attack from the Danes in the ninth century. Burgage plots were allocated to and maintained by important rural landowners, who thus acquired a foothold in the new towns. Bedford, Buckingham, Stafford and Warwick are examples of such creations (Beckinsale, 1977).

## 4. Scandinavian settlement

From the ninth century onwards the loose federations that formed the Saxon kingdoms were increasingly threatened by Danish raiders, and from the tenth century by the Norwegians. Penetration up river valleys was swift but eventual partition of the country led to a relatively stable distribution of English and Scandinavians under the reigns of Alfred and Cnut in the tenth century. Most Danish place names are confined to the north-east of Watling

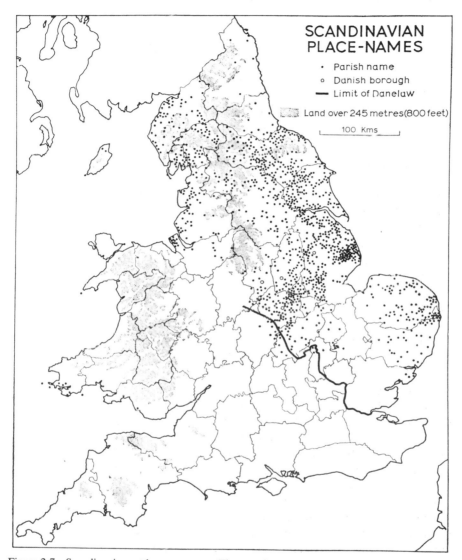

Figure 2.7   Scandinavian settlement pattern. Three main zones of penetration can be seen; the upper valleys of the Pennines, East Anglia and the southern and eastern parts of the Midlands. The conflict with Saxon kingdoms, especially Mercia and Wessex, was resolved by the establishment of a Danelaw boundary which ran from the Thames north-westward up the Lea Valley to the present site of Luton (Bedfordshire) and then roughly parallel with the routeway which forms the present A5 road. To the west of this border the Saxons occupied the country as far as the Offa's Dyke, which ran as a border with the Welsh along the Severn Valley and northwards towards Cheshire. (Source: Darby, 1976)

Street and the Lea Valley: roughly the line of the present A5 and A6 roads (see Figure 2.7). Often these 'burghs' were merely forts, although in the Midlands they sometimes became the nuclei of the new administrative shires, growing to become sizeable towns. Surviving central settlements of this type include Derby, Leicester, and the former Danish stronghold of Northampton.

It is likely, however, that although the local density of invaders might be high, as revealed by personal names in contemporary documents (totalling between 10% of the population in Norfolk and 50% in the northern part of the Danelaw) the total number of invaders was not great and their influence not long lasting. P. H. Sawyer (1976) believes that 'they settled where they could, most often on land left by the English or not yet occupied'.

Although the Danes entered Yorkshire in A.D. 876 and the East Midlands or Mercia in the next year, their hold lasted only a few decades and they were driven out in A.D. 919, so their settlements can be dated easily. Often the invaders took over existing villages and renamed them, so that it cannot be assumed that all settlements with place names of Danish extraction were Danish in origin. The attention of the Norwegians was limited to the north-west and the Lake District, where they left evidence in the distinctive *thwaite* (meaning 'clearing') suffix of many sites. Despite their invasion there is little evidence that the existing farming techniques or patterns were much disrupted; indeed it seems likely that those who stayed on adopted Saxon methods, which they found superior to the primitive shifting cultivation of their homeland. Later, more peaceable settlement, with English and Scandinavian living side by side, seems likely during the reigns of Alfred and Cnut. The early boroughs became prosperous because of the establishment of mints and markets. There were several 'moneyers', or coin makers in English cities by 1066, with half a dozen in many cathedral cities and twice as many in provincial capitals such as York. Increasingly the Crown tried to restrict trading to the boroughs, granting charters for fairs and markets, so that taxation could be more efficiently undertaken. Because of their rural connections through their burgesses, the towns had good access to rural hinterlands, guaranteeing produce for market and making them the logical administrative centres for the new *shires*. As yet there was little central government; the Saxon Council or wittan moved around the country from one shire town to another until 1065. Wallingford (Plate 2.8) remains a good example of the layout of a prosperous town of the period. Built within former Roman ramparts on a popular ford across the Thames, it occupied 45 hectares and had a population of some 2500 at the end of the Saxon period. A weekly market met there and it was the most important town in Berkshire, with its own mint (Beckinsale, 1977). This relative peace was disrupted by the invasion of William of Normandy in 1066, followed by the establishment of a system of military government covering the whole country, within twenty years.

34

Plate 2.8  Wallingford, Oxon. A fortified burgh laid out as part of the defence of Wessex in Saxon times. The defended ford, former walls, street grid and central church are clearly visible. In times of crisis towns such as this could call upon men from the surrounding countryside to guard them on a ratio of their land area to the number of soldiers needed for defence. It has been calculated that this system, the 'Burgage Hideage', enabled a part-time army of 27 000 men to be gathered together at short notice. (Photograph: Cambridge University Collection)

## 5. Norman and medieval settlement (1066–1550)

By the time that the Normans had established sufficient control to organise the Domesday survey of 1086, it is likely that almost all the villages of the pre-industrial period (many of which were later to disappear) had been established (see Figure 2.8). England had a population of some 1.25 million. Settlement density varied widely, from 4 per square mile in the north to over 80 near Yarmouth and Norwich in East Anglia. As population grew, despite high death rates and short life expectation for the average peasant, it became necessary to cultivate more and more land and to establish more settlements. Penelope Lively (1976) has described the resultant landscape:

> *... A peasant was entitled to a 'stint' – a ration or allowance – of grazing rights according to his general status and the size of his land-holding, a stint being composed of so many oxen or sheep, and as time goes on we see the number of animals allowed being more*

*sternly rationed. Obviously there was less waste available for them
to graze on: pressure of population had forced the village to clear
and cultivate it for growing crops. Ground cleared in this way is
called an 'assart' and once again the process is reflected in the
names of places.*

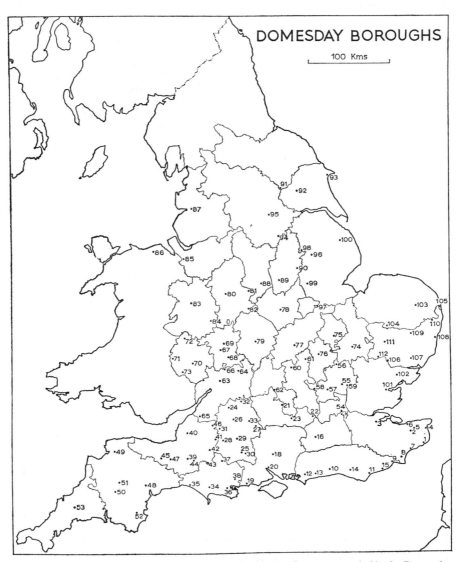

Figure 2.8 English boroughs in 1086. Over a hundred boroughs were recorded in the Domesday
book and their locations are shown on this map. Some declined because the estuaries upon which
they were sited silted up (Rye) and others declined because of plague (Ashwell) or because of
reduction in trade (Ewias Harold). Some, however, formed the nuclei for later expansion at the
centre of medieval shires (Shrewsbury). (Source: Darby, 1976)

36

During the three hundred years between the Conquest and the Black Death (1348) the population of England and Wales grew from 1.5 million to 4 million and this expansion was visible in the establishment of new towns under the Angevin kings, especially Edward I (see pages 38 to 40). These

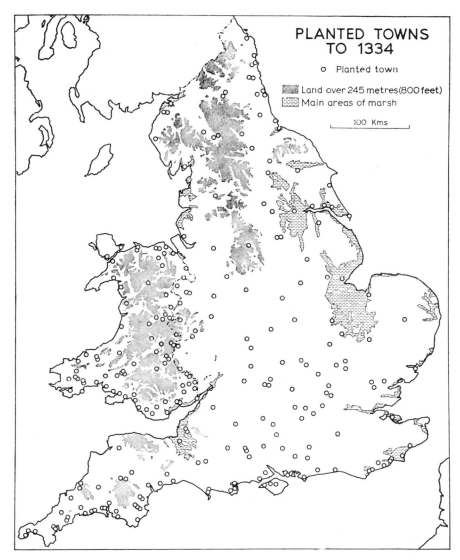

Figure 2.9   Planted towns before the Black Death. The expansion of town 'planting' was chiefly in the more peripheral areas in an attempt to establish control over the marchlands. Often a town wall was built, and a castle to garrison troops within it. The main street of the town grew up along the route from the gate to the castle, as at Monmouth and Caernarfon. The inland planted towns were often attempts at encouraging new market centres in agricultural areas. (Source: Darby, 1976)

included new ports at Portsmouth (1194) and Liverpool (1207), and after Edward's Welsh conquest in 1282, the 'chequerboard' designs of Flint, Caernarfon and Abergavenny, among others. Simultaneously villages expanded as their cultivated areas grew, and were promoted to borough status (e.g. Devizes). Old established towns also prospered, especially when markets and fairs were allocated to them by the king.

The strength of the monarchy and growing prosperity of the regions might have little significance for the peasant, but the effect on trade and building was remarkable. Between the Conquest and 1344 some 150 new boroughs were created (see Figure 2.9); almost half of them by the impoverished King John (1199–1216). The advantage to a settlement of achieving borough status was that the burgesses had freehold of their lands and the right to hold fairs and markets and to collect tolls. For these privileges they paid the monarch, so granting a charter was a speedy way for the king to obtain some ready money. The 'planted towns', mostly located as new service centres in areas of rural expansion, numbered some 160 in England and 80 in Wales by the mid fourteenth century. Many decayed after the Black Death and the subsequent decline in population. Thus of 23 new towns in Lancashire only four – Lancaster, Liverpool, Preston and Wigan – achieved real size.

The rapid growth in population before 1338 meant that there were now few areas where cultivation was not attempted, especially at the expense of forest land. New villages were founded in the twelfth and thirteenth centuries (e.g. Woodhouse Eaves, Leicestershire) as more and more land was parcelled out to barons. At the same time Royal Forests and Game Preserves were created, limiting further expansion in the south and east. In Henry II's reign, almost one-third of England was under Forest Law. Feudal affluence resulted in the annexation of land for parks (e.g. at Knowsley, 1299), although much unfarmed land was reclaimed as population grew. Parts of the Fens and Somerset Levels were drained and the huge sheep granges of the Cistercian monasteries began to tame the Cotswolds, Downs and Wolds. With increased forest clearance and marshland drainage the margin or profitable limit of arable land was rapidly being reached. This rising tide of population was stopped suddenly in the summer of 1348 by the introduction into Britain of bubonic plague. In the ensuing 30 years the population declined by 1.5 million people: between one-third and one-half of the total. The effect upon the rural landscape is shown in Figure 2.10.

At this turning point in population and settlement growth, it is helpful to take stock and see how the pattern of landscape occupance in the British countryside had changed.

One generalisation that can be made about the landscape by the medieval period is that, as in Roman times, a hierarchy of settlements and their regions had become re-established, now on a trading basis rather than a defensive one. The local village or town might be all that most people ever

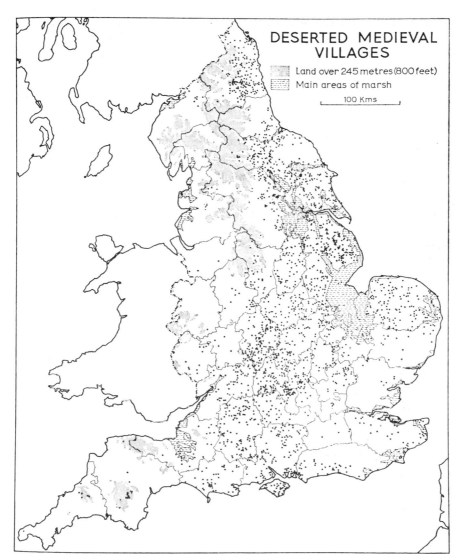

Figure 2.10   Deserted medieval settlements. The effect of the Black Death in decimating the population of villages and small towns is evident, although in some cases, even though the site was abandoned, the survivors relocated nearby and re-established their village. Isolated churches which continued in use after the mid fourteenth century often bear witness to a relocated village population who could not afford to rebuild. (Source: Darby, 1976)

dreamed of visiting but there was already evidence of movement among the upper levels of society to and from the major centres, especially to the pre-eminent centre of government: London. Growing agricultural prosperity and civil peace permitted a largely rural population to exist securely and to produce the surplus necessary to maintain about 4.5% of the population in towns where manufacturing and service activities were located. London was paramount in the hierarchy and this was reflected in government. Power descended through the county towns and their barons, while wealth in taxation and trade flowed upwards from the rural areas to support these urban centres. As Russell (1973) has commented,

> ... *The region of London in the thirteenth century enjoyed singular prosperity which was only slightly reduced by the worsening climate and the relative density of population at the end of the thirteenth century. The region was fortunate in that period to have suffered only one civil war of relatively small impact and, in the last half century, border warfare along the northern frontier.*

The prosperity of the towns was curtailed suddenly by the spread of plague during the 30 years after 1348. About a third of the population died but the boroughs lost more than the rural areas. For example, in Bedford nine out of ten priests died, and about two-thirds of the rest of the inhabitants, and this seems to have been fairly typical. As a result the town did not regain its former size for nearly 300 years. The decimation of the population as a result of the plagues meant that the expansion of agriculture and settlement ceased. The marginal lands were abandoned first, and it is reckoned that over 2000 villages became deserted (see Plate 2.9), either through depopulation or relocation for health reasons. Allied to this, landlords enclosed unprofitable arable fields and turned them over to pasture, thus causing more tenants to be displaced. The effects of this abandonment were several. In some cases abandoned lands were turned over to deer parks; in others the cultivated areas shrank as the market for food declined and thus pastoralism with its smaller labour force took over. There was no incentive to revert to corn production until the late eighteenth century and by then improved technology made it possible to release even more people from the land. By 1500 there were 8 million sheep in the country, but only 3 million people. Extensive farming seemed the only way for landowners to avoid bankruptcy, and drastic enclosing of open fields took place. During this period many boroughs perished or dwindled to become 'rotten' (i.e. they continued to send MPs to Parliament, despite a greatly reduced population). Although new churches and bridges were constructed few new settlements were built, unless for particular commercial purposes (e.g. Queensborough for wartime victualling, Staithes for fishing). The impetus for expansion would next come not from the agricultural sector but from the industrial, with the post-Reformation extension of trade in the wake of Elizabethan overseas discovery.

## 6. The rural landscape since 1550

The development of the leather and cloth trade, especially with the Low

Plate 2.9 Deserted medieval village. The modern farm and railway line disrupt the relic landscape but the original square house plots with their yards or 'tofts' can still be seen as can a possible green and meeting of pathways between the farm and the ford. Beyond the village site, ridge and furrow patterns in the old fields are also distinguishable. (Photograph: Cambridge University Collection)

Countries, increased demand for agricultural products. The yeoman farmer could be prosperous again, and there was a great upsurge in building in contrast to the depopulation and destruction of the previous century. As capital was required for the new industries of the towns, which were in turn the source of increased income, land became concentrated in fewer hands and more enclosures took place. The English village of today, and indeed the English market town (if it has been bypassed by the railway as was Stamford (Plate 2.10)) is largely a product of this period, when growing prosperity often found expression in the great 'wool churches' which were built by wealthy guilds or individuals. Again it was London which led the way in urban expansion, particularly in the late seventeenth and eighteenth centuries when the commercial success of England's colonies was providing

Plate 2.10  Stamford, Lincolnshire. Sited on the north side of the River Welland, the town was an important centre of learning in the late Middle Ages, but it stagnated after the eighteenth century when no industry or railway came there because of restrictions imposed by the Burghley family who owned the manor. (Author's photograph)

a bonus to seaports and financial interests. This increasing prosperity eventually meant more jobs for everyone, and the power of attraction of the city grew. Wrigley (1969) points out that London increased in size by some 275 000 between 1650 and 1750, despite the fact that the death rate in the city was higher than the birth rate, thus indicating substantial migration into the urban area.

Wrigley goes on to point out that, to sustain its growth rate, London must have been taking in half the natural increase of the whole country each year. The pressure of population on resources in rural areas was alleviated by migration to London, to other provincial cities and, from the late eighteenth century onwards, overseas.

For a long time the Settlement Laws prohibited the free movement of labour to stop vagrancy and to prevent parishes from abandoning their own poor in the hope that they would go away. Here again we must bear in mind the influence of local conditions, and especially the enclosure of common lands. Darby (1976) indicates the variety of rural settlement:

> *In old-enclosed country north of the Thames in Middlesex, in the Chilterns, in Essex, and in parts of East Anglia, farms were dispersed and hamlets, loosely ranged around spacious commons, at the edges of heaths or along roads, bore such names as '-end' and '-green'. ...*
>
> *In many parts of England, particularly in the Midlands, new farms were arising among old villages. In distant Northumberland,*

*where neither villages nor isolated houses had stood before, large farms were laid out with huts in rows to accommodate labourers. ...*

*Hamlets and isolated farms were characteristic not only of the uplands but also of formerly wooded districts in the English lowlands. Hamlets predominated in Cannock Chase, in Charnwood, in the Arden district of Warwickshire, in the Forest of Dean and in the well-wooded areas of southern and eastern England.*

By the mid nineteenth century, however, the obvious desire to migrate and the need of the new towns for labour had led to the repeal of the Settlement Laws with the result that new industrial towns, fed by immigrant population, were being built. The rise of the industrial town is a separate issue and will be dealt with in the next chapter. In the meantime it is worth noticing that the systems of land tenure in rural areas had, by this time, led to the establishment of very different types of village structure, which can be identified in the landscape today.

ASSIGNMENT
*Settlements can best be studied in the field. The previous exercises in this chapter should have given you some ideas about the way in which villages have developed, and it will be useful to see how the pattern of settlement has evolved in your local area. Very often students' attempts at village studies produce a great mass of data which is interesting but which is difficult to sort into a meaningful pattern. It may be helpful if you try to organise your information under headings for different periods, for example:*
*(a) Blogborough at Domesday,*
*(b) Medieval Blogborough,*
*(c) The effect of the Industrial Revolution,*
*rather than under topics such as buildings and industry. In addition to an investigation of those features of the local village which have survived from the past, documentary evidence is also valuable. One useful exercise is to identify buildings which remain from different periods to see how rebuilding and expansion have taken place. The* Illustrated Handbook of Vernacular Architecture *(Brunskill, 1970) is a valuable guide, and the British Council for Archaeology produce standard forms for logging industrial premises such as weavers' cottages, forges, corn mills, so that there is a permanent record of the fast-disappearing features of the pre-nineteenth-century landscape. (There is a list of sources of information on villages on page 54.)*

## C. Village Society

So far we have attempted to classify villages and other rural settlements on the basis of their *origins*, and their *physical form*. A third method of identifying the characteristics of particular settlements is in terms of the

43

*social form* of the settlement. Confining ourselves to the situation during the eighteenth and early nineteenth centuries in Britain we can distinguish a variety of different groups of people occupying these villages (see Table 2.1). This we refer to as the rural class structure. While all these groups would probably have been present in a large village, the proportion of different classes and activities would have varied. Work done by an historical geographer, Dennis Mills (1972), suggests that one of the basic factors which accounted for village social differences was the system of land ownership. He distinguishes between those settlements that were dominated by a single landlord, either living in the village or operating as an absentee landlord, and the settlements where no such control existed. The former category he refers to as 'closed villages' and the latter, which had no single important landowner, he terms 'open'. The pattern of class groups within these types of village he describes in terms of the relative numbers and proportional importance to the life of the community. Mills divides the open and closed village categories into those which are occupied by peasant owners of small plots, those where the residents are tenants (of one of several landlords), those where a major landlord is resident on the estate, and those where one is an absentee.

Table 2.1  Rural class structure

| Class | Description |
| --- | --- |
| The gentry | The landed family, members of the squirearchy or the aristocracy |
| Upper middle class | Professional men, e.g. clergy, doctors, bailiffs |
|  | Gentlemen farmers |
|  | Large tenant farmers |
| Lower or rural middle class | Yeoman farmers, i.e. small owner-occupiers |
|  | Tradespeople and craftsmen (masters) |
|  | Smaller tenant farmers |
| Artisan class | (a) Estate workers, e.g. carpenters, game-keepers, butlers |
|  | (b) Journeymen craftsmen |
|  | (c) Miscellaneous such as postmen, railway workers, police |
| Labourers | Farm labourers, gardeners, housemaids |

Source: Mills, 1972

# 1. Village classification based on land ownership

*(a)  Closed villages*

(i)  *Estate villages* (resident landlord). All aspects of village life were dominated by the landowner/squire. The estate was divided into a few large farms each with a tenant farmer employing a considerable force of labourers and having high socio-economic standing (see Plate 2.11).

Plate 2.11  Castle Ashby, Northamptonshire. An estate village built close to, but screened from, the great house. The church is actually within the park of the castle, which dominated the village economically and socially. The farms are large and prosperous but few in number, and building has been strictly controlled. (Photograph: Aerofilms)

(ii) *Closed villages with absentee landlord*. The landowner/squire exerted a less forceful impact.

### (b) Open peasant villages

These were characterised by fragmented land ownership and therefore a significant number of owner–occupiers each with the socio-economic standing of minor landlords. The average size of land holdings was necessarily restricted and therefore there was little opportunity for expansion of farming activities. This encouraged commercial/industrial enterprise and many land-owners developed side-lines (i.e. dual occupations). The small landowner had the advantage of being able to mortgage the property if necessary to raise capital for non-agricultural activities.

45

## (c) Divided villages

These were inhabited by a number of relatively small owner-occupiers but may also have contained the seat of a minor landed family. Divided villages were unlikely to have incorporated such a wide range of shops, workshops, Non-Conformist chapels and community organisations as the larger peasant villages.

## 2. Socio-economic relationships within villages

There would also be significant differences in the socio-economic relationships within the villages: greater security in the closed system, and greater freedom in the open.

### (a) Closed villages

In the closed village everyone knew his or her 'place'. The village worked as a closed economic, political and social system in which all parts were interdependent. The over-riding factor was the dependence of all the lower social strata on the resident family. Every aspect of life – economic, social, political, judicial, religious, educational – came under the scrutiny of the squire. In the open system, however, the interlocking network of economic, tenurial and social relationships was open to entry at many points, and villagers could move about the network playing many different roles. People might have dual occupations: could be both tenant and landlord; could be non-conformist and radical in their politics. They often paid for such 'privileges', however, by living in less attractive and less healthy housing.

We can now see why earlier reference was made to the importance of 'lordship' (Roberts, 1977) in discussions of village form, but the pervasive nature of the social and economic effects of concentrated land ownership were widespread, affecting control of church, school, social services, retailing and livestock. One effect was the restriction on industry which prevented alternative sources of employment forcing up the wage rate locally, thus keeping tenants dependent until well into the nineteenth century.

Landowners used their control of cottage accommodation to restrict the size of the labouring population. In this way the tenant farmers were protected from having to pay high Poor Rates, thus making it possible for them to pay higher than average rents to the landowner. The tenants were also subject to the close social control of the squire, parson and farmer and only respectable workers were allowed to remain in the closed community. For these reasons the population density of closed villages was relatively low. Few services developed in closed villages because of the reluctance of the large landowners to let properties to trades people. The class structure usually contained nothing to promote industry; large tenant farmers were expected to employ all their capital on their farms, while labourers had neither the time nor the money to begin serious side-lines.

## (b) Open villages

In contrast we may consider the characteristics of open villages, where dispersal of land ownership was the key to a freedom to experiment in new techniques and enterprises.

Social control was relatively lax and the population density of the open peasant villages was often high. Some labourers who lived in open villages found employment in nearby closed villages, walking many kilometres daily to their places of work.

The open villages were often more densely populated than the closed villages and therefore provided shops and related services with a bigger potential market. This attracted services to the open villages. Even so, many individuals needed to be involved in two or more services in order to make a reasonable living and this is reflected in nineteenth-century directories of the open villages which indicate many dual occupations (farmer/butcher; publican/grazier; miller/baker, etc.). The tendency for services to be concentrated into open villages may account for their growth in importance at the expense of the closed villages. It has been suggested that open villages were more likely to be situated along routeways of some significance and were thus more accessible and receptive to new ideas and external influences.

ASSIGNMENT

*Having read about the characteristics of open and closed villages, you may wish to test whether there are examples of such settlements in your own area. From the previous exercise you should have built up a clear idea of the history of local settlements, including their pattern of land ownership. The local record office should be able to assist you in this enquiry.*

*In some areas there is clear visual evidence in local housing: initials stamped on plaques, almshouses, and uniform colour of paintwork are still found in some closed estate villages. Such evidence can be mapped or photographed. A list of the common characteristics for closed villages is given in the appendix (page 53).*

*Using this as a guide, map the distribution of housing and facilities for one or more villages in your own area, paying particular attention to property built at the same time or over a period by an individual landlord. (Reference to your County or Borough Record Office should produce maps of the village over a period of several hundred years.) Discover how the village has grown, which landscape features survive from earlier estates and enclosure maps, and which have disappeared. Often roads will follow stream or field boundaries and names of fields will give a clue to former usage. The age of hedges in fields may be roughly determined by counting the number of species: as a guide, the hedge will be a century old for every species found in a 30 metre stretch. Using these methods you should be able to produce a map of the parish's development over time, and gain an idea of the history of its land ownership.*

## D. Villages in the Modern Period

### 1. Demographic changes in rural areas

Sadly, in the last quarter of the nineteenth century, agriculture suffered a severe slump, largely because of the import of cheap grain from North America, and the population of most villages and many small towns fell, as agricultural workers left to seek jobs in the industrial cities. The decline in rural population continued steadily and, as farmers increasingly mechanised their operations, the demand for labour continued to fall. There were brief revivals at the time of the two world wars but often the labour drafted in to increase food production was from the towns. The Womens Land Army numbered 18 000 in 1917 and reached a peak of 80 000 members in 1943. There were attempts at resettling former soldiers on smallholdings after the Second World War, but overall the spiral of population loss leading to loss of rural services continued inexorably until the 1950s.

The Town and Country Planning Act of 1947 was the first piece of national legislation to require local authorities to prepare plans of development in their areas. Previously there had been local initiatives to stabilise village population and prevent a drift to the towns: the replacement of tied cottages by council houses, the provision of water, gas and electricity and the subsidising of local bus services to encourage and sustain villages. But whereas before and during the Second World War the population in rural areas had continued to decline, in the post-war period it has grown as urban dwellers appreciate the attractions of rural life. Between 1951 and 1971 the rural population increased by around 25%, some 2.5 million people. At the same time, increasing private car ownership and the economies of scale which favour larger enterprises have seen the loss of local shops, the closure of village schools and the phasing out of cottage hospitals, so that the amenities in rural areas have been reduced. The effect of this on the non-mobile rural population has been largely overlooked, although a recent survey by the Standing Conference of Rural Community Councils entitled *The Decline of Rural Services* has highlighted the problems.

Even though retired people and commuters may be moving back into villages this does not mean that the problems of the rural communities are over, as Christopher Hall (1976) points out.

> *The impact of this reverse flow to the countryside is evident in the villages selected by planning authorities for expansion. New*

48

*speculative estates sprawl around the older village core. They house*
*the commuters – often newly-weds for whom such a home is a better*
*buy than its urban equivalent. In the old centre are more*
*commuters, retired people or week-enders – all people able to afford*
*the maintenance of desirable properties now beyond the purse of*
*indigenous villagers. The latter are likely to be living on the council*
*estate at the edge of the old village.*

As a result, local authorities (County and District Councils) have increasingly given attention to rural areas, often encouraging the development of redundant farm buildings for new 'craft' and 'hi-tech' industrial units, but problems remain, especially in the remote rural areas, and the resources available to organisations such as the Council for Industries in Rural Areas (CoSIRA) and the Rural Community Councils are inadequate to solve them. (For a fuller discussion of rural planning see Bull, Daniel & Hopkinson (1985).)

## 2. Planning at the local level

While general policy for what happens to villages is given in Development and Structure Plans, in many cases individual plans have been produced for particular villages. These may be villages where there are buildings of great architectural value, or villages which are scheduled for expansion, or renewal, or new 'planned' villages. Occasionally the impetus may come from local residents' associations or parish councils rather than from government. It seems possible to distinguish five approaches in formulating village plans although these are often combined.

### (a)  Outline structure approach

Instead of concentrating on infilling land to compact the shape of the village, development is permitted only in character with the historical morphology (linear, circular) of the village. This has been tried in north-east England where the traditional linear pattern is very strong. In Essex, design guides to ensure that new development is in keeping, not only in materials and styles but also in form with the old, have been introduced. There are obvious cost problems in the wholesale application of this approach, but often the inclusion of village greens and traditional patterns helps overcome the raw newness of housing estates.

### (b)  Capacity approach

The question of how to limit the village is a vexed one, and probably local rather than general answers are more appropriate. In the open framework of hamlets which is characteristic of parts of the south Midlands, the village

49

may have no focus, but consist of half a dozen or more 'ends' which bear a common linkage of name and lanes, whereas the compact narrow-streeted sheep villages of the old West Riding of Yorkshire have a much more definite 'edge'. However, the designing of an arbitrary limit to development, an 'envelope', is often used to indicate what are acceptable limits for growth. This may be on the basis of physical area, or the capacity of the village services.

### (c) Visual appraisal approach

This is a fairly subjective method, but one which is gaining popularity. The appropriateness of new building, or demolition, to the appearance of the existing village, and the evaluation of the physical appearance of hedges, walls and street signs are involved. This method has obviously been most commonly used in areas of particular character: the Cotswolds, Kent and Cambridgeshire.

### (d) Policy area approach

The method here has been to isolate the various components of the village either in functional or character terms and then decide which ones are to be altered or extended. This approach lends itself more to villages which are large, or contain a variety of clearly defined zones or periods of construction, or to new villages where it is desired to develop the character of individual neighbourhoods.

### (e) Conservation area approach

Perhaps the most commonly thought of method of controlling village growth is the designation (under the 1967 Civic Amenities Act) of conservation areas where, because of the particular interest of a group of buildings or streets, the scale of change is strictly limited. A village green, or belt of trees, may also be included. Some 4000 of these areas have been established in the last decade and it is likely that many more will be, especially as more old village centres are bypassed by new roads.

Conservation is a subject which is controversial, and the variety of approaches and subjective values of its practitioners illustrate that there is as yet little consensus over the objectives and methods that should be adopted if we wish to retain the quality of our landscape and its resources. However, it seems certain that the pressure of geographers and others interested in the environment will grow in the future, in the effort to ensure that planners do not adopt cheap short-term solutions to settlement problems.

Much will depend on the willingness of the government to invest in both the environmental quality and the economic future of rural communities, especially as the formerly paramount need for agricultural self-sufficiency has become less significant in the face of over-production of food in Europe. Early in 1987 the Conservative Government announced the withdrawal of some planning constraints in rural areas, but whether this will be enough to revitalise villages as working rather than dormitory settlements remains to be seen.

ASSIGNMENT
*Choose one or more villages in your own area and prepare a conservation strategy or village appraisal based upon one of the methods outlined above. Your local Rural Community Council will often be able to provide examples of the guidelines used in your area or the County Planning Department may have prepared criteria as part of its revision of the County Structure Plan which most county authorities undertook in the early 1980s. Often local schools and parish councillors are willing to co-operate in such an appraisal, and may already have collected some information as part of the BBC Domesday 900 Project which was completed for many rural areas in 1986.*

## E. Conclusion

Two related ideas may help us to explain the landscape in the light of the succession of settlers who came into Britain and either displaced earlier inhabitants or were assimilated by them. The first is the concept of *sequent occupance*: that gradually old centres were invaded by new inhabitants who added their own character. The second is that the landscape may be regarded as a *palimpsest*, i.e. composed of successive layers of new features superimposed upon the survivals of preceding generations. Deciphering the different levels is always complex and their persistence renders theoretical explanations of urban landscapes difficult. Only by archaeological survey is it possible to reveal all the levels of an area's development. The student must bear in mind the existence and persistence of earlier settlement features and land use decisions, as he or she seeks to explain a particular stage in the sequence of settlement.

## Key Ideas

*A. Geographical Concepts of Settlement Location and Morphology*

1. Relations between the physical and human environments at particular periods (e.g. availability of raw materials, grazing land, the level of technology) can be exemplified by the choice and development of settlement sites.
2. Too precise a construction should not be placed upon individual place-

name elements. Linguistic differences and the substitution of later names often complicate the picture of settlement thus gained.

3. Settlement nucleation and dispersal are often functions of the scale at which the settlement pattern is perceived, but certain general principles do govern their relative distribution of types.
4. Nucleated settlements are commonly associated with late enclosure of common land, a shortage of suitable sites and a need for defence.
5. Dispersed settlements are associated with early enclosure, agricultural specialisation and the break-up of large estates.
6. Enclosure is an important factor in landscape evolution, having social as well as economic consequences.

## B. Settlement Evolution in England and Wales

1. Each sequential wave of settlers has left behind landscape evidence which provides a cumulative picture (or palimpsest) of settlement history.
2. Celtic settlements are characterised by isolated clusters of housing, often remote and on easily defended sites, now found chiefly in northern and western Britain.
3. Roman remains are widespread, especially over southern England, where major villa colonies were established, many of which are preserved.
4. True Saxon settlement is largely located in south central England, many sites persisting as the nuclei of present-day villages, of distinct circular or linear shape.
5. In the east and north-east, place-name evidence acts as a good guide to the settlement location of invading Scandinavian settlers who occupied the Danelaw in the period up to the Norman Conquest.
6. In the early medieval period the market town grew to pre-eminence in Britain. Planted new towns acted as focal points for expansion as population grew.
7. After the Black Death, large numbers of settlements were abandoned, and can now be identified only by air photography or archaeological evidence.
8. Agricultural improvement and drainage led to the enclosure of large areas of common lands, especially in areas where monastic lands were broken up. This gave rise to a field pattern still extant today, with dispersed hamlets and farmsteads.

## C. Village Society

1. The arrangement of property and variety of functions within villages was largely controlled by landlords until the nineteenth century.
2. It is possible to construct models of traditional open and closed villages and to use these to test the experience of real settlements.

3. The web of social relationships within the village can also be measured by the use of models.

*D. Villages in the Modern Period*

1. Rural planning is constrained by the need to sustain village life and preserve the landscape on the one hand, and to provide services and homes at economic prices on the other, a problem which growing concern for the environment makes difficult.
2. At regional level, planning of rural communities and facilities is undertaken as part of major structure plans and, at local level, the economies of service provision mean that conservation is often restricted to limiting new developments, rather than arresting decay.

*E. Conclusion*

1. Sequent occupance implies that each successive wave of new settlers invaded old centres and added its own character.
2. Alternatively the landscape may be regarded as a palimpsest composed of successive layers of new features superimposed upon the survivals of preceding generations.

## Appendix 1. Characteristics of open and closed villages

Not all villages will still retain all the landscape features listed below, but enough should be present to enable you to come to a conclusion about the effect of land ownership on the history of a particular settlement.

## Closed estate village

Single large mansion with park, outbuildings and 'model' cottages or almshouses

Many of the buildings of a similar age

Layout of village often carefully planned

Influential Anglican church

Church containing family memorials, mausoleums, tombs, etc.

Village school may be voluntary aided (i.e. Church foundation)

Evidence of the squire as a social patron: almshouses, reading

## Open village

Possibly several medium-sized manor farmhouses

Wide variety of building ages and styles, including modern property

Several shops, often in converted residences

Small workshops

Irregular field boundaries and sizes

Evidence of encroachment on to greens and commons

Non-Conformist chapels

Little evidence of planning, shape not clear, often much infilling

| Closed estate village | Open village |
|---|---|
| room, cricket pitch, charities, etc. | Several smallholdings |
| Buildings purpose-built: little evidence of building conversion | In addition most of the features of closed villages are absent |
| Possibly a single public house | |
| Few other services: perhaps one general store | |
| No evidence of former cottage industry/crafts | |
| Probably no Non-Conformist chapels | |
| Arms of the manorial lord may be in evidence | |
| Land of parish divided into a few large farms | |
| Planned landscape, e.g. large regular-shaped fields with uniform field boundaries | |
| Coverts; woodland in regular stands to act as game preserve | |
| Little twentieth-century development | |

## Appendix 2. Sources for local historical landscape study

Again not all these materials will be available or relevant. A good starting point is the Victoria County History for your parish, available in most reference libraries, and any parish data or material produced for the BBC Domesday 900 Survey, which may be available at your local museum or record office.

Sources are discussed more fully in several local history texts (West, 1962; Rogers, 1977) and help can often be obtained from local history societies.

## 1. Legal

|  |  |
|---|---|
|  | Charters, Domesday, Lay Subsidy Rolls, Charter Sessions Rolls, Order and Minute Books, Calendars |
| **Clerk of the Peace:** | Parliamentary Enclosure Acts (award and maps) |
| **Gaol records:** | Test Act Certificates |
| (inc. photographs) | Toleration Act Certificates |
| **Magistrates' records:** | Toleration Act Certificates |
| (e.g. Settlement Books) | Registers of Papists' estates |

| | Road closure and diversion orders and maps |
| --- | --- |
| | Public utility plans and schemes |
| | Assessment lists (hearth tax, land tax) |
| | Population lists: Jurors, Electors, Pollbooks |

**Petty sessions records**

**Sheriff Court records**

**Lord Lieutenant's records** (especially for the seventeenth-century and eighteenth-century Revolutionary and Napoleonic Wars)

**Statutory Authority records:** Commissioners of Sewers
Turnpike Trusts/Railways
Boards of Guardians
Boards of Health
Highway Boards
School Societies and Boards
Improvement Commissioners
Census Returns (on microfilm)

**Borough Sessions/
Manorial Court records** .

## 2. Ecclesiastical

**Cathedral records**

**Diocesan and Archdiocesan records** (estates, cartullaries, Consistery courts, visitation books, 'cause' papers)
Tithe Awards and Maps
Bishops' transcripts (Parish registers)
Marriage Licences
Terriers
Faculties
Correspondence

**Non-Conformist records:** (e.g. membership lists, meeting house certificates, Society of Friends, Catholic Record Society)

## 3. Publications

Directories, journal articles, guide books, newspapers, travellers' accounts (e.g. Daniel Defoe's tour through England and Wales, 1720), local histories, etc. should be consulted with caution.

# 3 The Growth of Towns

## A. Pre-Industrial Towns

### 1. Medieval towns

The Norman Conquest brought stability and a strong centralised government to Britain and these facilitated the establishment of a new social and
economic order (see pages 35 to 40). Trade expanded and a greater
emphasis was placed on the specialisation of labour. The growth of towns
was a key factor in the fundamental changes which occurred. Many of the
towns which flourished during the Middle Ages grew organically from an
already established base, gradually and naturally as the need arose. These
towns developed within walls which could be extended relatively easily to
contain additional growth. The layout was amorphous and unplanned and
the buildings were linked and separated by a network of narrow winding
streets. Behind many of the town houses were long narrow plots which were
intensively cultivated so that, although the streets were often narrow and the
houses packed closely together, much open space was included within the
town walls. Population densities were, consequently, seldom high (Burke,
1975).

Bruges, in Belgium, provides a good example of the organic growth of a
medieval town, as the map illustrates (see Figure 3.1). The growth of Bruges
was closely associated with the development of the weaving industry in
Flanders in the twelfth century. The town prospered after a freak tidal wave
created a substantial harbour in what previously had been a narrow silted
channel connecting Bruges to the sea (Jones & Van Zandt, 1974). Even
today the medieval core of Bruges remains largely intact although the
network of canals which was formerly used for commerce is now neglected
and used only by pleasure boats.

Figure 3.1   A part of the unplanned medieval town of Bruges from Marcus Gerard's map of
1562. A section of the town walls is shown in the top right-hand corner of the photograph. Note
the network of narrow winding lanes which separated the irregularly shaped plots, many of which
were intensively developed with closely packed houses. The network of canals and many of the
fine medieval buildings have been preserved and form important features in contemporary
Bruges. (Source: part of Marcus Gerard's 1562 plan of Bruges)

Not all medieval towns, however, grew from an already well-established base. Some were planned or planted and built to a development plan in virtually a single operation. Such towns, known collectively as 'bastides' from the French *bâtir*, to build, were established by the monarch in newly conquered territories. For example, King Edward I established a number of new towns in Wales in the late thirteenth century after he conquered the country. Conwy provides a particularly fine example of such a town (see Plate 3.1). It was founded in 1284 to act as the regional focus for the Conwy Valley and the North Wales coast from Bangor to the south of the Clwyd (Conzen, 1968). The town was dominated by the castle from which extended

Plate 3.1 Conwy, North Wales, is a fine example of a planned medieval town. The town is still dominated by the castle from which extend the walls laid out in triangular form. One of the three gates which penetrated the walls, Porth Ulchaf, can be seen in the bottom right-hand corner of the photograph. The abbey church of St Mary still stands at the centre of the town and the medieval street pattern has been largely preserved. (Photograph: Aerofilms)

the walls laid out in triangular form. The town walls were penetrated by only three gates. The new town site had previously been occupied by the Cistercian abbey of Aberconwy and, although Edward I had caused the abbey to be moved to a new site higher up the valley, its church remained to serve the new borough. The medieval street pattern was arranged within the town walls and around the former abbey church. A sizeable market square was laid out and the remainder of the 21 acres divided into rectangular burgages.

During the Middle Ages scores of new towns were founded in Britain but not all of these prospered. For example, on the southern side of Poole Bay, Dorset, directly opposite the port of Poole, a site was chosen for the new town of Nova Villa (Hoskins, 1970). A charter was granted by King Edward I in 1286, two town planners were appointed and the town was marked out on the ground. The new town failed to develop, however, and it has left no mark on the landscape. Other planted medieval towns grew and flourished for a time but then stagnated. Such was the case with Longtown in Herefordshire. A very small population was recorded in Domesday Book of 1086, but by the thirteenth century a border castle had been established and a simple network of streets laid out just outside the earthworks of the castle (Beresford, 1967). By 1310, 100 burgages were recorded in Longtown but since then the borough has declined and a network of overgrown lanes and a few buildings are all that survive (see Plate 3.2).

Plate 3.2  Former High Street, Longtown, Herefordshire, now overgrown and neglected. A network of lanes still diverge from this 'street' which formerly was fronted by the Parish Church and a number of inns. (Author's photograph)

## 2. Renaissance towns

The Renaissance brought realisation of the intellectual limitations of the medieval world with the rebirth of a spirit of enquiry and a resurgence of individual creativity. This new mood affected architecture and town planning. The theory and form of Classical architecture were rediscovered (initially by Italians) in the latter part of the fifteenth century, and architects strove to impose order and symmetry on town planning and development. Neo-Classical buildings had to be placed in an ordered context and town extensions incorporated formal squares linked by broad tree-lined boulevards. Thus there developed a close relationship between landscape planning and town planning. Grandiose geometric plans for entire towns were devised such as that of Palma Nuova in Italy which was started in 1593 (see Figure 3.2). Existing towns and cities were improved and adapted, sometimes, as with Rome in the fifteenth, sixteenth and seventeenth centuries, comprehensively and to spectacular effect. It is little wonder that the Renaissance has been described as the golden age of town planning and development.

The Renaissance in architecture and town planning was slow to be

Figure 3.2   A simplified plan of Palma Nuova; founded in 1593. (Source: redrawn from an engraving in Braun and Hogenberg, *Civitates orbis terrarum* (1599))

adopted in Britain, where many towns, such as London, retained an essentially medieval appearance and layout right up to the early seventeenth century. Even during the seventeenth and eighteenth centuries few new towns were established in Britain and few large-scale extensions made to existing towns. Most of the neo-Classical developments in British towns were small piecemeal additions or arose from the redevelopment of slums and obsolete districts. There were exceptions, however, particularly where fire destroyed an existing city or town and a comprehensive programme of rebuilding had to be undertaken. Blandford Forum, in Dorset, provides such an example. It was virtually completely destroyed by fire in 1731 and rebuilt to a plan. The City of London is another, more obvious, example. The Great Fire of 1666 devastated the City; 13 200 dwellings, 89 churches and 400 streets were destroyed. Such a scale of destruction meant that a unique opportunity was presented for the remodelling of the City. Although Christopher Wren's plan for rebuilding the City (see Figure 3.3) was rejected, specific requirements were stipulated which went some way towards controlling the nature of the redevelopment. Building materials were regulated and the opportunity taken to widen and straighten many of the narrow medieval streets. Even an element of functional zoning was introduced (see page 115) as efforts were made to concentrate obnoxious smoke-creating industries and to prohibit them from other parts of the City (Burke, 1975).

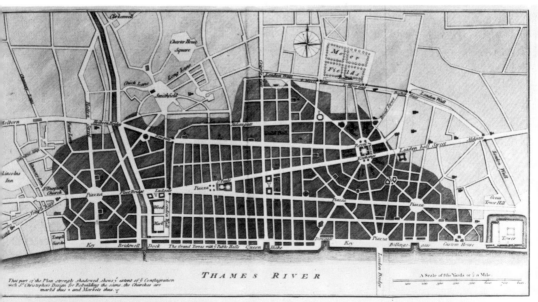

Figure 3.3   Wren's plan for rebuilding the City of London, after the Great Fire of 1666. (Source: *The Greater London History Library*)

Bath provides the pinnacle of the achievements in neo-Classical architecture and town planning in Britain. It was transformed from a small medieval walled town into an elegant and prosperous spa. John Wood was the surveyor, architect and builder who master-minded the development although he was aided by his son and numerous successors including Robert Adam, Thomas Baldwin and John Palmer. Together they created a unique townscape of elegant neo-Classical facades; avenues, crescents (see Plate 3.3) and squares; lawns, trees and greenery; and impressive public buildings including the Pump Rooms, Assembly Rooms, theatres and churches.

Many of the ideas adopted by John Palmer and his associates in Bath were later incorporated into other ambitious schemes for town improvement such as the spa towns of Cheltenham, Buxton and Leamington and the development of Edinburgh's 'New Town' from James Craig's plan, accepted by the City Council in 1767.

Unfortunately, urban development in Britain in the seventeenth and eighteenth centuries was not always aesthetically pleasing. Such developments were the preserve of the privileged rich who increasingly isolated

Plate 3.3 Lansdown Crescent, Bath, an architectural masterpiece designed by John Palmer and built between 1789 and 1793. (Author's photograph)

themselves from the urban poor. Working-class housing was often very poor, particularly where the unenclosed town fields prevented an extension of the built-up area. In parts of the English Midlands, in particular, the Lammas pasture rights, whereby burgesses had the right to graze their cattle and sheep over the open fields after the crops had been harvested, presented a disincentive to the enclosure of the open fields. In Nottingham, for example, the burgesses were particularly opposed to the reallocation of the strips of the surrounding town fields into large compact blocks of land (Hoskins, 1970). The enclosure of the open fields and the attendant changes in land tenure were, however, prerequisites for the extension of the built-up area of the town. While the open fields survived, the town could not expand

Figure 3.4   An eighteenth-century close in Nottingham. (Source: *Nottinghamshire Local Studies Library*)

outwards. Instead, any increase in population had to be contained within the existing built-up area. As a result, within the space of three generations Nottingham degenerated from one of the finest towns in Britain to a town which contained some of the country's most squalid slums (see Figure 3.4). Every bit of available open space was developed and densities were excessively high. Only after the open fields were enclosed in 1845 could Nottingham expand once more but by then it was largely too late; housing and public health conditions were among the worst in the country. Not infrequently, the slums and squalid housing conditions which became such a feature of urban growth in the nineteenth century had their origins in the eighteenth century.

Nevertheless, for the most part, the pre-industrial city remained relatively small and compact. The built-up area was confined and links with the surrounding countryside persisted. Although there were great variations in the quality of housing, there was little social segregation and families of different classes often lived close together.

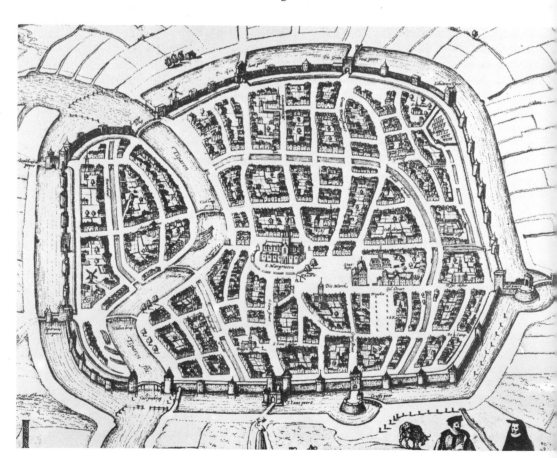

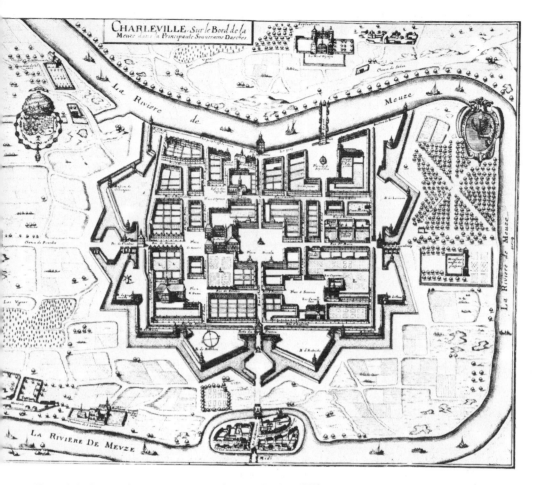

Figure 3.6    Plan of Charleville, France. (Source: Burke, 1975)

ASSIGNMENT
*Examine the plans of Haarlem (Netherlands) and Charleville (France) (see Figures 3.5 and 3.6). Each represents a good example of one of the following: adapted or organic medieval; planned or planted medieval; Renaissance. Decide which category best fits each map. Compare the street layout and morphology and justify your choice.*

◀ Figure 3.5    Plan of Haarlem, Netherlands, circa 1585.

## B. The Consequences of Rapid Nineteenth-Century Urban Growth

Although pre-nineteenth-century urban growth in Britain was significant, by the onset of the nineteenth century most of the population were still rural dwellers. In 1801 the population of England and Wales was less than 9 million and of these approximately 17% lived in the fifteen towns of over 20 000 inhabitants. Only London, with 865 000, had a population of more than 100 000. During the nineteenth century, however, urban growth was extremely rapid, particularly in the period from about 1840 to 1880. By 1891 the population had grown to over 29 million and nearly half lived in the 185 towns with populations in excess of 20 000. London's population had increased to a staggering 6.5 million, while the populations of such industrial giants as Birmingham and Manchester increased ten-fold during the nineteenth century to 760 000 and 645 000 respectively by 1901. The growth rates in some northern industrial towns were even more dramatic. For example, Middlesbrough, a hamlet of only 40 inhabitants in 1829, had a population of over 100 000 by the turn of the century.

Such rapid urbanisation was the result of a combination of natural increase – high death rates were exceeded by even higher birth rates – and rural–urban migration. Migration was encouraged by both 'push' and 'pull' factors. Changes in land tenure and agricultural improvements, including the development of farm machinery, helped to create a landless peasantry which, in turn, was attracted by the job prospects in the rapidly developing industries in the towns.

## 1. Planned growth

Birkenhead, situated on the Wirral peninsula on the south bank of the Mersey Estuary, provides a further good example of a town which grew rapidly from a very small base during the middle decades of the nineteenth century. In 1821 the township was a relatively remote hamlet of about 200 inhabitants and 60 dwellings (see Figure 3.7). About this time, however, a regular and reliable steam-powered ferry service was established which linked the settlement with Liverpool, and William Laird established a shipbuilding and repair industry in the adjoining Wallasey Pool. These events provided the impetus for urban growth and this was facilitated when William Laird purchased a considerable acreage of land in the centre of the township in 1824 and commissioned Gillespie Graham of Edinburgh fame to plan a new town. The streets were laid out in a grid pattern extending outwards from the elegant Hamilton Square. At first progress was relatively slow and the settlement grew to 2569 in 1831. The 1830s and 1840s, however, were two decades of particularly rapid urban growth (see Figure 3.8) and by 1851 the population exceeded 24 000.

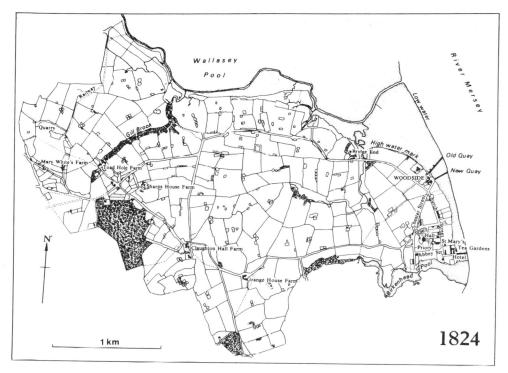

Figure 3.7   Birkenhead, 1824. (Source: Patmore & Hodgkiss, 1970)

Chambers' *Edinburgh Journal* of 17 May 1845 provides a graphic description of the building of Victorian Birkenhead.

> *When we had passed a mere frontier of streets overlooking the river we were at once launched into a mile's breadth of street building where unfinished houses, unmade roadways, brickfields, scaffolding, heaps of mortar, loaded wains and troops of busy workmen meet the eye in every direction. . . . Land which a few years ago hardly possessed a value is now selling £6 a square yard, and by good speculation in that line, large fortunes have been acquired.*

Birkenhead continued to grow rapidly and absorb neighbouring townships as it sprawled outwards from its planned nucleus, but the grand design of Gillespie Graham was never realised, as Sulley's description of 1888 makes clear.

> *Birkenhead possesses fine and broad streets, some of which merit the epithet of noble, and are unsurpassed in the United Kingdom; but the effect of these is marred and ruined by the paltry character of the greater part of the buildings which line them, by the undue*

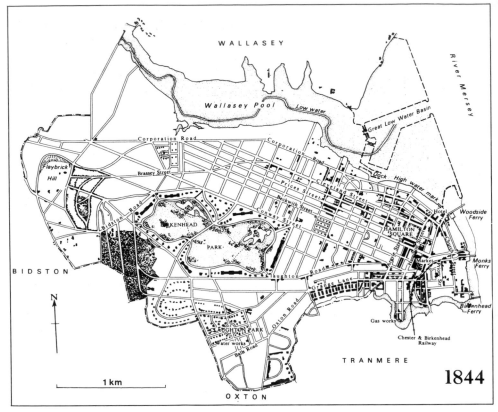

Figure 3.8   Birkenhead, 1844. Note the planned layout designed by Gillespie Graham. (Source: Patmore & Hodgkiss, 1970)

> *proportion of cottage property, and by the unsightly gaps and vacant spaces which occur in nearly every thoroughfare throughout the town. Laid out on a magnificent plan, on an extensive scale, the place has not grown to the anticipated extent (**Sulley, 1888**).*

## 2. Unplanned growth

The rapid rate of urbanisation in England and Wales during the nineteenth century meant that approximately 200 000 people had to be rehoused each year (Burke, 1975). There was no municipal housing, at least until the latter part of the century, and this considerable additional housing stock had to be provided almost exclusively by speculative builders. Housing conditions, particularly for the unskilled worker, were all too frequently appallingly bad. Housing densities were high and overcrowding commonplace. In the worst housing districts of many of the industrial towns such as London, Leeds, Nottingham and Liverpool, houses were built back-to-back and arranged around enclosed unpaved courts. The only entrances to many of these courts were by narrow tunnels which penetrated the rows of terraced houses which lined the streets (look back at Figure 3.4).

There was no sewerage provision and at the end of the courts were open earth middens. Refuse was not collected and no piped water was available. The houses themselves were extremely simple and provided only the most rudimentary accommodation. In Liverpool a common regional house type was a dwelling three storeys high, each floor consisting of a single room approximately 4 metres square, and a cellar. It was not uncommon for families to occupy single rooms or even the cellars which were pervaded by damp polluted air.

It is hardly surprising that in these conditions diseases such as typhoid fever and tuberculosis were rife and frequent epidemics took a heavy toll. For example the cholera epidemic in London in 1849 was responsible for 14 000 deaths (Burke, 1975). Life expectancy was extremely low and infant mortality rates tragically high. In Liverpool during the period 1839 to 1844 the average age at death was only seventeen years and more than half the children born failed to reach five years of age (Taylor, 1970).

Andrew Mearns' (1883) description of the appalling housing conditions of London's poorest families provides us with some indication of the dreadful squalor in which they struggled to survive.

> *To get to the house you have to penetrate courts reeking with poisonous and malodorous gases arising from accumulations of sewage and refuse scattered in all directions and often flowing beneath your feet: courts, many of them which the sun never penetrates, which are never visited by a breath of fresh air, and which rarely know the virtues of a drop of cleansing water. You have to descend rotten staircases. ... You have to grope your way along dark and filthy passages swarming with vermin. Then, if you are not driven back by the intolerable stench, you may gain admittance to the dens in which these thousands of beings. ... herd together. ... Eight feet square – that is about the average size of very many of these rooms. Walls and ceilings are black with the accretions of filth which have gathered upon them through long years of neglect. It is exuding through cracks in the boards overhead; it is running down the walls; it is everywhere.*

Another vivid description of the human misery arising from these dreadful housing conditions is contained in Arthur Morrison's novel, *A Child of the Jago* which was first published in 1897 and describes the notorious Jago district of court houses in Shoreditch in the East End of London.

> *It was past the mid of a summer night in the Old Jago. ... Below, the hot, heavy air lay, a rank oppression on the contorted forms of*

*those who made for sleep on the pavement: and in it, and through it all, there rose from the foul earth and the grimed walls a close, mingled stink – the odour of the Jago....*

*... A square of two hundred and fifty yards or less – that was all there was of the Jago. But in that square the human population swarmed in thousands. ... On the pavement some writhed wearily, longing for sleep; others, despairing of it, sat and lolled, and a few talked. They were not there for lack of shelter, but because in this weather repose was less unlikely in the street than within doors; and the lodgings of the few who nevertheless abode at home were marked here and there by the lights visible from the windows. For in this place none ever slept without a light, because of three kinds of vermin that light in some sort keeps at bay. ... (**Morrison, 1897**).*

## 3. Municipal involvement

It was only after a close correlation had been demonstrated between sub-standard housing, polluted water supply and the spread of disease that legislation was enacted in an attempt to improve working-class housing conditions. Liverpool, which had the unenviable reputation of being the unhealthiest town in Britain, pioneered the way with its 1842 Act to Improve the Health of the Inhabitants of Liverpool (White, 1951). This stipulated a minimum width for streets and courts and minimum dimensions for house buildings. Under the Act, courts had to be open at one end, their surfaces flagged and kept clean, and privies had to be provided and maintained. Cellars in court houses were no longer to be used as separate dwellings. The 1844 Public Health Act, championed by Edwin Chadwick, aimed to secure the provision of adequate water supply, drainage and sewerage to combat waterborne diseases although, in the event, the Act proved largely ineffective because the local authorities were not obliged to adopt it. There followed a spate of health and housing legislation in the latter half of the nineteenth century which aimed at the provision of improved sanitary conditions, established minimum standards for house building and empowered local authorities to make by-laws governing town growth. The local authorities responded by making it illegal to build courts and back-to-back houses (in Liverpool under a by-law of 1864), and rows of improved terraces, *by-law housing*, became the universal house type for working-class families throughout England and Wales. These were usually arranged in a grid pattern of streets as this was the most convenient way of subdividing land for sale before building (see Plate 3.4).

The introduction of building restrictions and minimum standards, how-ever, had unfortunate consequences for many of the poorest families. For, as building specifications improved and building costs rose, so rents also

Plate 3.4  High-density nineteenth-century terraced housing in Preston constructed on a grid-iron plan. Note how the houses are interspersed with industry thereby minimising journeys to work. (Photograph: Aerofilms)

increased. The poorest families thus found themselves evicted from their condemned cellar dwellings or the victims of slum clearance programmes, but unable to afford the higher rents of the newly built and improved by-law housing. In addition much of the working-class housing was financed by small-scale speculators, often drawn from the ranks of the skilled artisans and the lower middle classes. The term 'the shopocracy' has been coined to describe them. For example, in Liverpool in the 1840s the average holding of working-class property exceeded eight houses per landlord in only three wards (Treble, 1971). Such small-scale speculators were frequently unable to afford the much greater outlay necessary to meet the increased building specifications, and investment in working-class housing became a less attractive proposition. Thus the improvement Acts interfered with market forces but at the same time provided no alternative form of housing for the least advantaged families. It was against such a background that certain local authorities somewhat reluctantly became involved in direct provision of housing.

The way in which local authorities almost stumbled into municipal housing involvement is well illustrated by the case of Liverpool, where the first council house dwellings in Britain were built in 1867 (White, 1951). By the 1860s the City Council was beginning to realise that, without some positive measures to ensure provision of new and improved housing, other parts of its housing policy, such as the demolition of the courts and the eviction of families from cellar dwellings, were not likely to be successful. A sub-committee was thus set up to look into the provision of working-class dwellings. The committee suggested that a plot of land should be leased out of the Corporation Estate for the development of labourers' dwellings approved by the health committee. Members of the council subsequently advertised for a developer but received no offer and decided to go ahead themselves. As a result St Martin's Cottages, which still stand beside the Vauxhall Road in Liverpool, were completed in 1869 (see Plate 3.5). The development, which comprised 124 dwellings was, by contemporary standards, built to a high specification, so much so that they eventually came to be occupied by persons of a higher income level than those for whom they were intended. St Martin's Cottages were built essentially as an example to

Plate 3.5 St Martin's Cottages, Liverpool. Completed in 1869, these were the first council houses to be built in England. (Author's photograph)

private developers and were not intended as the first instalment of a municipal building programme. In fact no further council dwellings were erected in Liverpool until 1885 and it was only from about 1895 onwards that municipal housing started to play a significant role in the rehousing of Liverpool's most disadvantaged families. This was in part a result of the Housing of the Working Classes Act of 1890 which extended the Corporation's powers to provide housing. Between 1895 and 1914, 2392 corporation dwellings were built in Liverpool without any government subsidy (White, 1951). Moreover they were mostly occupied by the families for whom they were intended, that is the most disadvantaged. This meant that the Corporation could not charge economic rents. In fact the rents charged were hardly sufficient to cover maintenance charges and the Corporation had a substantial housing deficit annually. Thus by 1914 the Corporation had accepted the principle of a housing subsidy, that is charging uneconomic rents to house some of the poorest families in the city. Nevertheless, by 1914 only 1.31% of Liverpool's total population rented their houses from the local authority and, although this was a higher proportion than any other city in Britain (Swansea was second with 0.93%), it was not until the housing legislation of the inter-war period had been passed that a nation-wide boom in local authority house building took place (White, 1951).

ASSIGNMENTS

1. Look carefully at Figures 3.7 and 3.8 and describe the changes that occurred in Birkenhead between 1824 and 1844. Describe the form of the new and rapidly growing town and consider how the town plan was influenced by natural features such as lines of drainage, the coast and tidal creeks.

2. Figure 3.9 is an O.S. 1 : 2500 plan extract of a part of the 1908 edition of Scotland Ward, Liverpool. A section of the Leeds–Liverpool Canal, with its associated industry, is shown on the western edge of the map which is also close to the Liverpool dock system.
   (a) With the aid of sketches, describe the layout of housing shown on the map.
   (b) Work out the housing density for 1 hectare for the southern part of the map.
   (c) St Martin's Cottages are situated at the junction of Vauxhall Road and Silvester Street. Describe the relative advantages of their site and neighbourhood.

3. Try to find out how the local authority of your town or district first became involved in providing houses for working-class families. When were the first council houses built?

4. Compare the descriptions of nineteenth-century Birkenhead and the Old Jago. In what respects may both be regarded as failures?

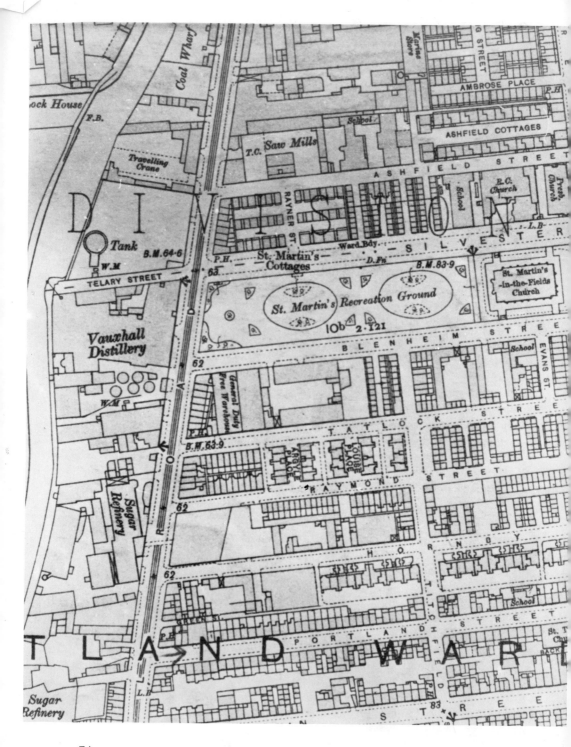

## C. The Origins of the Garden City Movement

### 1. Middle-class philanthropy

In the previous section, you discovered how, with some reluctance, local government became involved in both providing and managing houses for working-class families. During the nineteenth and early twentieth centuries there was a parallel movement, initiated by a number of unconnected philanthropic employers who saw in the creation of new settlements a solution to the problem of the appalling slums, which were a product of rapid urbanisation. Among the most important were the following people.

*Intro*

#### (a) *Robert Owen* (1771–1858)

Owen took over a cotton mill and industrial village at New Lanark in Scotland in 1799 and devoted all the surplus profits of the enterprise to the provision of social services. He enlarged houses to minimise overcrowding, opened a co-operative shop, abolished child labour in his mills and also set up a school. Owen's writings included *Villages of unity and mutual co-operation* in which he proposed model villages of 800–1200 inhabitants, but only New Lanark (now a museum) was ever built.

#### (b) *James Silk Buckingham* (1786–1855)

Buckingham published in 1849 an elaborate proposal for a new town of not more than 10 000 called Victoria, in his book *National Evils and Practical Remedies*. The settlement was not built because of lack of finance.

#### (c) *Titus Salt* (1803–1876)

Salt established a factory employing 3000 people on a site near Bradford in the 1840s. He provided housing, water supply and drainage, a chapel, church, club, library and many other public buildings in the village of Saltaire (see Plate 3.6).

Robert Owen's experiment at New Lanark (1799) and Titus Salt's model village near Bradford were designed to accommodate relatively small numbers of people but, by 1875, B. W. Richardson had proposed a city of 100 000 people: Hygea, the City of Health. He aimed to provide a healthy city, large enough to contain a cross-section of the national population and offering a wide range of employment opportunities. It is interesting to notice

*Con*

◀ Figure 3.9 An extract from the 1908 edition of a 1 : 2500 OS map showing part of Scotland Ward, Liverpool.

Plate 3.6   Saltaire: a north-east view of the village and works in 1895. The settlement is still occupied, and almost all of Sir Titus Salt's original dwellings and social buildings have survived; together with the original lions from Trafalgar Square. (Photograph: Bradford Central Library)

that at this early date there was already realisation that the *size* and *self-sufficiency* of any new towns were to be important factors in their chance of development. Finance was also a stumbling block to building. In the meantime it remained for individual enlightened factory owners to provide for their workers. This was done by the Cadbury family at Bournville, in the Midlands and by W. H. Lever, who established Port Sunlight (Plate 3.7) near Liverpool in 1889. Lever wanted to socialise and Christianise business relations and get back again in the office, factory and workshop to the close family brotherhood that had existed in the days of hand labour. Inspired by the 'model cottages' built for workers at the nearby Price candle factory, he constructed 900 houses with a church, hotel, social club, bowling greens, swimming pools and a now famous art gallery. The entire 130 acre site was completed just before the First World War and the low-density semi-rural or 'garden city' layout of only seven houses to the acre set new standards for urban housing. It bore obvious fruit in terms of the health of the inhabitants, as Table 3.1 indicates.

Table 3.1   Death rates and infant mortality rates

| 1907 | Death rate per 1000 of population | Infant mortality rate per 1000 |
| --- | --- | --- |
| England and Wales | 16 | 119 |
| Liverpool | 20 | 140 |
| Port Sunlight | 9 | 70 |

Plate 3.7  Port Sunlight. The model village with its church, adjacent social club, hotel and art gallery is sited between the main road and railway routes, affording access to Chester and Liverpool. The factory is separately zoned away from the houses which are arranged in short rows and crescents with their own rear gardens. A central green boulevard runs through the site, an idea used later by Louis de Soissons at Welwyn. The large proportion of open space and numbers of trees give a rural atmosphere to what is actually an industrial suburb. (Photograph: UML Ltd)

While such new housing schemes directly benefited the employees' individual cases, their spread was limited by their dependence upon entrepreneurial generosity and a general belief that they could not be financially self-supporting. It needed an economist to argue the case for large-scale new development and dispersal to begin a genuine widespread zeal for a new form of settlement.

## 2. Garden cities

Ebenezer Howard's *Garden Cities of Tomorrow* was published in 1898 and revised in 1902. His argument was that high city land values and rents encouraged overcrowded high-density building, and discouraged the provision of social amenities. On the other hand rural life, despite the advantages of clean air and spaciousness, was lacking in transport, employment and

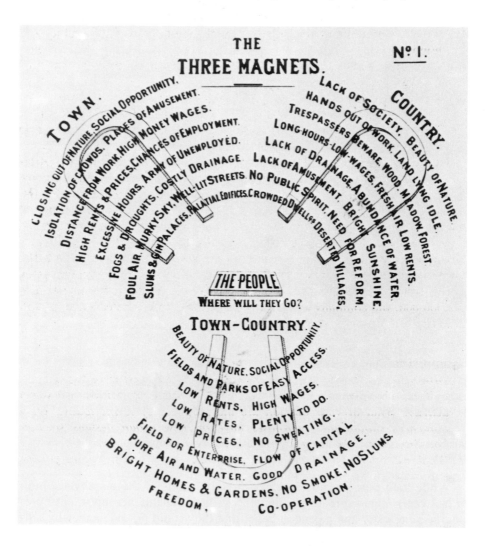

housing. Why not combine the advantages of both environments in the 'garden city'? (See Figure 3.10.)

Howard considered 30 000 people as the optimum town-estate size and that further growth would be by planned decentralisation to new centres grouped around and linked to the central city. It is of interest to note that, although he was probably unaware of the work of Von Thünen, and Christaller's ideas on central place were published much later, Howard's diagrammatic representation combined aspects of the Von Thünen principle of economic rent with the Christaller theory of central places and market areas (Christaller, 1933).

The features emphasised in Howard's proposals were:

(a) The town would be built on agricultural land acquired at a low cost.
(b) All land would be held in trust by 'gentlemen of undoubted probity and honour'.
(c) The town would contain 30 000 people and have a wide range of facilities and employment opportunities.
(d) The town estate would incorporate agricultural activities (farms, cow pastures and allotments). These would utilise the refuse of the town.
(e) The process of growth would be by establishing another new town near to the original town, directly connected by rail and road links.

Howard stressed the need for links between established and new settlements and the need for balanced economic growth rather than mere re-housing, '... after being once started it ought to be self supporting for the cost of carriage ... would be less than the saving made in rent. [There would be] much passive resistance at first. Ultimately all would gain, but most the landowners and the rail-roads connected with the colony' (Howard, 1902).

The ideas which Howard advanced were put into practice through the formation in 1901 of the Garden City Association, which was the precursor of the Town and Country Planning Association. In 1903, with a capital sum of £300 000, the company started work on its first town, Letchworth, and in 1920 the second town, Welwyn, was begun.

ASSIGNMENTS

1. *Howard's ideas of how new towns should be designed were based upon philosophical perceptions of what towns are for: their purpose for social activity. What in your opinion are the purposes of towns today? What influences should these purposes have on new urban designs such as housing estates, shopping centres and industrial areas?*

2. *What were the advantages and disadvantages of relying upon private enterprise for the designing of the first new towns?*

Figure 3.10   Howard's magnet diagram. (Source: Hertfordshire County Council)

## D. Residential Segregation

The middle-class response to the squalor and unhealthiness of the exploding nineteenth-century towns was to take refuge in the emerging suburbs which developed rapidly from about the 1840s on the edge of the built-up areas. Increasingly, members of the middle class were no longer content to live in a socially heterogeneous community in the heart of the town where the poor were unobtrusively screened off in nearby courts. They were all too conscious of the risks of disease and periodic epidemics and wished to seek out a healthier environment on the edge of the town. The suburb thus evolved as a highly efficient means of permitting both functional and social segregation; functional in that it enabled homelife and work to be carried out in two discrete and often relatively distant places, and social in that it provided the means whereby middle-class families could live in physically separate, socially homogeneous and exclusive neighbourhoods. Furthermore, as had been observed by Engels during his stay in Manchester in the 1840s, the towns were constructed in such a way that the middle classes remained oblivious to working-class housing conditions on their journeys to work. In his *The Condition of the Working Class in England* he describes a main thoroughfare linking central Manchester with middle-class suburbs.

> *So Market Street running south-east from the Exchange; at first brilliant shops of the best sort, with counting houses and warehouses above; in the continuation, Piccadilly, immense hotels and warehouses; in the further continuation, London Road, in the neighbourhood of the Medlock, factories, beerhouses, shops for the humbler bourgeoisie and the working population; and from this point onward, large gardens and villas of the wealthier merchants and manufacturers ... one is seldom in a position to catch from the street a glimpse of the real labouring districts (**Engels, 1969**).*

So began the accentuation of segregation between classes in the growing Victorian towns of Britain, and the erosion of a sense of community. Villages within easy reach of the towns became engulfed by the burgeoning suburbs and removal to these new districts became a mark of social distinction, echoed in the ringing names which adorn streets of this period: Burlington, Montague, Addington, Melbourne, Devonshire and Bedford. Suburban development was characterised by detached and semi-detached villas each constructed on relatively spacious plots. The low-density development was possible because of the availability and relatively low cost of suburban land. Most of the occupiers could not afford to live in architect-designed houses and so the estates acquired a degree of uniformity, although variations on the basic house designs were achieved by projecting bays, gable ends, ornamental brickwork and other devices and these gave to the estates a degree of individuality, as befitted the spirit of the Victorian age.

# 1. The influence of transport technology

Suburban development was made possible through the availability of capital for house purchasing and by transport innovation which enabled people to travel farther to work. The aspiring middle classes were able to buy their new healthier homes by the growth of building societies that developed out of the small banks and friendly societies of northern England, which were to be found in almost every town in the country by the mid nineteenth century (Price, 1958). Another important contributory factor was the setting up of freehold housing estates by entrepreneurs who bought large plots of farm-land for subsequent resale.

The first important intra-urban innovation in public transport was the horse-drawn omnibus, a Parisian development imported by George Shilli-beer in 1829. It provided a genteel alternative to the private carriage, which enabled the gentleman with limited means to live beyond walking distance from his place of work (Dyos, 1966). Regular omnibus services were established to the growing London suburbs from about the mid 1830s and provided the only means of public transport to the City for some time. The success of suburban development often depended on easy access to an omnibus route. For example, in the south London suburb of Camberwell from 1835 to 1862 the omnibus was the only form of public passenger transport available (Dyos, 1966). Although omnibus fares were gradually reduced, they remained relatively high, beyond the reach of all but the better off. The omnibus became predominantly a one-class vehicle con-veying the middle classes to their places of work (Olsen, 1976).

By the mid 1860s the construction of suburban railways had become an economical proposition. A railway mania followed whereby numerous sub-urban lines were built (see Figure 3.11). The first underground railway in the world, the Metropolitan Line, was opened in the early 1860s to link Paddington with Farringdon Street and Moorgate (Olsen, 1976). The rail-ways reduced travelling time and enabled people to live farther away from their places of work than the omnibus had. They pushed out the suburban frontier and enabled towns to sprawl deeper into the surrounding country-side. At first, however, like the omnibuses, fares were expensive and put the railways, as a means of daily travel, well beyond the means of all but the well-paid. There is some dispute over the relative importance of the sub-urban railway as an instigator of suburban development. It is of course unwise to generalise from specific case studies as each town had its own peculiar problems and responded to these differently, but it has been demonstrated that, at least for certain London suburbs, railway extensions usually *followed* rather than preceded suburban development. At best they served to rein-force population movements already in progress (Dyos, 1966).

In the latter part of the nineteenth century attempts were made to reduce the cost of commuting, so that more people could live beyond walking

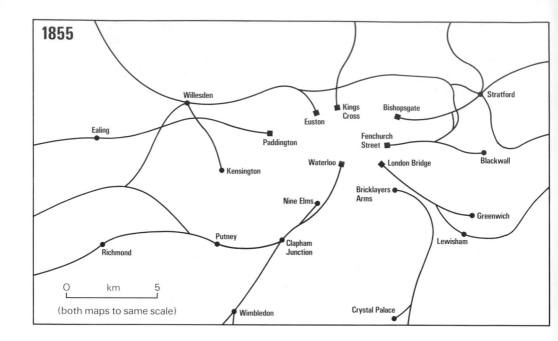

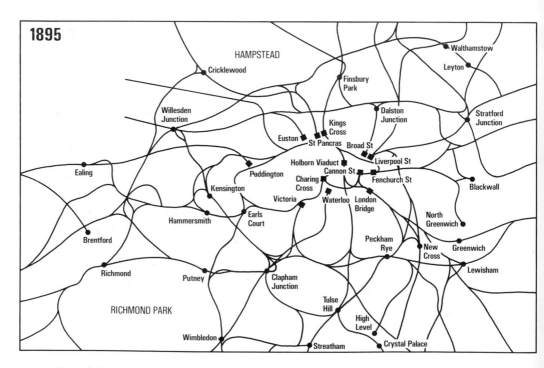

Figure 3.11  London railways, 1855 and 1895. (Source: Olsen, 1976)

distance from their work places. The horse-drawn tramways introduced in the late 1860s went some way towards achieving this. In Camberwell, for instance, a network of routes was operational by 1872 and the fares were only a fraction of the cost of comparable rail fares (Dyos, 1966). The inner suburbs became even more accessible to workers with the passing of the Cheap Trains Act in 1882, which compelled all railway companies to introduce workers' fares as and when required by the Board of Trade. This was seen as a means of alleviating the housing problem which persisted in the heart of the cities. It certainly encouraged the filling up of the inner suburbs, which underwent a process of invasion-succession or filtering. Houses formerly occupied by middle-class families were subdivided into multi-occupation tenements for working people (see page 119). The process is aptly described by a contemporary writer, Charles Booth, who wrote, 'North of Peckham Road [Camberwell] is a large district becoming steadily poorer as the fairly comfortable move south and immigrants from Walworth arrive' (Dyos, 1966). We shall see in Chapter 5 that this process of invasion-succession was later to be recognised as the fundamental means by which towns grow, exerting a considerable influence on the structure of towns (see page 123).

## 2. The effects of land ownership

The Victorian suburbs were not subject to positive planning constraints. The layout and morphology of an individual estate was influenced by a combination of factors such as its relative proximity and accessibility to the city centre, the characteristics of the site and its ownership prior to development. In general the more distant suburbs (which incurred higher commuting costs) attracted only the better off. Likewise an elevated, well-drained site with pleasant views could command high land prices and this also influenced the way in which it was developed (see page 122). Land which had formed part of an extensive estate before its development was often developed quite differently from land where ownership had been fragmented. Where land had been in multi-ownership, development was likely to be more haphazard and of higher density, whereas when land which had formed part of a large estate was released for building the ensuing development was often carefully controlled. Covenants and stipulations in the leases on such lands were imposed to control housing densities and influence building standards. This is well illustrated in the case of Oxton, a suburb of Birkenhead within easy commuting distance of central Liverpool, which was developed particularly rapidly in the 1840s. The land had previously formed part of the estate of the Earl of Shrewsbury, who controlled the character of its development in the manner described by a contemporary writer. 'Although the land has been greatly divided among small holders on building leases, the principal portion yet remains subject to restrictions on the style and character of the houses whereby a pleasing appearance will be preserved, and a guarantee offered for the future well condition of the township' (Mortimore, 1847). And so it proved to be.

ASSIGNMENTS
*Figure 3.12 is a section of Toxteth, Liverpool, as shown on the 1908 edition of the O.S. 1 : 2500 map.*
*(a) Describe the style and layout of the houses.*
*(b) Measure the density of housing per hectare and compare it with the housing density in Scotland Ward, Liverpool (Figure 3.9).*

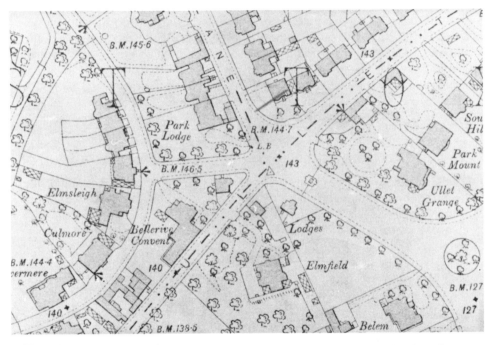

Figure 3.12 An extract from the 1908 edition of a 1 : 2500 OS map showing part of Toxteth, Liverpool.

# Key Ideas

*A. Pre-Industrial Towns*

1. The establishment of a new social and economic order in medieval times encouraged the growth of towns.
2. It is possible to distinguish unplanned or organic medieval towns from those which were planned or planted.

3. Not all of the planted medieval towns flourished. Some failed to grow at all, while others prospered for a time and then declined.
4. The Renaissance was characterised by attempts to impose order and symmetry on town planning and development, and a close relationship developed between landscape planning and town planning.
5. The Renaissance probably marks the pinnacle of achievement in town planning in Western Europe, as exemplified at Rome, London and Bath.
6. Most of the neo-Classical developments in British towns took the form of piecemeal extensions to existing towns.
7. Restrictions in land ownership sometimes resulted in developments of excessively high densities, and contrasts in the quality of housing were accentuated.

## B. The Consequences of Rapid Nineteenth-Century Urban Growth

1. The historical phenomenon of rapid urban growth has never been more dramatically represented than in nineteenth-century Britain.
2. Urbanisation changed fundamentally the pre-existing patterns of settlement. It was concentrated in particular areas in response to chance locations and the exploitation of resources and the development of industry and trade.
3. Urbanisation was partly a consequence of migration into the towns, a process which had appalling consequences for the migrants in terms of squalid housing conditions, gross overcrowding and a debilitating environment.
4. Measures to improve the quality of working-class housing were introduced only after a clear correlation had been demonstrated between bad housing conditions and the spread of disease. This encouraged the involvement of central government and legislation in the areas of housing, public health and education.
5. Improved housing standards and pressures on space led, however, to rising rents and evictions, making worse the problems of poorer sections of the community.
6. It rapidly became clear that housing subsidies were essential if local authorities were to provide housing for the most disadvantaged families.

## C. The Origins of the Garden City Movement

1. The new town movement has its base in nineteenth-century industrial philanthropy.
2. Certain fundamental principles of social equality and harmony guided the early movement and its creations.
3. Howard aimed to combine the most favourable aspects of town and country living in the Garden City.

## D. Residential Segregation

1. In early nineteenth-century Britain, the different social classes of the towns, though identifiable as separate groups, tended to live in relatively close proximity.
2. As urban transport facilities developed, the more well-to-do groups increasingly moved outwards (centrifugally), while incoming poorer social groups colonised the property which had been left (a centripetal movement).
3. Thus exclusive socially homogeneous neighbourhoods developed, where levels of rent and costs of commuting provided selecting mechanisms.
4. Factors influencing 'exclusiveness' included social distance (as well as distance on the ground) and physical aspects of site (well-drained, commanding situation, etc.).
5. Land ownership before development frequently exerted a significant influence on the type of development which occurred, i.e. the density and quality of housing.

# 4 The Evolution of Urban Planning and Housing Policies

House building all but ceased during the First World War and consequently the housing problem was exacerbated. After 1918 the demand for houses with gardens in suburban locations continued to increase as average wages rose and changes in family structure occurred (Strachan, 1974). (In general, there were more smaller families and therefore more housing units were required.) The introduction of more flexible forms of public transport such as electric trams from about 1900 and motorbus services from about 1918 made it increasingly possible for families to move to the suburbs on the edge of the towns.

## A. Suburban Sprawl and the Beginnings of Town Planning

### 1. Inter-war council estates

With the exception of the occupiers of certain working-class suburbs such as West Ham in London, which had been developed in the nineteenth century, only the better paid could afford a house in the suburbs. It was, however, becoming increasingly recognised that working-class families had housing aspirations similar to those of their middle-class counterparts and that the housing problems of the congested town centres could be solved successfully only if more of the working-class families moved to suburban estates. This was made possible by the Housing and Town Planning Act of 1919 which made provision for a state subsidy to be paid to local authorities towards the cost of slum clearance and municipal housing development (Liverpool Corporation, 1951). Up to that time all council house developments had been financed entirely by the local authorities themselves. The Act provided the necessary incentive for local authorities to become more involved. The Report of the Tudor Walters Committee on the Housing of the Working Classes, published in 1918, had advocated housing densities of only twelve houses per net acre (Burke, 1975), thus it was inevitable that much of the municipal housing development of the inter-war period would be in the form of low-density suburban estates (Figure 4.1). The development of council estates in the inter-war period added a new dimension to suburban growth

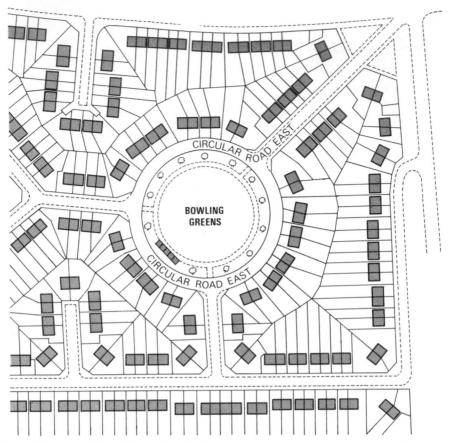

Figure 4.1   Part of Norris Green, Liverpool, a low-density suburban council estate built between the wars.

and helped to continue and accentuate the Victorian trend of keeping social groups apart.

The inter-war council estates were not without their problems. The sheer speed of development created its own problems. Thus the vast Norris Green Estate in Liverpool, housing over 25 000 people, was built up in four years (Williams, 1939). The lack of constructive planning meant that the estates were often developed without adequate provision of shops, schools, clinics and other essential services. The houses themselves tended to be a standard, three-bedroom type, which created particular difficulties as young families grew up and other changes occurred within the family cycle. When the houses became too small or too large for family requirements, there was no suitable alternative accommodation in the area. The position was improved very little by the Housing Act of 1936 which stipulated the number of houses of different sizes which were to be incorporated in the new estates, for 82% were still to be three-bedroom houses (Liverpool Corporation, 1951). The lack of local employment opportunities and increased length of journey to work also created problems for many of the families and probably contributed to the above average rates of unemployment on many of the estates during the Great Depression. Nevertheless, the spaciously laid out inter-war council estates did provide an environment vastly superior to much of the inner city. Many of the estates developed at that time remain some of the most successful attempts at large-scale public housing provision.

## 2. The need for planning

The inter-war period was a phase of unprecedented urban growth. Much private building, in particular, sprawled along main roads leading from the towns in the form of ribbon development, putting the agricultural land between the roads under considerable pressure. The urban frontier penetrated deeper and deeper into the surrounding countryside and it became increasingly recognised that it was necessary to introduce planning controls to contain urban growth. The 1930 Housing Act aimed at limiting suburban growth by attempting to encourage the more intensive development of the inner areas of cities while a Ministry Circular of 1933 required all local authorities to submit programmes of slum clearance. Much of the inter-war redevelopment was, however, unimaginative. Massive four-storey and five-storey blocks of flats were often built with little awareness of their environmental context. Nevertheless even the most intensive redevelopment schemes left a surplus of population to be rehoused in the suburbs. Planning legislation was necessary if town growth was to be contained. There had been certain early legislation such as the Housing, Town Planning, etc. Act of 1909 which tried to regularise suburban development, but it was during the inter-war period that the foundations for later comprehensive planning legislation were laid. The 1932 Town and Country Planning Act proved largely ineffectual because local authorities were put under no obligation to prepare town planning schemes. A similar fate befell the Restriction of Ribbon Development Act of 1935 which attempted to restrict urban sprawl along main routes, and the Green Belt (London and Home Counties) Act of 1938 which tried to curtail London's growth. Nevertheless an attempt to control development within the urban system had been made, if somewhat belatedly. The extremely low-density inter-war suburban development which consumed so much space was, at least in part, responsible for some of the less desirable later developments.

Inter-war planning legislation was largely ineffectual because it tried to grapple with particular problems that arose within the urban system rather than to treat the system as a whole. The first comprehensive piece of planning legislation was the Town and Country Planning Act of 1947 which put all local authorities in England and Wales under a statutory obligation to prepare Development Plans and submit these to the appropriate Minister for approval or amendment (Strachan, 1974). The Development Plans were to state the general use to which each plot of land and building was to be put. The Act aimed at controlling future development by requiring each potential developer to submit detailed plans of his proposals for consideration by a Planning Committee. Local authorities could thus refuse applications for what were considered to be undesirable proposals. Previously they could do this only by purchasing the land on which the proposal was planned. The 1947 Act provided the legislative framework for the development of an effective planning system in Britain, which uses development control as its main weapon.

ASSIGNMENTS
1. *Compare the map extract of part of the Norris Green estate (see Figure 4.1) with that of Scotland Ward (Figure 3.9), Liverpool, in 1908. Describe differences in house types and layouts; the pattern of streets; landscape planning and housing densities.*
2. *Outline the advantages and disadvantages of suburban estate development compared with inner city redevelopment.*
3. *Why was it necessary to introduce planning legislation in the 1930s? How effective was it?*

## 3. New town planning

Another piece of far-reaching planning legislation which had a major impact on urban development in post-war Britain was the 1946 New Towns Act. You have already seen how the development of new towns in Britain has its roots in the Garden City Movement. The Marley Committee was appointed in 1935 to consider if the provision of Garden Cities and satellite towns could be extended and the Committee advocated the 'fullest adoption' of new towns as an alternative to the suburban sprawl and ribbon development so characteristic of the inter-war period. No action was taken because of the Second World War, but in 1944 Abercrombie's Greater London Plan proposed a constraining Green Belt around London and the establishment of 10 new towns each 30 to 50 kilometres from central London (Abercrombie, 1945). The first generation of new towns were designated between 1946 and 1949 and incorporated many of the principles which had been advocated by Ebenezer Howard at the beginning of the century. The principal planning concepts which the first generation of New Town Development Corporations aimed to achieve can be summarised as follows.

*(a) The towns should grow rapidly to an optimum or ideal size from a small initial base population*

Hence there must be controls on the size of the settlement, but paradoxically in the early years there must be incentives for people to move there. The New Towns Committee in 1946 was not dogmatic about the optimum size of new towns but suggested from 20 000 to 60 000 people. The Committee considered that constraints to size included: (i) the need for dwellings to be within walking or cycling distance of work; (ii) that contact with countryside was essential for the whole community; (iii) that it was difficult to attain a sense of civic consciousness in very large towns; and (iv) that smaller units could be built more quickly.

During the period up to the early 1950s the concept of small, dispersed, concentrically planned towns isolated by Green Belts became a familiar and popular one. However, by 1955 projections of future population growth indicated a need for larger units, and increasing car ownership cast doubts on the scale of distance which was needed for settlements to be independent. Despite this the new town lobby, led by the writings of F.J. Osborn, continued to be favoured. His basic tenets were two-fold (although the number and size of towns varied between 1918 and 1946, the dates when his book *New Towns after the War* was first printed and reissued). Osborn argued that (i) a town should be large enough for efficient industrial organisation and full social activity but no larger, and (ii) the whole of the land both urban and rural should be owned and administered in the interest of the community (Osborn, 1918). Populations of around 40 000 and areas of 2000 acres were envisaged. This philosophy was coupled to Howard's ideas that:

*(b) The towns should be comprehensively planned by a development agency*

Under the 1946 Act the Minister for Town and Country Planning could designate the site of a proposed new town and establish a development corporation to implement the proposal. Under the Act the development corporations have the powers to: 'acquire, hold, manage and dispose of land and other property, to carry out building and other operations, to provide water, electricity, gas, sewerage and other services, to carry on any business or undertaking in or for the purposes of the New Town, and generally to do anything necessary or expedient for the purposes of the New Town'. A third principle was that:

*(c) The town should be spatially separate from the parent city and be built on land which has been acquired at lower cost than has that at the periphery of the built-up area*

Land values decrease with distance from the city centre and eventually level off where land is in agricultural use. This means that land some distance from the edge of the built-up area is cheaper than land adjacent to the built-up area. The First Garden City Co. Ltd. was able to purchase land at a distance of 56 kilometres from central London from fifteen different owners at an average cost of only £42 per acre.

Even today the development agency of a new town has the right to acquire land compulsorily at the price that would have applied if the new town did *not* exist. This is necessary because there will have been much public discussion of the plans for the new town and, without such provision, land prices in the designated area and surrounding area would rocket upwards in anticipation of the growth of the town.

### (d) A large proportion of the property in the town should remain in the ownership of a non-profit-making public body

Ebenezer Howard envisaged that all property in the town would be rented. In fact in new towns present building can be sold or let. Note that for the first two decades after the passing of the New Towns Act in 1946, only one in five dwellings in new towns could be sold for owner-occupation. But the current policy is to sell Development Corporation houses built for rent and to put new towns more in line with the national average of owner-occupation.

### (e) New towns should be self-contained

The adjective self-contained is taken to have three meanings:
(i)   Describing the physical form of the town. New towns were in part a reaction against inter-war ribbon development and other forms of suburban sprawl. Also their sites were chosen to avoid as far as possible high-quality agricultural land.
(ii)  Relating to the provision of facilities. Ideally the town should be self-contained for its requirements of shopping, schools, hospitals, entertainment, and so on.
(iii) Having a sociological definition. New towns were built some distance from overspill cities in the expectation of their residents becoming independent of their old home bases, and setting up new community groups.
Finally, it was intended that:

### (f) New towns should be socially balanced

They should have a range of age, income and social groups within them; a point made initially by Richardson over a century ago.

The conflicting aims of these principles – optimum size versus self-sufficiency, social balance versus full employment and the provision of some public housing – have led to a variety of practical problems which we shall consider in a later section (see pages 101 to 104).

*Select a new town which you can either visit or obtain information on and try to evaluate how far the planning concepts summarised in Section 3 have been implemented.*

## 4. Green Belt policy

Ebenezer Howard had advocated the need to contain the growth of large cities by restricting housing and other development on land adjacent to the built-up area and directing it to new planned settlements which would be located beyond this fringe of conserved countryside. Howard's ideas were developed subsequently by Raymond Unwin and Patrick Abercrombie. Unwin, in 1929, argued that a narrow girdle of undeveloped land should surround Greater London and form a Green Belt of recreational space, while Abercrombie, in his 1944 Greater London Plan, advocated the need to establish a Green Belt of between 8 and 15 kilometres wide around the built-up area. The function of Abercrombie's Green Belt ring was 'to provide primarily for recreation and fresh food for the Londoner, and prevent further continuous suburban outward growth' (Abercrombie, 1945).

In the post-war period, the establishment and maintenance of a Metro-politan Green Belt around Greater London has been a key planning objective. The function of the Green Belt was outlined in a Ministry Circular of 1955 (MHLG Circular 42/1955) which stated that Green Belts were intended to
(a) check the growth of the urban area,
(b) prevent the coalescence of neighbouring towns,
(c) preserve the special character of a town.
The function of Green Belts has remained unaltered since then, although a recent Department of Environment (DoE) Circular also recognises that a Green Belt policy, strictly implemented, can help to direct development from edge-of-town to inner-city locations (DoE Circular 14/84).

The function of the Green Belt is thus seen purely as a means of containing urban growth by restricting development land immediately be-yond the built-up area. Green Belt policies have not advocated how this undeveloped land should be used. In practice a significant proportion of land surrounding the Metropolitan Green Belt has become under-used and, in some cases, semi-derelict, and attempts have been made to introduce land management measures in an attempt to counteract this trend (Munton, 1988): see Plate 4.1 and page 320.

*Why are countryside management measures necessary in London's Green Belt? Plate 4.1 illustrates two such measures. What others might be used to reduce conflict between the different users?*

Plate 4.1  Countryside management measures in London's Green Belt introduced by the Hertfordshire and Barnet Countryside Management Service.

(a) Reclaimed road chippings are laid over the polythene sheeting to provide a free draining surface for horses and walkers. (b) Erecting an orientation board for walkers using the Ver-Colne Way, a medium-distant route. (Photographs: Hertfordshire and Barnet Countryside Management Service)

## B. Post-War Housing Policies

## 1. Slum clearance and overspill

In the immediate post-war period, Britain's major cities faced housing problems of gargantuan proportions. Many, such as the East End of London and Liverpool, had suffered serious war damage. There had been very little house building during and immediately after the war and the housing stock had deteriorated markedly with the number of unfit dwellings increasing at an alarming rate. Solutions to the housing crisis were sought in massive slum clearance and council house building programmes. In the 1950s, inner city redevelopment was typified by low-rise flats, most commonly five storeys high and with balcony access (see Plate 4.2). Developments in building technology, in particular tower cranes and concrete technology, made high-rise flats feasible from the late 1950s and these were encouraged by the 1956 Housing Act through which central government paid local authorities increased subsidies if they built high-rise flats as opposed to conventional housing.

At the same time very large council housing estates were developed on the edge of the built-up area. The housing estates were built quickly and incorporated experimental housing which used new building techniques and

Plate 4.2   Five-storey, balcony-access flats in Liverpool's inner city. Large blocks similar to this were built between about 1930 and 1955 until being replaced by notorious tower blocks. (Author's photograph)

materials. Shortages of building land and rising land prices encouraged high-density development, and the semi-detached houses with front and rear gardens that typified the inter-war housing estates gave way to maisonettes and, from the late 1950s, high-rise flats. Open spaces were included but they tended to be communal and sometimes suffered from neglect. In some cases, blocks of flats were linked by aerial walkways which were difficult, if not impossible, to police and attracted high levels of vandalism. These vast suburban estates provided little other than housing and lacked the balance of functions which the new towns aimed to provide.

Families which could not be housed in either redeveloped areas in the inner city or the suburban housing estates may have found accommodation in one of the designated new towns or in one of the 'expanded towns' which were designated under the 1952 Town Development Act. The expanded towns provided houses and jobs for the overspill families and, in return, received financial help from central government and a housing subsidy paid over a number of years by the city from which the family had moved (Liverpool Corporation, 1967). Some of the expanded towns were situated far away from the cities from which they received overspill families. For example, Liverpool had an arrangement with Burnley, in north-east Lancashire, while Huntingdon, in Cambridgeshire, received families from inner London boroughs.

Even with the introduction of overspill policies, the housing problem

95

Figure 4.2   Carla Ostrer's satirical comment on the lack of consultation that occurred in the 1960s between the architects who designed the high-rise flats and the families who occupied them (Source: *The Guardian*, 22 June 1984)

remained because slums were created as quickly as they were cleared. Surveys conducted in the mid 1960s into housing conditions in Liverpool and Manchester revealed that approximately 40% of the total housing stock in each city was unfit for habitation (Manchester Corporation, 1970; Liverpool Corporation, 1970). It was information such as this that encouraged the local authorities to make even more stringent efforts to get to grips with their housing problems. Slum clearance programmes were stepped up so that in the late 1960s many thousands of houses were being demolished each year in Britain's industrial cities.

The 'Utopian' solutions to the post-war housing crisis were conceived by experts, including architects and planners, with little or no attempt being made to find out what sort of accommodation the families being rehoused would have preferred (see Figure 4.2). It is hardly surprising, therefore, that many of the attempts made in the 1950s and 1960s to grapple with the problems of a housing shortage and a deteriorating housing stock now stand condemned. The vast suburban council estates have been singled out for particular criticism and a number of recent studies have revealed that, in many respects, those who live on one of these estates face even more intractable problems than inner city dwellers. One such comparative study looked at four 'outer estates' in Britain: Kirby on Merseyside; Easterhouse in Glasgow; East Middlesbrough and Orchard Park in Hull, and concluded that these have become Britain's 'forgotten areas of deprivation' with unemployment rates at three times the national average and 70% of the households on housing benefit (CES Ltd, 1985). The sheer size of the estates is in itself a problem. Some contain up to 50 000 people. They are essentially one-class estates with virtually all land and property in public sector ownership. Typically, they are situated several kilometres from the centres of the towns which spawned them and their relative remoteness

Plate 4.3   Ronan Point. In 1968 a gas cooker exploded in one of the flats, causing the entire south-east corner of this 23-storey block to collapse, killing several people. The structural weakness of this sort of system building was demonstrated and there was great public outcry, particularly as these were council flats in Canning Town, London. The future of high-rise blocks then under construction began to be seriously questioned and councils subsequently abandoned this solution to housing shortage problems. (Photograph: Keystone Press)

means that the estate dwellers are often faced with long and costly journeys to shop, to work, and, for example, to receive specialised medical treatment. The situation is exacerbated because 70% of these households do not have access to a car.

Another feature of late 1950s and 1960s public sector housing development was the construction of systems-built high-rise flats. These went out of favour after the Ronan Point disaster in 1968, when a 23-storey tower block in Newham partially collapsed after a gas explosion, killing five people (Plate 4.3). The accident occurred within only one month of the block being officially opened. Ronan Point was only the beginning of a problem which has reached catastrophic proportions. In some of the blocks, vandalism proved to be such a problem that they became virtually unmanageable. Two such blocks in Birkenhead were built in the 1950s and demolished twenty years later; while two other notorious blocks in the Everton district of Liverpool became known as the 'piggeries' and were virtually given to a private developer in 1978 (see Plate 4.4). The experimental nature of the design and construction of many of the blocks has also subsequently created enormous problems for the local authorities which built them and many have had to spend vast sums on essential structural repairs. For example, in October 1984, an official report confirmed that all nine towers in the Ronan Point group were unsafe and should be evacuated.

Alice Coleman in her research study of the design and layout of post-war council estates is particularly condemnatory.

Plate 4.4   The demolition of Oak and Eldon Gardens, Birkenhead. These massive double tower blocks were built in the late 1950s and demolished on 30 September 1979. (Photograph: Liverpool Daily Post and Echo)

*Why should Utopia have been such an all-pervading failure, when it was envisaged as a form of national salvation? It was conceived in compassion but has been born and bred in authoritarianism, profligacy and frustration. It aimed to liberate people from the slums but has come to represent an even worse form of bondage. It aspired to beautify the urban environment, but has been transmogrified into the epitome of ugliness (**Coleman, 1985**).*

## 2. The rehabilitation of older property

In the late 1960s, housing policies moved away from an emphasis on slum clearance and overspill to policies which encouraged the rehabilitation of older property and, following from that, the retention of existing communities. The policy change can be traced back to the 1969 Housing Act which increased the level of grant aid available to the owners of older property for renovating and modernising their houses. Under the Act, in Development Areas, grants paid to house owners for improvements to their properties increased to 75% of the total costs incurred and at the same time the scope of the grants was increased to cover inter-war property. In addition local authorities were empowered to create General Improvement Areas (GIAs) in districts of older property and, within these, house owners were obliged to make improvements to their property, while the local authority undertook to enhance the urban environment by measures such as landscaping and pedestrianisation. As a result of the 1969 Act local authorities reappraised their housing stocks and many houses which previously had been designated for demolition under slum clearance programmes were reprieved and rehabilitated instead (Plate 4.5). This radical change in policy which occurred in the late 1960s was brought about by a number of interdependent factors which included:

(a) A realisation of the effects of overspill policies on inner city areas. In the period 1961–71 the populations of nearly all Britain's largest cities declined substantially. For example Greater London's population fell from 7 997 234 to 7 452 346; Liverpool's from 745 750 to 610 113 and Manchester's from 662 030 to 543 868. The population loss continued in the succeeding decade, with all British cities over 250 000, with the exception of Plymouth, losing population. The population losses in the conurbations continued to be acute with Glasgow losing 22% of its population and Liverpool and Manchester 16.4% and 17.5% respectively (Champion, Coombes & Openshaw, 1983). In addition, many jobs in manufacturing industry were also lost as the manufacturers followed, or even preceded, the overspill families to the new and expanded towns. Thus the overspill policies were a major contributory factor to the malaise of the inner city.

(b) Demographic changes meant that, after a period of continuous post-war

Plate 4.5 King Street in Southsea, Portsmouth, which is part of both a General Improvement Area and a Conservation Area. The houses have been rehabilitated with the help of improvement grants while the City Council has greatly improved the appearance of the street. (Photograph: Portsmouth City Council)

growth, the population stabilised in the mid 1970s to reach a situation of zero growth by 1976. Thus many overspill schemes and new town development projects which had been designed in the 1950s or early 1960s to take account of projected continuing increases in Britain's population were based on false assumptions.

(c) There was a growing awareness that the massive slum clearance programmes carried out in the 1960s had destroyed not only unfit dwellings but also working-class communities which had developed over a number of generations. It was also evident that a comparable sense of community could not be replicated in a new housing estate and that many families which had been rehoused felt alienated by their new surroundings.

(d) Since the late 1960s, there has been a re-evaluation of the quality of much Victorian vernacular architecture and the terraced houses built originally for the artisan classes have become desirable residences.

The 1974 Housing Act gave further encouragement to the rehabilitation of older property. Under this Act, local authorities were encouraged to design-

100

ate Housing Action Areas (HAAs), districts of around 300–400 houses which were comprehensively redeveloped and environmentally enhanced with the aid of government grants. At the same time, Comprehensive Community Programmes (CCPs) were established in inner city areas in which integrated programmes were introduced to deal with a whole battery of social, economic and environmental problems within a set time-scale.

ASSIGNMENTS
1. *What point is Carla Ostrer trying to make through her cartoon (Figure 4.2)?*
2. *Find out from your district planning department if the town nearest to you has any general improvement areas and, if so, where they are located. Visit one of these and look for evidence of house improvements, such as new roofs, double glazing, rendering, etc. Look out for evidence of environmental enhancement in the form of tree planting, improved street furniture and floorscapes; traffic management schemes, etc.*

## C. An Evaluation of the New Town Movement in Britain

Sufficient time has elapsed since the passing of the 1946 New Towns Act for an attempt to be made to evaluate how successful new towns have been and how far they have departed from the planning and development concepts originally envisaged by Ebenezer Howard and later enshrined in the 1946 Act. The first generation of new towns most closely incorporated at least some of Howard's ideals. Between 1946 and 1949, eight new towns were designated for the Greater London area: Stevenage, Crawley, Hemel Hempstead, Harlow, Hatfield, Welwyn, Basildon and Bracknell. The Development Corporation plans for these towns have been completed and the Development Corporations have been dissolved, the last, Basildon, in 1985. Without exception, this first generation of new towns grew from relatively small population bases, varying from 4500 in the case of Harlow to 25 000 in the case of Basildon. By 1985, only Basildon (with a population of 103 000) had grown to over 100 000, the population of the others varying from 25 200 (Hatfield) to 78 000 (Harlow) (Potter, 1985).

The growth patterns of the new towns designated in the late 1960s have been very different. A number of the towns already had substantial populations when they were designated as new towns. For example, Northampton increased its population from 133 000 to 168 000 between 1968, its date of designation, and 1985; while Warrington grew from 122 300 to 142 000 in the same period and Peterborough from 81 000 in 1967 to 128 125 in 1985. The reason why many of the later designated new towns were grafted on to towns which had already attained relatively large populations was a recognition of the problems which arose when people moved to new towns before

101

the shops and health, leisure and other services could be provided. In the first generation of new towns there was often a time lag of many years between the first families being housed and, for example, a hospital or a cinema being built. By grafting a new town on to an existing town, the newcomers could use the shopping centre and other facilities which were already there and which could be gradually increased as the population grew.

Many of the new towns designated in the 1960s were set very high target populations. For example, it was envisaged that Milton Keynes would eventually attain a population in excess of 250 000 and the Central Lancashire New Town, which was based on Preston, Chorley, Leyland, would reach half a million. These high target figures were set in response to population projections made in the early 1950s which envisaged continuing steady growth of Britain's population. In the event, new birth control methods brought about a rapid decline in the birth rate in the 1960s and the high target populations were subsequently considerably reduced. In fact Central Lancashire's target population was later set at 260 000, only 25 500 above its 1970 population when it was designated as a new town. With the slowing down of the national population growth rate to zero, no new towns have been designated since 1970, nor are they likely to be in the foreseeable future.

Not all Britain's new towns were designated in response to the pressures of metropolitan growth. For example, Corby was designated a new town in 1950, so that steel works could be developed which could tap the local resource of low-grade Jurassic iron ore. Hardly surprisingly, the town became very largely a one-industry town and suffered greatly when the steel works closed in the early 1980s, although since then various government-inspired initiatives have helped to pull the town's economy round. A number of new towns, such as Peterlee and Washington in the north-east, were designated in an attempt to revitalise depressed regions, while Newtown in Mid Wales, with a target population of only 10 000, was designated a new town in an attempt to reverse population out-migration from that region. Milton Keynes has developed in a part of England which lacked a major regional and shopping centre and has gone some way to meeting this need since its designation in 1967 (see Plate 4.6).

The internal characteristics of new towns have also changed over time. The first generation of new towns were planned on a neighbourhood principle and strenuous attempts were made to try to ensure that each neighbourhood was socially mixed and reflected the class structure of Britain as a whole. This often proved difficult as, in many of the new towns, the extremes of the social spectrum, that is the professional and managerial classes on the one hand and the unskilled manual workers on the other were under-represented, while the skilled and semi-skilled manual workers tended to be relatively over-represented. Attempts at social engineering by, for

102

Plate 4.6  Milton Keynes shopping centre, a vast shopping mall surrounded by extensive free parking spaces, has been very successful and now attracts shoppers from a wide area. (Photograph: The Creative Company, Milton Keynes Development Corporation)

example, implementing policies aimed at creating neighbourhoods which were socially heterogeneous have not always met with success and, gradually, certain neighbourhoods have been perceived by the town's inhabitants as being more prestigious than others. Thus, some of the later new towns, such as Milton Keynes, partly abandoned neighbourhood planning principles, adopting instead a cellular structure and tacitly accepting the reality of social zoning.

The balance of ownership in new towns has also shifted dramatically during the 1980s. Public investment has been substantially reduced but has been replaced by increased private investment. For example, between 1983 and 1985, the proportion of private investment in Britain's new towns increased from 52% to 65%. This shift from public to private investment was most marked in the house building sector in which private house building increased from 52% to 67% and that in the public sector decreased from 40% to 14%. The switch in the balance of housing tenure was further increased by the sale of over 34 000 council and development corporation rented houses in new towns between 1981 and 1985.

By the mid 1980s, Britain's new towns contained about 2.1 million people and provided nearly 900 000 jobs. Although some, such as Glenrothes in Scotland and Runcorn on Merseyside, have unemployment rates persistently above the national average, many of Britain's new towns continue to act as growth poles, attracting new investment, including considerable overseas investment, and expanding employment opportunities. A number of Howard's original planning and development concepts may have been modified or, in some cases, abandoned but, nevertheless, a case can be made for the relative success of the new town movement in post-war Britain.

## D. Housing Policies since 1979 and their Effects

The main aims of post-1979 housing policies can be summarised as follows:

## 1. An extension of home ownership

In the post-war period, there has been a political consensus over the desirability of increasing levels of home ownership, and the proportion of owner-occupiers increased steadily up to 1979. Since then, successive Conservative governments, under Mrs Thatcher, have accelerated this trend by extending opportunities for home ownership to lower-income groups. One way in which this has been achieved is through the 'right to buy' clause introduced in the 1980 Housing Act. This gave all council house and flat occupiers of more than three years standing the right to buy their homes and, under the legislation, local authorities were required to notify all their tenants of this right. The houses were offered at prices below the assessed market value, with discounts varying from 33% after three years tenancy to 50% for those who had lived in their council homes for more than 20 years.

These discounts are forfeited, at least in part, if the new owners sell the property within five years of purchase. The Housing and Building Control Act of 1984 reduced the qualification period from three years to two and increased the maximum discount to 68% after 30 years of tenancy (Roberts, 1984).

The 1980 Housing Act also encourages local authorities to sell tenement blocks or groups of houses to tenants forming community ownership co-operatives. This has been done in Glasgow where tenants have grouped together to buy a block of properties with finance provided through a building society mortgage. The co-operative pays back the mortgage by levying a rent from all its members and, when a property becomes vacant, it is allocated to a new co-operative member, who continues to pay the rent. The new owners take on responsibility for managing and maintaining their properties (Edgington, 1984).

The 1984 Housing and Building Control Act also introduced the concept of shared ownership, whereby it is possible for someone to buy a 50% stake in a property. This idea has also been extended to new 'starter homes' built by private developers in partnership with a local authority. Under such schemes those on council waiting lists or those who are council tenants can pay what they can afford on a mortgage and the rest in rent. Such encouragements to home ownership have increased considerably the proportion of owner-occupiers so that by 1987 approximately 66% of all homes in Britain were privately owned.

## 2. The targeting of home improvement grants

The commitment to the rehabilitation of older property has remained intact, although the amount of money available from year to year has varied markedly, with expenditure on grant aid reaching record levels in 1984. The most significant change has been to try to ensure that grants are targeted to those most in need; so that on a means-tested basis, mandatory grants of up to 90% of the cost and up to a maximum of about £10 000 per house are available where a house is lacking a basic amenity or where a notice has been served by the local authority. A 1985 Green Paper, *Home Improvement: a New Approach*, suggested other forms of loan including discretionary equity sharing loans whereby a local authority, in return for financing improvement work, would have a share in the enhanced value of the property when it was sold. At the time of writing, however, these grants have not been introduced.

## 3. A reduction in council house building

In the post-war period, successive governments, both Conservative and Labour, have been committed to extensive programmes of council house building, the number of council dwelling completions reaching a peak of over 180 000 in 1968. The Conservative administrations, under Mrs Thatcher, have queried to what extent the state and local authorities are the appropriate agents for building and managing houses. They have seen, instead, a more residual role for public sector housing providing accommodation for those who cannot afford, even under more favourable arrangements, to buy their own homes. In the period from 1979 to 1983 housing took the brunt of public expenditure cuts. During this period, central government spending on housing was cut by 50%, and the number of house completions by the local authorities fell by 57.3% (Malpass, 1986). Some critics have seen this policy as inevitably leading to a downgrading of the status of local authority housing; Forest & Williams (1984) suggested that 'we are moving towards a situation where state housing will become stigmatised welfare housing'.

The 1988 Housing Act will further reduce the number of council houses by permitting council-house dwellers to choose their own landlords. It is expected that one of the outcomes of the Act will be a significant transfer of council houses to Housing Association ownership and control.

## 4. Measures to reverse the decline of the private rented housing sector

In 1918, 90% of Britain's households rented from private landlords. With the inter-war and post-war increase in local authority housing and owner-occupation, the private rented sector has dwindled in importance. Legislation to control rents and provide security of tenure to tenants through obligatory lease agreements have made it less attractive for people to invest in the private rented sector. It is argued, however, that private rented accommodation is important for certain groups in society such as students, young people working away from home and the elderly who choose to live in sheltered accommodation. The 1980 Housing Act tried to reverse the trend of a diminishing private rented housing sector by introducing short-hold tenancies, making it possible for landlords to rent their accommodation for periods of one year or longer. More recently rent controls in the private rented housing sector have come under scrutiny and there are proposals to ease these in an attempt to increase the number of houses and flats available for rent in the private sector.

## 5. Some undesirable outcomes of housing policies

Owner-occupation in the UK now stands at about 66% of all households and it has been extended to include categories which previously would not have aspired to home ownership. One of the effects of this has been to increase significantly the number of people who fail to meet mortgage repayments. In the first six months of 1987 a record number of home owners faced eviction and 11 700 homes were repossessed. This compares with a total of 2500 for the whole of 1979. Furthermore, in October 1987, an estimated 50 000 people were more than six months behind with their mortgage repayments (Hughes, 1987). The reduction in the number of council houses and flats, arising from a combination of the sale of council houses and a great reduction in the number of new houses being built by local authorities, has contributed to an increase in council house waiting lists and the number of homeless people (see Plate 4.7). Between 1982 and 1987 there was a 47% increase in homelessness in the UK while the number of homeless in London nearly doubled (Bramley & Price, 1987). Where local authorities have a legal obligation to provide accommodation for homeless families with children, a number have had to use private hotels which often prove to be an expensive and unsatisfactory solution to their housing problem.

Plate 4.7   One of London's homeless sleeping rough by the Embankment underground station. The number of homeless in London nearly doubled between 1982 and 1987. (Photograph: Reflex Picture Agency/Andrew Moore)

It can be argued that the government's emphasis on free market forces in the housing sector has contributed to an increase in regional differences in house prices. There have been marked regional differences in house prices in the UK for some time but, until recently, the gap between house prices in different parts of the country had been fairly static. For example, between 1970 and 1984, the annual average rise in house prices was between 12.8% and 14.4% in every region. Since then, however, differentials have been widening rapidly. Prices in Greater London rose 22.9% during 1987, while, for the same year, the East Anglia region recorded the highest increase of 30.4%. The lowest house price rises occurred in Northern Ireland (0.4%), Scotland (5.6%) and the North region of England (7.1%). It is significant that these regions are the most peripheral to the south-east core (see Figure 4.3).

The widening regional divide in house prices has serious implications for the mobility of labour. As recently as 1982 the average price of a house in Yorkshire and Humberside was 65% of that in Greater London, but since then the differential has increased sharply so that, in 1988, the average house price in Yorkshire and Humberside had fallen to only 36% of that in Greater London (Counsell, 1988). The differential in house prices not only makes it almost impossible for people living in modest accommodation in the north to contemplate moving to jobs in southern England but it also acts as a deterrent to people moving north, if they fear that it will make it very difficult for them to return south in the future.

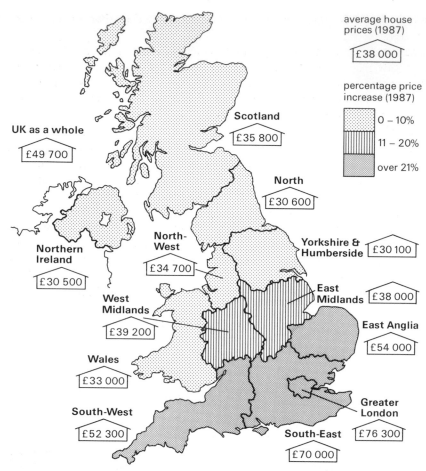

average house prices (1987)

£38 000

percentage price increase (1987)

| | |
|---|---|
| | 0 – 10% |
| | 11 – 20% |
| | over 21% |

Scotland £35 800

UK as a whole £49 700

North £30 600

North-West £34 700

Yorkshire & Humberside £30 100

Northern Ireland £30 500

West Midlands £39 200

East Midlands £38 000

East Anglia £54 000

Wales £33 000

Greater London £76 300

South-West £52 300

South-East £70 000

Figure 4.3   The average price of houses and the annual increase in house prices in the standard regions of the UK in 1987. (Source: Halifax Building Society)

## 6. The impact of housing policies on urban morphology

Housing policies pursued by successive governments have had a profound effect on the appearance of Britain's towns and cities. The Utopian solutions of the 1950s and 1960s have left a legacy of vast council estates and high-rise flats. Since then, new council building has been on a more human scale and, often, much more integrated with private sector housing. The development of Housing Associations since the mid 1970s has provided alternative forms of rented accommodation. The Housing Associations receive an annual grant from the government financed through the Housing Corporation and provide accommodation for such categories as the elderly and single-parent families. Many Housing Associations have a good record of rehabilitating older property, in particular large Victorian and Edwardian villas, close to town centres.

The availability of housing improvement grants for properties below a certain rateable value has also made its mark on the townscape. Most towns have a number of designated General Improvement Areas where environmental enhancement in the form of tree planting and better-quality street furniture and floorscapes is much in evidence.

The sale of council houses is also making an impact, particularly on estates where a significant proportion of former tenants have bought their houses. Many of the new owner-occupiers have wanted to confer a degree of individuality on their houses through, for example, installing new front doors, double glazed windows or by painting the exterior a different colour.

Changes are also occurring in the layout of the private housing estates. The semi-pedestrianised layouts of the 1960s and early 1970s have often been replaced by more interesting layouts which make use of curved roads and strategically placed high garden walls to interrupt a view. Floorscapes are far more varied with tarmacadam and grey concrete paving flags being replaced by materials of a variety of shapes, colours and textures. In general, the houses are no longer built in straight rows, but some are likely to be built at right angles to one another. The building styles may be

Plate 4.8   This new housing development in Brentwood, Essex, has been based on the so-called Essex Design Guide. This encourages developers to break away from the uniformity of house design and estate layout, and to include a variety of house styles which incorporate features of local vernacular architecture. The use of traditional building materials is encouraged, as are curved roads and floor surfaces of different textures and colours. The layout of buildings is designed to imitate a village form with some houses at right angles to the road. (Author's photograph)

imitative of vernacular architecture of a former age, such as mock tudor or neo-Georgian. Such layouts were first adopted in Essex, following what became known as the Essex Design Guide, but they have been copied elsewhere, partly in an attempt to recreate the interest and variety of an English village but also as a means of increasing housing densities in an acceptable fashion (see Plate 4.8).

## E. Understanding and Evaluating Housing Policies

Increasingly, geographers have come to appreciate that in order to analyse the processes which contribute to changes in urban morphology, some attention must be paid to the prevailing ideologies that underpinned the policies which influenced the nature of that change. Thus it is with housing. You have seen in both Chapters 3 and 4 how housing policies have been subjected to constant modification as contrasting political ideologies have been dominant. It is important to appreciate that ideologies cannot necessarily be equated with a single political party. For example, the liberal democratic pluralist model, which aims through rational discussion and consultation to arrive at consensus and develop policies which will benefit the majority, has, until relatively recently, been adopted by successive post-war governments, both Conservative and Labour. Furthermore, the Labour Party, which is sometimes referred to as a 'broad church', embraces a spectrum of political views and includes Fabians and neo-Marxists. Inevitably, the labels which are used to describe ideologies are inadequate and can be confusing. In the section which follows, housing policy is examined from the stand point of three contrasting ideologies, laissez-faire anti-collectivism, pluralism and neo-Marxism (Barratt Brown, 1984). This is by no means an exhaustive list but provides us with a useful framework to understand better the underlying rationale of housing policies.

## 1. Laissez-faire anti-collectivism

Since 1979, successive Conservative governments have adopted a laissez-faire approach, believing that housing is a commodity which can be met most effectively and efficiently by the private sector. Owner-occupation has been favoured because it encourages individualism and self-reliance and provides the maximum choice of housing for the majority. Policies have been pursued which have encouraged an extension of owner-occupation through subsidising the sale of council houses and flats and providing continued support, in the form of income tax relief, to mortgage holders. Council housing has been relegated to a more residual role, still necessary for those families who cannot afford to buy their own homes, but regarded as a less efficient means of providing housing. The so-called anti-collectivist New Right points to the bureaucracy which public sector housing inevitably generates, the frustrations which many council tenants experience when they try to get repairs done and the patronising paternalistic attitudes that public sector housing tends to encourage. It is their contention that owner-occupation provides the best value for money and greatest degree of householder satisfaction.

## 2. Neo-Marxism

Neo-Marxism takes a quite contrary view of attempts to extend home ownership. They are seen as a means of encumbering working-class families with debt in the form of a mortgage and thereby making them more pliant and less inclined to withdraw their labour. Neo-Marxism recognises that owner-occupation encourages individualism rather than collectivism and points out that the private housing sector is fuelled by competition with the participants competing unequally. It is inevitable that those with lower incomes and earning capacity will finish up with the poorest-quality housing.

Neo-Marxists envisage public sector housing dominating housing provision, contending that public sector housing can be allocated on the basis of need rather than ability to pay, particularly if rents are subsidised. Neo-Marxists have a particular antipathy to the private rented sector, contending that landlords can, and sometimes will, exploit their tenants through charging inflated rates and denying them security of tenure.

Neo-Marxists interpret reductions in public expenditure on housing and the sale of council houses as attacks on the welfare state. They are aware of the deficiencies of some public sector housing but claim that council housing has invariably been relegated to inferior sites and locations and that untested experimental building methods used in the 1960s by private sector construction companies have given council housing a bad name which is unjustified.

## 3. Pluralism

Pluralists take a more pragmatic view of housing policy and argue that housing policies must adjust to changing demand. People's expectations have increased and more people now aspire to home ownership. Housing policies should recognise this while at the same time making adequate provision for those families who will never be in a position to own their own homes. Pluralists point out that it was only with some reluctance that local authorities first became involved in providing housing for the least well off, when the private sector failed to provide them with suitable accommodation at rents which they could afford. Public housing is seen as a response to an identified housing need which the private sector is either unable or unwilling to meet.

Pluralists acknowledge that much of public sector housing that exists is not what families might have chosen had they been more involved in its design or choice of location. They consider the lack of consultation in the 1950s and 1960s between the local authorities who were providing housing and the families being rehoused as a root cause of some of the mistakes that were made at that time. They, therefore, favour greater public participation at the development stage and more responsive forms of housing management once the properties have been let.

Pluralists are not antipathetic to either the private or public housing sectors and consider that the totality of housing needs can best be met through mixed tenure with the balance between the public and private sectors changing as demand dictates.

ASSIGNMENTS

1. *It has been suggested that what is important about housing is not what it is but what it does to people's lives (Turner, 1976). What is Turner getting at? Do you agree with him and if so why?*
2. *What could be the attitude of laissez-faire anti-collectivists; neo-Marxists, and pluralists to the following housing policy issues? Give reasons to support your views.*
   *(a) The sale of council flats in a high-rise block.*
   *(b) Releasing local authority land for an estate of council houses.*
   *(c) A housing association's planning application to convert a large Victorian villa for sheltered housing for the elderly.*
   *(d) A house owner's application to convert her large property into student bedsits for rent.*
   *(e) A housing development financed jointly by a private house builder and a local authority to enable people on relatively low incomes to buy a stake in their house with the possibility of increasing it later.*

## Key Ideas

*A. Suburban Sprawl and the Beginnings of Town Planning*

1. In this century, demands for suburban living space have increased the pressure on rural areas around the towns.
2. Cheaper fares from the late nineteenth century have made it increasingly possible for less affluent people to commute, again increasing demands on suburban space.
3. Additional pressure has come from twentieth-century slum clearance programmes, moving less well-to-do groups out to suburban council estates.
4. Building of estates has not generally been accompanied by adequate planning for employment and social facilities.

5. Inter-war suburban development took place with a minimum of planning constraints and this resulted in much private development sprawling along roads out of the city centre, as ribbon development.
6. The consequences of these pressures have been an alarming increase in urban sprawl, towns becoming conurbations, and conurbations joining to form a megalopolis.
7. Since 1930 legislation has been introduced to limit suburban growth, leading to the establishment of Green Belts.
8. The designation of new towns under the 1945 Act was part of a strategy to control London's growth.
9. The early new towns aimed to incorporate the following key planning concepts:
   (a) rapid growth from a small initial population and settlement base,
   (b) comprehensively planned by a development agency,
   (c) spatially separate from the parent city,
   (d) built on land which could be compulsorily purchased at pre-development prices,
   (e) the development agencies became substantial land and property owners,
   (f) the new towns aimed to be self-contained physically, in the range of functions they provided and as free-standing communities,
   (g) the new towns aimed at a social balance which reflected that of the nation as a whole.
10. Green Belts were also designated to contain urban growth.
11. More recently Green Belts have also been seen as a means of deflecting some development from edge of town to inner city locations.

## B. Post-War Housing Policies

1. In the 1950s and 1960s solutions to the housing crisis were sought in massive slum clearance and council house building programmes.
2. Some overspill families were rehoused in new towns and expanded towns.
3. Many of the housing programmes of the 1950s and 1960s have created their own problems through the scale and nature of the housing developments and the lack of consultation that took place.
4. In the late 1960s housing policies changed to emphasise the rehabilitation of older property and the retention of existing communities.
5. This change of policy resulted from:
   (a) a rapid loss of population from inner city areas,
   (b) a slowing down of population growth nationally,
   (c) a realisation that communities had been destroyed which could not easily be re-created,
   (d) a re-evaluation of the value of Victorian artisan housing.

## C. An Evaluation of the New Town Movement in Britain

1. A number of later designated new towns were grafted on to existing towns.
2. Some of the later designated new towns had much larger target populations.
3. Some of the new towns were designated for reasons other than that of containing metropolitan growth.
4. The neighbourhood principles were diluted in the later designated new towns.
5. Since 1980, the balance of ownership has shifted in new towns from the public to the private sector.

## D. Housing Policies since 1979 and their Effects

1. The main thrusts of housing policy have been to:
   (a) extend home ownership,
   (b) target home improvement grants to those with low incomes,
   (c) reduce the volume of council house building,
   (d) reverse the decline of the number of houses in the private rented housing sector.
2. There have been some undesirable outcomes of a more market-orientated approach to housing including:
   (a) an increase in default in mortgage repayments and the number of homeless families,
   (b) a sharp increase in the differential between house prices in London and south and east England compared with other regions.
3. Housing policies have an effect on urban morphology including house design and street layout.

## E. Understanding and Evaluating Housing Policies

1. Increasingly geographers have come to appreciate that housing policies reflect prevailing political ideologies.
2. There are marked contrasts in housing policies advocated by those who adopt different political perspectives.

# 5 Urban Morphology

## A. Functional Zones

We have seen in Chapter 3 that until the nineteenth century urban growth in Britain was a relatively slow and gradual process. We have also observed that during the nineteenth century urbanisation rates increased dramatically. This rapid urban growth often coincided with the development in towns of factory industry which required a considerable workforce living near the factories. Transport innovations encouraged the expansion of towns. It became easier for people to move within towns, and for many to live farther from their places of work and from certain essential services which were available only in the town centre.

The pattern of urban growth was frequently influenced and sometimes constrained by natural barriers and both existing and new lines of communication. For example, land which was liable to flooding could not be built on and was, therefore, often preserved as open space. Similarly a very sharp break of slope may have restricted development, while land of contrasting physical qualities may have attracted different types of urban development. The expensive low-density residential area may require free-draining sites commanding attractive views, while heavy industry may favour extensive areas of flat land offering scope for future expansion. Canals and railway lines frequently exerted considerable influence on town growth, acting as barriers to movement so that different functions often developed on either side of them. More recently, the development of dual carriageways, inner ring roads and even urban motorways have all provided further constraints on town growth.

As a town grows, there is a tendency for different functions to occupy different areas within the town so that housing, industry or commercial activities become the dominant functions in different parts of the town. These broadly dissimilar *functional areas* or *zones* are readily recognisable. Residential areas can be distinguished from the town centre where commercial activities dominate, and from extensive industrial estates (see Figure 5.1). Sometimes, the barriers to development described in the previous paragraph also act as boundaries to the functional zones, in which case the

115

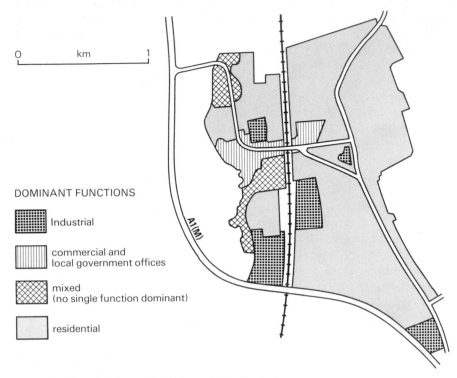

DOMINANT FUNCTIONS

Industrial

commercial and
local government offices

mixed
(no single function dominant)

residential

Figure 5.1   Functional zones in Biggleswade, Bedfordshire

zones may be quite discrete and easily distinguished. This is by no means
always the case, however, and careful mapping of building function may
have to precede any attempt to distinguish functional zones within a town.
Even then it might be discovered that in part of the town the types of
building are inextricably mixed, and it will not then be easy to designate
such areas with a single descriptive name.

Fieldwork and map work will also reveal that frequently within zones of
broadly similar function more subtle spatial contrasts can be discerned. For
example, an extensive residential area may contain a number of contrasting
districts based on ownership and housing age and quality. Thus council
housing estates are often physically separate from private housing estates,
and districts of high-density nineteenth-century terraces are readily distinguishable from those of low-density expensive modern housing. Similarly,
within a large town centre, where commercial activities dominate, it may be
possible to distinguish different sub-areas. Different specialist functions,
such as department and specialist stores, banks and insurance offices, and
places of entertainment, are dominant here. These functional contrasts are
often reflected in the arrangement and layout of the buildings and in the

street patterns. The large-scale Ordnance Survey map extracts which you used in Chapter 3 (see Figures 3.9, 3.12) clearly illustrate contrasts in the patterns of high-density nineteenth-century, as against low-density villa and inter-war, council residential areas.

The arrangement and layout of the buildings and the function or use of land and buildings in a town are collectively described as the town's *morphology*. The search for pattern and order in a town inevitably involves an attempt to distinguish clearly identifiable *morphological zones*. In order to gain some understanding of the spatial relationships that exist within the complexities of a town, we must use some form of simplification. The distinguishing of morphological or, at a simpler level, functional zones provides a useful starting point in this respect. Furthermore, the development of such zones results from a variety of processes and, if we are to understand how these processes operate, we must study their effects.

## B. Models of Urban Growth

The study of *urban structure* attempts to emphasise significant spatial relationships between the broad land use zones in a town. A number of descriptive models have been developed which summarise these. They seek to identify certain spatial characteristics which are common to all towns and provide some understanding of the processes which bring these about.

E. W. Burgess's concentric zone model is one of the earliest attempts to provide some insight into urban structure and this will be considered first (see Figure 5.2).

## 1. The concentric zone model

*(a) The model described*

The concentric nature of the rapidly growing nineteenth-century industrial towns was apparent to the keen observer even in the relatively early stages of their development. For example, Frederick Engels included the following description of Manchester in the 1840s in his *The Condition of the Working Class in England*.

> *Manchester contains, at its heart, a rather extended commercial district, perhaps half a mile long and about as broad consisting almost wholly of offices and warehouses. ... The district is cut through by certain main thoroughfares ... lined with brilliant shops ... unmixed working people's quarters stretch like a girdle, averaging a mile and a half in breadth, around the commercial district. Outside, beyond this girdle, lives the upper and middle bourgeoisie, the middle bourgeoisie in regularly laid out streets in*

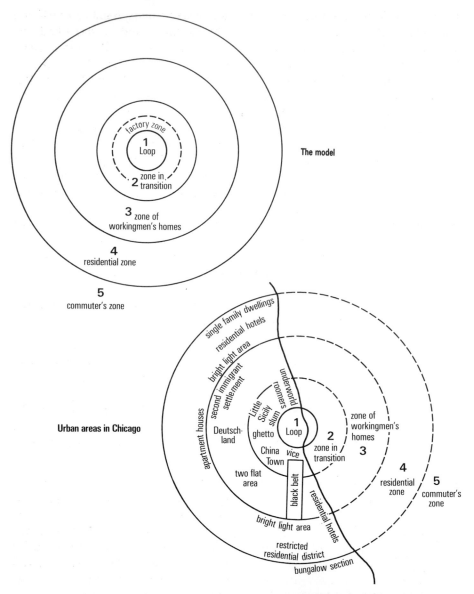

Figure 5.2   Burgess's concentric model of urban structure. (Source: original appeared in Park, Burgess & McKenzie, 1925)

*the vicinity of the working quarters ..., the upper bourgeoisie in remoter villas with gardens ...* (**Engels, 1969**).

It was, however, left to E. W. Burgess and his associates, who made comparable observations almost a century later (in the 1920s), to develop the concentric zone model. The model was based on empirical research in a number of American cities, particularly Chicago, and it described the concentric arrangement of functional zones within a city. Burgess claimed that although no one city that he studied perfectly exemplified the concentric zone model, all 'approximate in greater or lesser degree to this ideal construction' (Burgess, 1925). He acknowledged, however, that the model would probably not hold for all cities throughout the world.

In his search for a greater understanding of a complex urban system, Burgess adopted some of the fundamental concepts used by the plant ecologists (the ideas of competition, dominance, invasion, succession) in their study of plant associations. He envisaged that, within the city, people *competed* for limited space. Those who were best able to pay achieved the most desirable locations for their homes, and businesses. Those individuals and functions with the lowest level of economic competence had the least choice and were, therefore, left with the poorest locations. Burgess suggested that this process led to *functional zoning* and *residential segregation* within cities. In other words, within different areas of the city different single functions formed the *dominant* element.

Burgess observed that the zones are arranged concentrically around the city centre, and that each is distinctive in age and character.

(i) *Central business district (CBD)*. At the heart of the city is the central business district (CBD) which forms the commercial, social and cultural hub (see Chapter 7). The CBD is the most accessible part of the city, being at the focus of the urban transport network. Here are situated mainly offices, large departmental stores, specialist and variety goods shops as well as the main theatres, cinemas and best hotels. These activities can best afford to pay the high property values and rents required for such advantageous sites (see Plate 5.1).

(ii) *Zone in transition*. Surrounding the CBD there is a zone in transition or deterioration, where the land use is very mixed and is constantly changing. It is too inaccessible to be sought after by prosperous commercial enterprises, such as department stores, variety goods stores and large office blocks, but too near to the noise and grime of the city to provide sites for anything but the poorest residential buildings where the most deprived social groups live. It is an unwanted zone, often characterised by blight (i.e. decay) and abandonment, and probably contains retail services such as poor-quality cafés, vacant and derelict buildings and barren spaces where slums have recently been demolished. In addition, being a zone of change, it will probably include many large and formerly fine houses, often Georgian or Victorian, which are now used for other purposes. Some may have been renovated and divided into offices, others may now be occupied by light industries, while those which still serve as dwellings are likely to have degenerated into overcrowded slums (see Plate 5.2).

Plate 5.1 The central business district, Sheffield. The commercial core is the most intensively developed part of the urban system and contains many multi-storey buildings. (Photograph: Aerofilms)

Plate 5.3 High-density nineteenth-century housing in Burgess's zone of working men's houses. Note the juxtaposition of houses and heavy industry. (Author's photograph)

(iii) *Working-class zone.* The zone in transition is surrounded by a zone of working-class houses. This zone contains some of the older residential buildings in the city and, in particular, rows of Victorian terraced houses (see Plate 5.3). These originally housed families who moved from poorer-quality property in the zone in transition, but who were still compelled by travelling costs and rents to live near to their places of work.

(iv) *Middle-class zone.* Adjacent to this zone of working-class houses is what Burgess described as a zone of better residences, where the terrace has been replaced by semi-detached and detached houses of the middle class (see Plate 5.4). Some light industry will also probably be situated here, perhaps in industrial estates which have developed near the edge of the built-up area (although this was not integral to the original model).

(v) *Commuters' zone.* The Burgess model also recognises a rural–urban fringe zone, the commuters' zone, beyond the continuous built-up area. Dormitory suburbs have developed there and certain space-consuming but nonetheless essential urban functions are also situated there. These include

◄ Plate 5.2 The zone in transition is characterised by blight and neglect. Former prosperous residences have been subdivided to form small workshops and these are intermixed with warehouses, vacant and derelict sites and poor-quality housing. (Author's photographs)

Plate 5.4 Middle-class housing. The Burgess model envisages this sort of low-density housing development occurring in the outer suburbs. (Author's photograph)

public utilities, such as sewage disposal plants and refuse tips, and recreational facilities, such as golf courses. These urban functions will probably be interspersed with non-urban land use such as agricultural land and woodland (see Plate 5.5 and pages 316 to 322).

To summarise, Burgess envisaged that the lower-status groups are to be found near the city centre and the high-status groups at its periphery.

Burgess also acknowledged the likely occurrence of what his co-worker R. E. Park had described as *natural areas* within the broader zones. These are districts which are culturally distinct and are occupied by people of similar race, language and socio-economic status. For example, in his original model of the structure of Chicago, Burgess indicates a 'black belt', wedging out from the zone in transition (Figure 5.2). These 'natural areas' might be bounded by physical constraints such as topographical features or main lines of communication.

Burgess noted that his idealised concentric zones would be modified by *opposing factors*. These included such features as high ground, which might offer good views and provide a slightly more favourable micro-climate (including less winter fog), which would lead to the persistence of a high-class residential area within the inner zone. He also acknowledged that the distribution of heavy industry might act as a distorting factor on zoning. It is more likely to be concentrated in areas of poor-quality cheap land, such as on river floodplains or, as with portside industry, at points of break of bulk, rather than to be distributed in a concentric arrangement.

122

Plate 5.5 The commuters' zone or rural–urban fringe on the edge of Glasgow. Note how low-density housing development is interspersed with playing fields, a golf course and farmland. (Photograph: Aerofilms)

The Burgess model 'was also intended to serve as a mechanistic framework for urban growth and change' (Herbert, 1972). Burgess saw the mechanism of urban growth as similar to the ecological process of invasion and succession, by which population groups gradually filtered outwards from the centre as their status and level of assimilation improved. By this means, higher-status residential areas came to be occupied by lower-income groups and ethnic areas of one type were overtaken by people of a different ethnic stock. This invasion/succession process was also the mechanism by which residential areas were taken over by commercial and business undertakings, a process which can still be identified in contemporary British cities (see Figure 5.3).

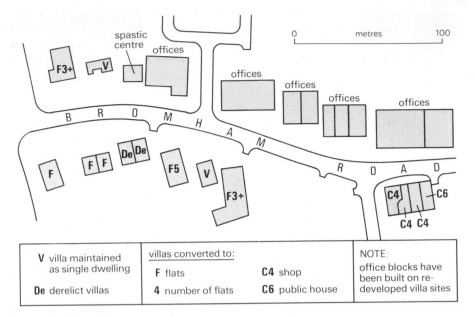

| V villa maintained as single dwelling | villas converted to: | | NOTE: |
|---|---|---|---|
| | F flats | C4 shop | office blocks have been built on re- |
| De derelict villas | 4 number of flats | C6 public house | developed villa sites |

Figure 5.3   Villa conversion and replacement, Bromham Road, Bedford. The process of invasion and succession envisaged by Burgess is in evidence on the edge of the CBD. Commercial functions are penetrating a district which until relatively recently was a residential one. (Source: based on an OS map. Crown Copyright Reserved)

## (b) Criticisms of the concentric zone model

Since E. W. Burgess first outlined his concentric zone model in the 1920s a number of criticisms have been levelled at it. These include the following.

(i)    The model considers ground floor functions only, and little attention is paid to the height of buildings and variations of function on. different floors.

(ii)   The model emphasises clear-cut boundaries between the concentric zones. These cannot, however, be justified by gradient studies which suggest no abrupt division between zones but rather that they merge gradually from one to another (see page 143). But if the gradients are as continuous as some research has demonstrated, this implies that zonal lines can be drawn at random at any radius from the centre.

(iii)  The concentric zones are displayed as distinctive ecological areas but field studies confirm that, where the zones can be identified, they lack homogeneity. In fact they display a significant degree of internal heterogeneity.

(iv)   The model pays scant attention to the distribution of industry. Burgess merely regards heavy industry as a distorting factor. It could be argued that in any model of urban structure, greater consideration should be given to the location of industry within the urban system.

(v)  In suggesting invasion/succession as the dominant process by which towns grow, Burgess was insufficiently aware of the *forces of inertia* that exist within a city. Some buildings simply do not lend themselves to conversion as readily as others. It is perhaps no accident that the process is often best observed in districts of decaying Georgian terraces or Victorian villas.

(vi)  Above all else, the model has been criticised because it is rooted in a specific historical and cultural context (i.e. the USA of the 1920s). It is limited 'to a particular situation, at a particular time in a particular country' (Carter, 1976), and this inevitably limits its universality. It can, therefore, be argued that it is most applicable to cities of the developed Western world but certain trends operating since the 1920s make the model less appropriate than it was. These include:

(a)  the decline of the CBD, and the emergence of suburban business centres, a process most in evidence in North America;

(b)  transport innovations, in particular widespread car ownership which has increased the mobility of a growing proportion of the urban population; and

(c)  the increasing level of public intervention, for example development control, and the provision of public sector housing in the UK, and the Zoning Laws of the USA which regulate 'types of use, density of use and height of buildings' (Hoyt, 1971).

Hardly surprisingly, the model has been demonstrated to be of little value in attempting to interpret the internal structure of the pre-industrial city, either past or present. G. Sjoberg (1965) has demonstrated that within the feudal city there was no clear-cut functional differentiation of land use. For example, merchants and craftsmen often lived at their place of work. Where a zonal pattern of land use could be identified, however, it was in many respects the inverse of that identified by Burgess in North American cities in the 1920s. The market place and certain status functions were situated at the centre of the feudal city and the surrounding residential areas declined in terms of residential prestige towards the periphery, the poorest families living outside the city walls (see Figure 5.4).

One of the main reasons why the concentric zone model has been so criticised is that Burgess failed to state the pre-conditions which must exist if the model is to be applicable without modification. It was left to J. A. Quinn (1950) and L. F. Schnøre (1965) to describe these later. They suggested that the following conditions must apply if the concentric zones envisaged by Burgess are to develop.

(i)  A uniform land surface, i.e. no differences in the physical qualities of land in different parts of the city;

(ii)  A mixed industrial-commercial base.

(iii)  A single commercial focus situated at the city's most accessible part, the centre. There is much competition for central area sites because

125

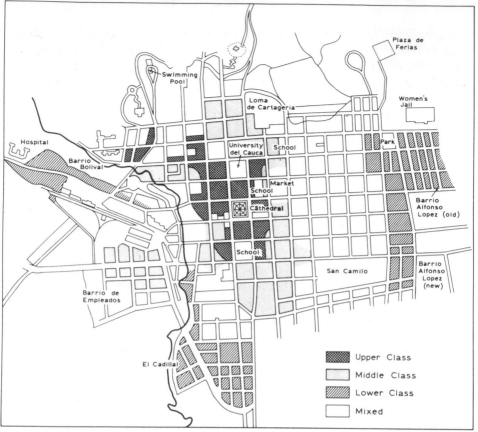

Figure 5.4  The distribution of social classes in Popáyan, Colombia. (Source: Carter, 1976, p. 169; after A. H. Whiteford, *Two Cities of Latin America*, New York)

space at the centre of the city is restricted. Thus central area sites are highly valued.

(iv) Property privately owned. Economic competition and an efficient transport system which is equally easy, cheap and rapid in every direction within the city (i.e. the conditions which appertained in the USA in the 1920s).

(v) A heterogeneous population living in the city: contrasts in race, degree of cultural assimilation, social class and occupations. The standard of living and, by implication, volume of purchasing power, differ greatly.

(vi) The higher socio-economic groups have a greater degree of freedom of choice as against the very restricted choice of the poor.

In the absence of any of these conditions, the concentric zones will develop in, at best, a modified form.

Much of the criticism of the model perhaps misses the point of what the model is trying to achieve. It is not an attempt to provide a pattern which can be applied to all cities throughout the world in an unmodified form.

Burgess recognised that in any town there will be a number of opposing factors which will prevent this from happening. The model is important rather because it represents a pioneer attempt to give some meaning to the complexities of morphological zones within an urban system and to suggest a process of urban growth which might give rise to these. It provides a refreshingly novel way of looking at cities and a yardstick with which the structure of any city can be compared.

ASSIGNMENTS
1. *List the factors which Burgess considered might distort the development of concentric zones in a town. Summarise other 'opposing factors'.*
2. *Why does the concentric zone model lack 'universality' (i.e. it cannot be applied to any city throughout the world)?*

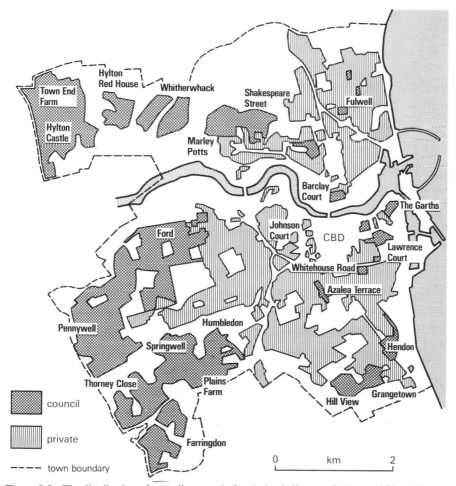

Figure 5.5   The distribution of council estates in Sunderland. (Source: Robson, 1975, p. 97)

127

3. *How far does the distribution of council estates in Sunderland (see Figure 5.5) comply with the key concepts of residential segregation envisaged in the Burgess model? Account for the discrepancy.*
4. *Devise a simple generalised model to illustrate social structures within the town of Popáyan, Colombia (Figure 5.4). In what respects does your model differ from the Burgess model? Try to account for the differences.*
5. *(a) Why is it necessary to make the simplifying assumptions suggested by Quinn and Schnøre?*
   *(b) Consider each of the simplifying assumptions in turn. Suggest how the model would need to be modified if it did not apply.*

## 2. The sector model

The concentric zone model has proved to be remarkably persistent and has acted as a point of reference for much later research into urban structure, the most notable example being Homer Hoyt's sector model (Hoyt, 1939) (see Figure 5.6).

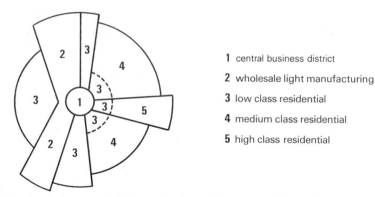

1 central business district

2 wholesale light manufacturing

3 low class residential

4 medium class residential

5 high class residential

Figure 5.6   Hoyt's sector model of urban land use. (Source: after Hoyt, 1939)

The sector model should be seen as an extension of the Burgess concentric zone model. It was developed from research conducted by Hoyt into residential rent patterns which were mapped by blocks in 64 widely distributed American cities. Hoyt's findings were first published in 1939 in a volume of the US Federal Housing Administration, *The Structure and Growth of Residential Neighbourhoods in American Cities.*

Hoyt concluded that 'there is a general pattern of rent that applies to all cities...rent areas in American cities tend to conform to a pattern of sectors rather than of concentric circles' (Hoyt, 1939). In other words, residential areas of a particular class develop outwards from the city centre in the form of wedges or sectors. Thus a residential district of a particular class in one sector of the city would migrate outwards in that direction by new growth on its outer edge. He further suggested that because the high-

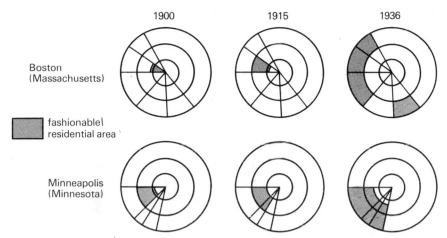

Figure 5.7   A theoretical pattern of the migration of 'high-rent' residential areas over time in two US cities. (Source: after Hoyt, 1939, p. 115)

income groups could afford to pay for the most desirable sites the 'high-grade residential areas pre-empted the most desirable space and were powerful forces in the pattern of urban growth' (Herbert, 1972). Other grades of residential areas were arranged around the high-grade areas, the poorest occupying the least desirable land in the zone in transition or adjacent to manufacturing districts (see Figure 5.7).

Hoyt suggested that sectors, rather than concentric zones, developed because of differences in accessibility from outlying districts to the city centre. The high-class housing estates were built in those sectors where transport links with the city were particularly good as, for example, along a suburban railway line. He contended that sectors were most likely to develop in towns which had a radial network of routes diverging from the city centre. Hoyt also found that sectors of high-class residential areas were particularly well pronounced towards: (a) high ground and open spaces; (b) existing outlying smaller settlements; (c) the homes of influential leaders within the community.

The process of sector development is well exemplified by Pritchard's sequence of maps of the social geography of Leicester 1870–1958 which are reproduced in Figure 5.8. They clearly demonstrate the development of a high-class residential district in the south-east of the town which migrated outwards as the town grew. By 1911 it had reached the town boundary and could shift no farther. Thereafter, gradually, it was virtually surrounded by housing districts of only slightly lesser quality which acted as a buffer, shielding the exclusive residential district from the 'encroachment' of working-class property.

The sector model has been criticised on the grounds that it is constrained by its narrow focus on housing and rent. There have, however, been a

129

Figure 5.8    The social geography of Leicester 1870–1938. (Source: Pritchard, 1976, pp. 81, 83, 84, 87)

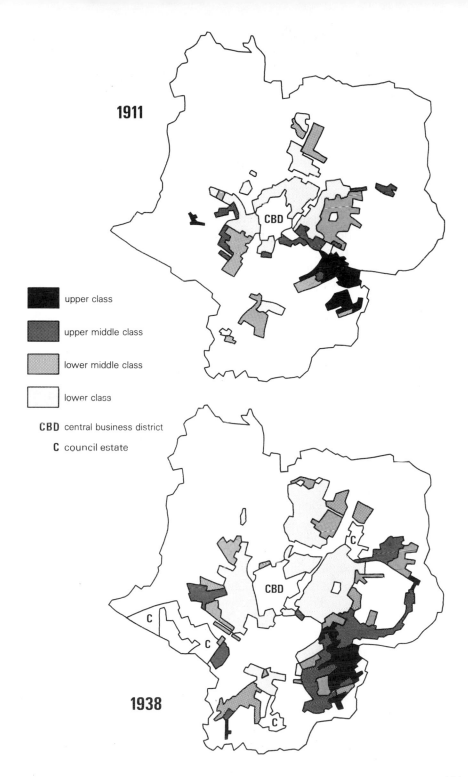

**1911**

upper class

upper middle class

lower middle class

lower class

**CBD** central business district

**C** council estate

**1938**

number of attempts to extend the scope of the model. R. L. Morrill, for example, suggests that a variety of complementary uses occurs within each sector, with the intensity of land use decreasing with distance from the CBD.

> *Thus, within the upper-class sector, for instance, the gradient will go from wealthy shops, to expensive high-rise apartments, to older upper-class apartments, through newer upper-class residential suburbs and industries that utilize professional skills, such as research laboratories (**Morrill, 1970**).*

The sector model complements rather than contradicts the concentric zone model by adding a *directional element* while not discounting the distance variable. It pays more attention than the Burgess model to the importance of transport in the functioning of a city, and has proved to be a more useful tool in incorporating industrial districts into an analysis of urban structure.

It has been suggested that the two models are essentially complementary because each describes a different facet of urban social structure. Hoyt's research into rents and house values was essentially concerned with the distribution of the socio-economic variable, social status and class, within the city and this was found to be sectoral. In contrast, Burgess's research was based primarily on the density of settlement and the distribution of different house types. Both these elements are indicative of stages in the family life cycle, i.e. family size and composition, and this was found to be zonal.

ASSIGNMENTS

1. *How does the evidence presented in Figure 5.8 support Hoyt's sector theory?*
2. *Which factors did Hoyt suggest influenced the directional movement of the sectors of high-class housing in a city?*
3. *(a) In what ways does Morrill envisage a decrease in the intensity of land use the farther it is from the CBD?*
   *(b) How does Morrill's modified sector model differ from that devised by Hoyt?*
4. *How far do the criticisms of the concentric zone model developed on pages 124 to 127 also apply to the sector model?*

## 3. Composite models

*(a) The multiple nuclei model*

Both the concentric and sector models envisage zones developing outwards

132

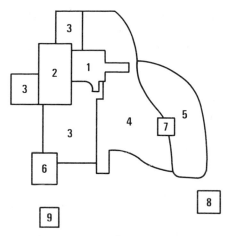

1 central business district

2 wholesale light manufacturing

3 low class residential

4 medium class residential

5 high class

6 heavy manufacturing

7 outlying business district

8 residential suburb

9 industrial suburb

Figure 5.9   Harris and Ullman's multiple nuclei theory of urban structure. (Source: after Harris & Ullman, 1945)

from a single centre. C. D. Harris and E. L. Ullman challenged this idea, abandoning the CBD as the sole focal point, and suggesting alternatively that the zones will develop around a number of quite separate discrete nuclei in addition to the CBD (Harris & Ullman, 1945) (see Figure 5.9). The number of nuclei will depend on the size of the city, and the larger the city the more numerous and specialised are the nuclei. Some of the nuclei, such as some of the suburban shopping centres, could be quite recent developments, while others will have been former village and small-town centres which have been enveloped by the city's growth. Harris and Ullman suggested that the reasons for the development of functional zones were combinations of the following.

(i) *Specialised requirements of certain activities.* For example, shops need to be accessible to their customers; industry requires large blocks of relatively cheap land.

(ii) *Tendency for like activities to group together.* With this arrangement shops benefit through an increase in the number of potential customers and the customers benefit because they can compare goods and prices in nearby shops before making a purchase.

(iii) *The repulsion of some activities by others.* Certain unlike activities such as heavy industry and high-class housing are detrimental to each other and are, therefore, unlikely to be located close together.

(iv) *Differences in the ability of various activities to pay rents and high property prices.* Only large prosperous commercial enterprises can afford to pay the high site values demanded in the city centre whereas warehousing, which requires much space, is commercially feasible only on cheaper sites.

133

The multiple nuclei model envisages that the city will neither develop along zonal nor sectoral lines but will take on a cellular structure in which distinctive forms of land use have developed around certain nuclei within the urban area. Thus heavy industry may be concentrated on the floor of a low-lying valley; zones of light industry may develop along the main road and rail routes and better residential areas may be concentrated on higher ground away from noxious industry.

## (b) The Mann model

Both the concentric zone and sector models were developed from research conducted in American cities. As a result of empirical studies in Hudders-field, Nottingham and Sheffield, P. H. Mann (1965) combined both models to produce a revised model which applies to a medium-sized British city which is not part of a conurbation but which is large enough to depict functional zones (see Figure 5.10).

The model identifies a CBD surrounded by a transitional zone which, Mann contends, may be seen best on the sides of cities which lead to the more middle-class residential areas. Extending outwards from the CBD are sectors of different social status, where industry is associated with the 'lowest working-class sector'. The model assumes that the prevailing wind is south-westerly and, therefore, the most expensive residential sectors are in the west, and the industrial sectors in the east. He suggested that the sectors of working-class houses are likely to be more extensive or more numerous than those of middle-class houses as the working-class population out-numbers that of the middle-class by 3 to 1.

Mann saw the concentric element in his model as being largely a reflec-

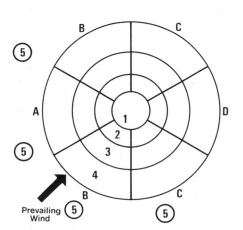

1 central business district

2 Transitional zone

3 zone of small terrace houses in sectors C, D; larger by-law housing in sector B; large old houses in sector A

4 post-1918 residential areas, with post 1945 development mainly on the periphery

5 commuting distance 'dormitory' towns

A middle-class sector

B lower-middle-class sector

C working-class sector (and main council estates)

D industry and lowest working-class sector

Figure 5.10   Mann's model of the structure of a hypothetical British city. (Source: after Mann, 1965)

tion of houses of a particular age rather than a particular type. Thus houses become progressively newer the farther they are from the CBD. In zone 4, both council and private houses will probably occur but their distribution is likely to reinforce the class sectors which already existed.

### (c) The Rees model

Rees, basing his conclusions on detailed work conducted in Chicago which is developed further on pages 146 to 150, adds another element, *ethnicity*, in the development of his composite model (see Figure 5.11) (Rees, 1970). Socio-economic status again takes on a sectoral form (A) and stages in the family life cycle a concentric form (B), related to housing of different age and type. The ethnic areas form nuclei (C) which are superimposed on the other forms to produce a simple structure (D and E). The composite model (I) has been developed to reflect the shape of the physical growth of Chicago (F) and to take account of the existence of industrial concentrations (H).

### (d) The Lawton model

The Mann model is a useful descriptive tool but it throws little light on the processes of urban growth which interact to create the urban structure. In contrast, Professor R. Lawton's model (see Figure 5.12), which is largely derived from research into social and demographic conditions in Liverpool, examines the processes of urban development in the nineteenth century. The model identifies a historic nucleus with 'successive belts of housing wrapped around the older city' and within these are 'sectors of individuality, derived from the character of adjacent areas' (Lawton, 1973). The concentric development of the city (stages A, A1 and A2) reflects its cyclical growth: the city growing rapidly during phases of prosperity but consolidating or even stagnating during periods of recession. On Merseyside, for example, the pre-1914 building booms occurred in the 1840s (associated with Irish immigration), the early 1860s, the late 1870s and the 1900s. Within these successive belts of housing the morphological details of development were greatly influenced by topography and pre-existing patterns of land owner-ship. Villages, and even small towns, were overtaken by the outward growth of the city and became absorbed within the built-up area as inliers of older buildings with more varied functions.

These rapid phases of growth were made possible initially by in-migration from surrounding rural areas and neighbouring small towns. The intensity of migration into different sectors of the city was influenced by the competition from other centres of attraction which presented 'intervening opportunities' to the migrant. Many of the migrants at first moved to the poorest housing conditions in or close to the historic core of the city, while some moved straight away to the relatively cheap working-class houses which were being

135

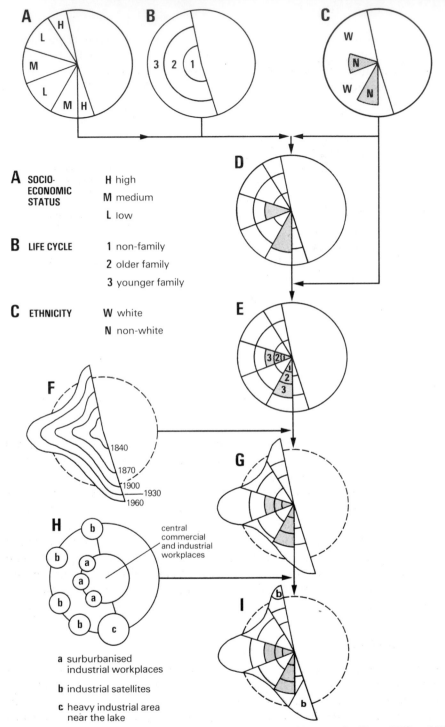

Figure 5.11   An integrated model of the structure of Chicago. (Source: after Rees, 1970, p. 310)

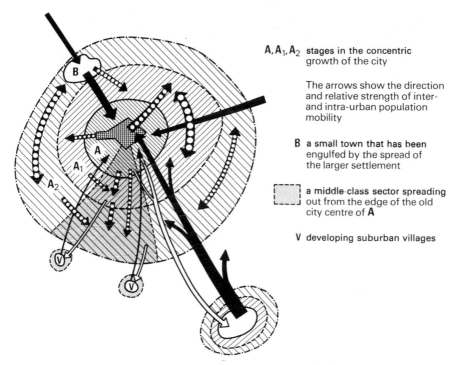

A, A₁, A₂ stages in the concentric growth of the city

The arrows show the direction and relative strength of inter- and intra-urban population mobility

B a small town that has been engulfed by the spread of the larger settlement

a middle-class sector spreading out from the edge of the old city centre of A

V developing suburban villages

Figure 5.12 Lawton's model of urban development in the nineteenth century. (Source: Lawton, 1973)

developed in new estates on the edge of the built-up area. There was also a much less intensive counter current of dissatisfied migrants, many of whom returned to their places of origin.

The model also considers the role of intra-urban movement in the development of the city. Some of the poorer working-class families eventually moved into better residential districts in a form of classic invasion-succession while the middle class developed, through contiguous outward growth, a distinct sector of more advantaged houses. Contemporary with this sector development, some of the more affluent and adventurous families established homes in peripheral villages which, consequently, took on a suburban role.

*(e) The Hopkinson model*

Another attempt at devising a model of urban zoning to take account of conditions in Britain and Europe was made by Hopkinson (1985). One of the problems of theoretical morphological models is that they often do not take account of existing and persistent landscape features built in previous periods of urban design. Two such common features in European towns are

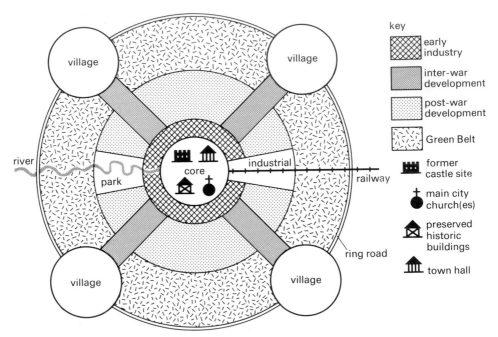

Figure 5.13   A composite model of the European town. From a defensive core, the town has expanded in a concentric manner, but individual land uses have tended to dominate particular sectors around the industrial ring. This is especially true of public open space and industrial land which tend to be river and railway oriented respectively. A Green Belt has now been penetrated by radial development along main roads, drawing the surrounding villages into the town's residential network since the 1960s.

the tight-knit street layout of the former walled defensive core of the city, often dating back over a thousand years, and the conversion of formerly private estates into public open space. Moreover transport technology has changed rapidly since the 1960s, so many historic towns are now bypassed or surrounded by ring roads, the intersections of which provide new nodes for industrial development. To a greater extent than in North America, European towns have preserved buildings in their central areas beyond their economic lifetimes, to maintain an attractive environment, and this cultural heart of the city has often been responsible for the retention of middle-class families close to the core. Hopkinson's model tries to incorporate these and other processes at work in the contemporary European city to give an explanation of land use which reflects the pattern of development in provincial towns (see Figure 5.13).

### (f)   An empirical study of the structure of Sunderland

Figure 5.14 illustrates B. T. Robson's idealised model of the patterns of residential segregation in Sunderland. It was obtained by superimposing

138

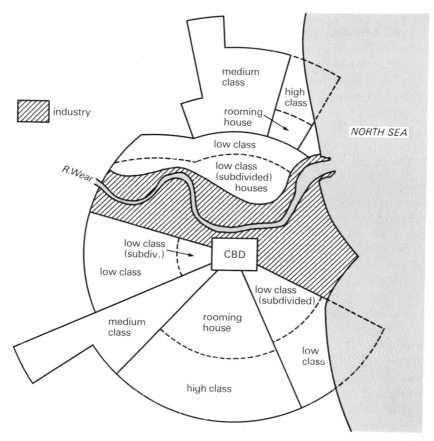

Figure 5.14   A model of patterns of residential segregation in Sunderland, 1963. (Source: Robson, 1975, p. 12)

rateable values of houses, which are based on the amenities of a property and its general location, and the degree of subdivided houses in the private sector. Robson describes his model as follows:

> *The Central Business District lies to the south of the river with industrial areas following both banks of the river and extending south along the coast to the south of the river mouth. The residential pattern in the north has some elements of the sectoral developments suggested by Hoyt (in that the highest rated area forms a partial sector adjacent to the amenity area of the seaboard), but in the main the northern area is in the form of a series of concentric rings of the Burgess type, progressing outwards from a poor, subdivided zone adjacent to the industrial area flanking the river, through a medium-rated area extending to the east–west railway line, and to a higher rated zone north of this and running to the boundary of the*

139

*town. To the south of the river, the residential areas have developed
a pattern closely akin to the sectoral model of Hoyt with four
principal sectors: a low-class sector in the east which is highly
subdivided at its northern apex; a highly rated sector next to it
which reaches out from the inner areas in an expanding area to the
southern boundary; a middle-class sector running out to the west;
and finally, a second low-rated sector flanking the industrial areas
of the river. As Hoyt's model would suggest, a rooming-house area
has developed at the townward apexes of both of the highly rated
sectors, one to the north of the river, the other, more extensive, to the
south (**Robson, 1975**).*

Robson refers to the juxtaposition of sectoral development in one part of
the town with concentric ring development in another and suggests that
neither the Burgess nor the Hoyt model can provide a total explanation of
the patterns of residential segregation.

Robson contends that the location of the high-class residential areas
exerts great influence in the total urban structure. He suggests that the two
principal factors which determine their location are:

1. *maximum accessibility* to the CBD while meeting certain other requirements such as a good site, nearness to amenity land and access to the sea
   front;
2. *avoidance of industrial areas*, particularly, as in Sunderland, where much
   local manufacturing industry is heavy and noxious.

Collectively these two factors are primarily responsible for determining
the residential pattern and help to explain the development of sectors and
concentric zones on opposite sides of the river. To the south, direct access to
the CBD could be achieved by residential sectors which were not in contact
with the industrial belt fringing the river. This, however, was not possible to
the north of the river where a concentric zone of lower-rated housing
developed to act as a buffer between the industrial belt and the area of
better-quality housing.


### (g) The residential mosaic

This chapter has examined attempts that have been made to develop a
number of models, based on empirical research, of the internal structure of
cities in advanced capitalist countries in which people can exercise varying
degrees of choice about where they live. It is possible to pick out certain
common elements within these models and to develop a general model
which provides, at least, a partial explanation of the residential mosaic (see
Figure 5.15). Superimposed on the physical space of roads and buildings are
three dimensions of social space: socio-economic status; family status; and
ethnic status (Murdie, 1969).

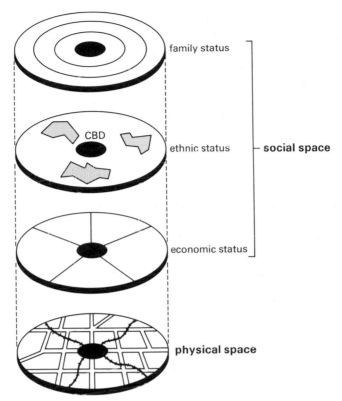

Figure 5.15 The elements which contribute to the residential mosaic. Superimposed on physical space are three aspects of social space: economic status which has a sector pattern; family status which has a concentric pattern; and ethnic status, leading to ethnic and racial concentrations. (Source: Murdie, 1969)

(i) *Socio-economic status* takes on a broadly sectoral pattern. People's choice of residential areas is restricted by their level of income. Those with the highest incomes can exercise the greatest amount of choice and will seek out the most desirable neighbourhoods. Others, with lower family incomes, will be more restricted in their choice of houses and will live in neighbourhoods which provide accommodation commensurate with their ability to pay a rent or mortgage (Short, 1984).

(ii) *Family status* acknowledges that, at different stages in their life cycle, people's housing needs will differ. When a young person leaves home for the first time, he/she is likely to seek out cheap rented accommodation which is most likely to be provided in bedsits in the large Victorian/Edwardian property in the inner residential zone. The accommodation needs will change on marriage, when a larger flat or cheap starter home is likely to be sought. A family with children will require more space and, perhaps, move to a larger property, with garden, in the newer suburbs. When the family

141

has grown up and left home, accommodation needs will change once again and many elderly people will move to smaller accommodation which is, perhaps, more conveniently situated close to the shops and other services of the town centre. This propensity to move house at different stages in the life cycle gives a concentric element to the urban mosaic, reflecting the fact that towns, in general, have developed outwards through concentric growth and that different types of accommodation are to be found at varying distances from the town centre.

(iii) *Ethnic status* applies to those towns and cities which have accommodated immigrant families. As we shall see in Chapter 6, ethnic minorities cluster together for a variety of reasons, some voluntary and some imposed. The ethnic clustering may be relatively short lived, with the families dispersing as they become economically established, or it may persist. Whatever the ultimate outcome, ethnic status is a dimension of social space that cannot be ignored and is an important element in the residential mosaic of many cities.

In the private housing sector of cities in advanced capitalist countries, these three dimensions of social space interact and impose constraints on people's choice of housing and neighbourhood. In countries such as Sweden and the UK, however, there is a substantial *public housing sector* and this introduces a further dimension which has to be taken into account in any analysis of the residential mosaic. In the public housing sector residential mobility will depend on the size and variety of the housing stock and people's ability to move within this sector may be quite restricted. Clearly, any study of the internal structure of British cities must pay special attention to the distribution of council estates and other public sector housing.

ASSIGNMENTS
1. *Do observations made in your nearest large town support Mann's contention that the zone in transition can be seen best in those sides of towns which lead to the more middle-class residential areas? Why is this likely to be the case?*
2. *What influence does the prevailing south-westerly wind exert in localising certain functional zones within a city?*
3. *Discuss the modifications which need to be made to Professor Lawton's model to take into account twentieth-century urban growth. Consider the development of municipal estates; new town development; overspill into expanding towns; urban growth; urban renewal.*
4. *From your parents and/or grandparents, find out how often they have moved house and their motives for moving. Did changes in the family life cycle contribute directly to any of the moves?*
5. *With members of your geography group, discuss the influence that socio-economic status, family status, ethnic status and housing tenure exert on residential patterns in your nearest town.*

142

# C. Interpretations of the Internal Structure of Cities

## 1. Interpretations based on contrasts in urban land values

Early attempts to explain differences in the internal structure of towns and cities concentrated on economic explanations. As early as 1903, R. M. Hurd recognised that, within an urban system, there are marked contrasts in land values and it is the varying ability of different functions, firms and families to compete for space that leads to both functional zoning and residential segregation. It was Hurd's contention that, as a city grows, so remoter and therefore inferior locations are brought into use. This has the effect of increasing the value of the more accessible central sites as more potential users compete for a convenient site which can minimise transport costs or the costs of *friction of distance*. This competition for land finds expression in terms of economic rent: the price potential users are prepared to pay for accessibility. Thus patterns of land use within cities are arrived at through the competition of functions for favourable locations. 'The use that can extract the greatest return from a given site will be the successful bidder' (Ratcliffe, 1947). This gives rise to the development of an orderly pattern of land use within an urban system, spatially organised so that the various functions which are integral to urban life can be carried out most efficiently.

Figure 5.16 illustrates the rent-paying ability (i.e. 'bid rents') of each broad category of land user, against distance from a single, most accessible

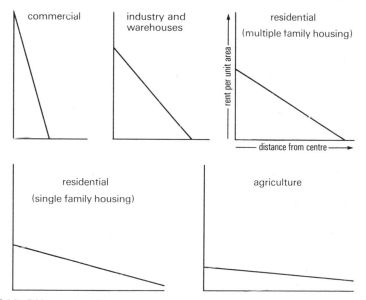

Figure 5.16   Bid rents for different users of urban land in relation to distance from the city centre. (Source: after Berry, 1959)

143

central core. Retail users will compete for the most accessible central sites which will provide them with the greatest customer potential and thereby enable them to maximise profits. Offices also require accessibility and a central location in order to assemble their substantial workforces, but these can avoid the very high rents of the peak land value intersection (see page 221), and can afford to be located in a more marginal central location. Likewise, multi-storey flats will give larger returns per unit area of land than single houses for families and will, therefore, be able to compete for more accessible locations. They will not, however, be able to compete with the rent-paying ability of commercial enterprises. Agricultural uses are the least intensive and are, therefore, outbid by all urban uses. If the separate graphs are superimposed, some indication of the dominant land use in relation to distance from the city centre can be obtained (see Figure 5.17).

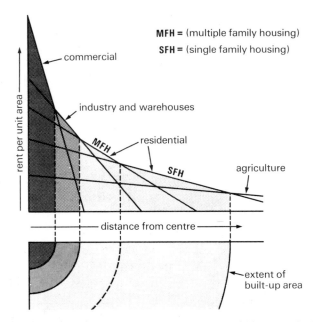

Figure 5.17   Graphs to show the idealised relationship between bid rents and urban land use. (Source: Fielding, 1975, p. 166)

The urban land market can thus be visualised as a rent or land-value surface. The market centre will be the point of the highest site value. As rent declines with distance, value falls and land uses change. If sites of equal value are connected in the form of a series of contours, then a configuration of a cone-like structure emerges (see Figure 5.18). Note the extremely high value attached to the city centre sites in Topeka and the very steep decline of these values with distance from the centre.

144

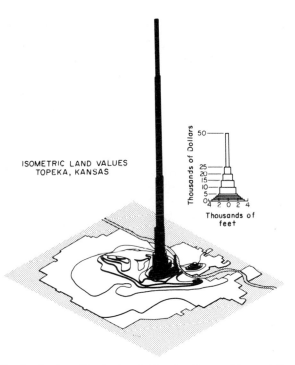

ISOMETRIC LAND VALUES
TOPEKA, KANSAS

Thousands of Dollars

Thousands of feet

Figure 5.18    The distribution of land values in Topeka, Kansas. (Source: after Knoss, 1962)

Similar research conducted in a number of cities has enabled a generalised picture of the average land-value surface to be obtained. The highest values occur in the city centre and decrease towards the periphery. The surface is modified, however, by two additional elements:
(a) main traffic arteries that have higher land values;
(b) the intersections of main arteries where secondary commercial centres develop.

The development of additional nuclei causes the surface to be modified in a way illustrated in Figure 5.19.

Distance from the market centre has been the only variable so far considered. W. Alonso (1964) suggested that, in reality, the rent bid curve is derived from a whole series of factors. He highlights just two of these.
(a) The quantity of land which each user wishes to acquire. For example, the house purchaser or industrialist may prefer to purchase larger plots of land in less convenient locations.
(b) Individual tastes and preferences which determine how users spend their disposable income. In this case, the amount spent on land and travel as a proportion of that spent on all goods and services. Some will choose to devote a higher proportion of their disposable income to travel costs in order to secure the advantages of a suburban environment.

145

(a) Small single centre town

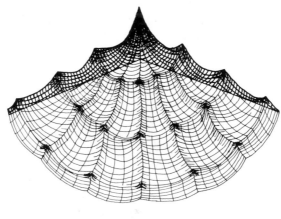

(b) Large city

Figure 5.19  The pattern of land values in relation to main roads and secondary commercial centres. (Source: after J. Simmons, 1964)

Alonso suggests that it is through the complex interaction of each of these variables, as well as others not identified, that the individual arrives at an equilibrium solution to the problem of the optimum location of home or business. This will depend on how the user values convenience as opposed to amenity, the priorities by which he or she allocates any disposable income, and so on.

ASSIGNMENTS
1. *Look at Figure 5.17 (page 144). How far do the zones projected from the idealised gradient of land rent as a function of distance from the CBD conform to those envisaged by Burgess in his concentric zone model?*
2. *How does the development of secondary commercial centres cause the idealised gradient of land rent to be modified?*

## 2. Interpretations arising from the use of factor analysis

In the 1960s urban geographers employed computer technology to experiment with sophisticated methods of analysing urban residential patterns.

146

Factor analysis enabled researchers to examine a large number of variables, which are in some way related to social characteristics within towns. These are then collapsed into a smaller range of significantly associated variables, which indicate underlying components of social characteristics (Herbert & Thomas, 1982).

Factor analysis summarises the inter-relationships between the input variables which are fed into the computer. If variables 'a' to 'm' are fed in, it may be shown that 'a', 'f', 'g' and 'l' are grouped and therefore explain 60% of the phenomenon. For example, they might be indices of socio-economic status, such as the proportion of white-collar workers; the proportion continuing on to some form of higher education and the proportion of professional and managerial employees.

P. H. Rees used 57 variables in his factor analysis of Chicago (Rees, 1970). These were collapsed to ten factors which are shown, in decreasing order of significance, in Table 5.1. The table shows the proportion of the total variance which can be accounted for by each factor. In Rees's study, therefore, the first four factors cumulatively account for 55.9% of the total variance. Most studies employing factor analysis have produced similar results – the first two, three, or four factors generally account for between half and two-thirds of the total variance. This means that attention can be focused on those factors which are most important and (collectively) significantly influence social patterning within cities.

Table 5.1 Factor analysis of Chicago

| Factor | Variance % | Cumulative % |
|---|---|---|
| 1. Socio-economic status | 17.8 | 17.8 |
| 2. Stage in life cycle | 14.2 | 32.0 |
| 3. Race and resources | 13.1 | 45.1 |
| 4. Immigrant/Catholic status | 10.8 | 55.9 |
| 5. Population size and density | 7.5 | 63.4 |
| 6. Jewish/Russian population | 3.8 | 67.2 |
| 7. Housing built in 1940s; workers commute by car | 3.0 | 70.2 |
| 8. Irish/Swedish population | 2.6 | 72.8 |
| 9. Mobility | 2.4 | 75.2 |
| 10. Other non-whites/Italians | 2.1 | 77.3 |

Source: Rees, 1970

Variation in each factor can be mapped using census tracts or enumeration districts as the areal unit. P. H. Rees did this in his study of Chicago and in Figure 5.20 spatial variations in the socio-economic status of the population (factor I) are shown. The low-status districts in the inner city and 'black belt' can be easily distinguished from the high-status suburbs. The factor scores can also be plotted on to a two-dimensional social space diagram. In Figure 5.21 this has been done for factor I. By this means the

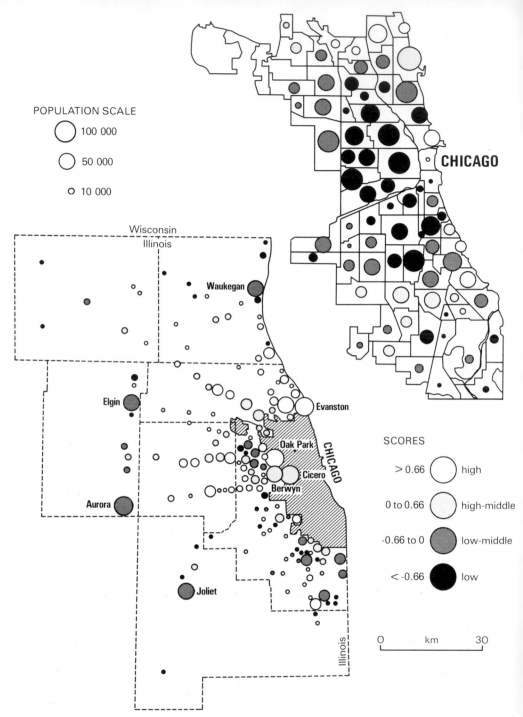

POPULATION SCALE

100 000

50 000

10 000

Wisconsin
Illinois

Waukegan

Elgin

Evanston

Oak Park

CHICAGO

Cicero

Berwyn

Aurora

Joliet

CHICAGO

SCORES

> 0.66        high

0 to 0.66     high-middle

-0.66 to 0    low-middle

< -0.66       low

Illinois

0        km        30

Figure 5.20   The distribution of four socio-economic status groups in metropolitan Chicago, 1960. (Source: Rees, 1968)

148

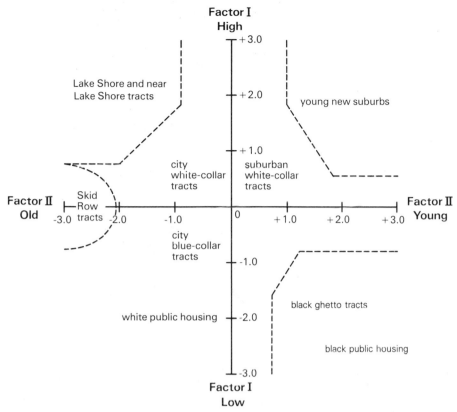

Figure 5.21   Social space diagram for Chicago. Each census tract can be plotted on the diagram which has as its axes factor I socio-economic status and factor II stage in the life cycle. (Source: Rees, 1968)

enumeration districts can be divided into four broad categories: (i) high-status older small families; (ii) high-status younger large families; (iii) low-status older small families, and (iv) low-status younger large families. The information so derived has been used to construct a model of the social areas of the Chicago metropolis (Figure 5.22) which includes both concentric and sectoral elements.

In both factor analysis and principal component analysis the selection of the input variables is of the utmost importance, as they will determine the results obtained. In his study of Sunderland, B. T. Robson (1975) selected a total of 30 variables 'with an eye to their possible theoretical import', the aim being to select a sufficient cross-section of variables so as not to give undue weight to any one aspect of urban social structure. Nevertheless the selection of the variables does introduce an element of subjectivity into the technique. A further problem is posed by the interpretation of the principal components, that is, giving meaning to what are really no more than mathematical artefacts.

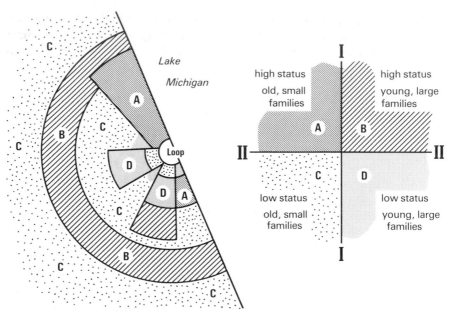

Figure 5.22  Social areas of Chicago. The groupings of census tracts obtained from Figure 5.21 are used as the basis for Rees's model. (Source: Rees, 1968)

It must be remembered that factor analysis is no more than an analytical technique which enables vast amounts of data to be handled for small areal units within towns and cities. Nevertheless, provided the input variables are selected carefully and the results interpreted shrewdly it is a technique which does make it possible to offer at least a partial explanation of patterns of residential segregation.

## 3. Structuralist interpretations

Structuralists regard residential segregation as a symptom of the way in which society is organised. It is their contention that the major variable determining the residential patterning of cities in a capitalist society is the class system. An important function of the class system is to act as a procedure for the allocation of rewards in the form of income, including accumulated wealth; the power that an individual can exert to manipulate society towards certain ends, and status, 'a largely intangible indication of the standing of an individual, a family, a group or a class within their society' (Johnston, 1984). These 'rewards' are seen as interdependent and any one can be used to advance claims for the others.

Within a capitalist system a degree of social mobility is an essential ingredient, so that individuals can strive to improve their position through the acquisition of increased income, status and power. For many people, the

150

optimum way of obtaining upward social mobility is through the acquisition of marketable skills through education and training. This leads to 'conflict between classes over access to educational and other resources which is strongly reflected in intra-urban residential patterns' (Johnston, 1984, p. 155).

Immigration allows established urban dwellers to maintain and enhance their position in the class structure. Migration, at first rural-to-urban but more recently from overseas, has been an important component of urban growth. Newly arrived migrants will take a time to become economically established and, at first, will be prepared to take on lower-paid more menial jobs. The established urban dwellers will set up barriers, often subtle and difficult to pinpoint, to slow down the process of assimilation and thereby protect their own positions in society. It is the structuralists' contention that 'these two themes, of conflict between classes over educational opportunity and between immigrants and their hosts, are crucial to the discussion of residential patterns' (Johnston, 1984, p. 163).

Different classes use a mechanism of *distancing*, that is, living in socially cohesive neighbourhoods physically separate from families of different social standing, to protect their position in the class structure. The contrasting neighbourhoods are affected by a number of *external economies* or *externalities* which Johnston defines as 'aspects of the local environment which contribute to the quality of life of an individual, family or household resident there, but which are not purchased directly by them' (Johnson, 1984, p. 164). Externalities may be either relatively good or bad and include such factors as the quality of the local schools and aspects of the physical environment such as the availability of open spaces or the intrusion of polluting industry or aspects of dereliction. Property prices reflect, not only the quality of the accommodation itself, but also the *positive and negative externalities* that exist within the neighbourhood. The urban residential mosaic arises from individuals competing for space but also from unequal positions of income, status and power. It is this inequality in society, which the class system perpetuates, which results in residential segregation.

ASSIGNMENT

*Discuss which of the following features act as (a) positive and (b) negative externalities. Consider how far it is possible for certain external economies to have both positive and negative properties.*

- *An urban motorway*
- *A school playing field*
- *A disused dock*
- *A superstore or hypermarket*
- *A drive-in Macdonalds*
- *A student hall of residence*
- *A suburban railway station*

# D. Conclusion

There is much empirical evidence to demonstrate that functional zoning and residential segregation exist in towns of even quite modest size. Various attempts have been made to devise models to examine the shape of those zones and the way in which they relate to one another. It has been contended, however, that these empirical models are largely descriptive and fail to provide satisfactory explanations of the internal structure of cities (Johnston, 1982). For more adequate explanations, it is necessary to look beyond the residential mosaic that can be observed through field studies or by an analysis of census enumeration districts to urban land ownership and land values and to the way in which society is structured. It is necessary to have some knowledge of the way in which the housing market operates and the role, for example, of estate agents and housing officers in acting as gatekeepers, filtering the information which they pass on to those in search of new accommodation. In short, many variables interact to contribute to the internal structuring of cities. This chapter should have provided you with some insights into a selection of these but any explanations can, at best, be only partial.

# Key Ideas

*A. Functional Zones*

1. The pattern of urban growth is influenced and, at times, constrained by natural barriers and lines of communication.
2. There is a tendency for different functions to occupy different areas within the town.
3. Within the broad functional zones, more subtle spatial contrasts can often be identified, based on, for example, building age, ownership, environmental quality or categories of function.
4. A town's morphology includes both the arrangement and layout of buildings and the function of land and buildings.
5. Urban structure describes the significant spatial relationships that exist between broad land use zones.

*B. Models of Urban Growth*
*The concentric zone model (Burgess)*

1. Within the city different functions compete for limited space.
2. In certain areas of the city, single functions dominate to form distinctive functional zones.
3. The functional zones are arranged concentrically around the city centre.

4. Lower-status groups are to be found near the city centre and the high-status groups at the periphery.
5. Both within and traversing the concentric zones are natural areas, that is districts which are culturally distinctive.
6. The idealised concentric zones will be modified by 'opposing factors'.
7. Towns grow by a process of invasion and succession whereby population groups gradually filter outwards as their status and level of assimilation improve.

*Criticisms of the concentric zone model*

1. The model emphasises clear-cut boundaries between the concentric zones but gradient studies indicate no such abrupt divisions.
2. The model is rooted in a specific historical and cultural context and, therefore, lacks universality.
3. Since the 1930s, fundamental changes have occurred in Western cities and these make the model less appropriate.
4. In the pre-industrial city both past and present, high-status groups frequently live near the city centre and the poorest families on the edge of the built-up area.
5. Only if certain conditions are met will the idealised concentric zones develop in a town.

*The sector model (Hoyt)*

1. The sector model envisages that residential areas of a particular class develop outwards from the city centre in the form of wedges or sectors.
2. The model adds a directional element while not discounting the distance variable.
3. High-grade residential areas pre-empt the most desirable locations and are powerful forces in urban growth.
4. Differences in accessibility within a town influence the location of sectors of different status.
5. The Burgess and Hoyt models are complementary and describe different facets of urban social structure.

*Composite models*

1. *The multiple nuclei model (Harris and Ullman)*

The multiple nuclei model envisages a city with a cellular structure with distinctive forms of land use developing around a number of discrete nuclei.

## 2. *The Mann model*

The Mann model combines sectors and concentric zones to produce a model applicable to a medium-sized British town. Robson suggests that the structure of British cities is derived from the inter-relationship of socio-economic status, stages in the family life cycle and housing tenure. In broad terms, socio-economic status is arranged sectorally and stages in the family life cycle concentrically.

## 3. *The Rees model*

Rees considers also the influence of ethnicity as a factor influencing urban structure.

## 4. *The Lawton model*

(a) During the nineteenth century urban growth was cyclical, periods of rapid development alternating with periods of little growth. This accounts for the concentric element within the city.
(b) A middle-class sector developed through contiguous outward growth and beyond this peripheral villages acquired a suburban role.

## 5. *The Hopkinson model*

Hopkinson examines the influence of persistent landscape and townscape features on the internal structure of the contemporary European city.

*General considerations*

6. Any model which attempts to provide explanations of the residential mosaic must take into account dimensions of social space (socio-economic status; family status; and ethnic status) which are superimposed on the physical space.
7. The effects of public sector housing must also be taken into account in those countries where it forms a significant element of housing tenure.

*C. Interpretations of the Internal Structure of Cities*
*Contrasts in land values*

1. In a town, land users compete for a convenient site in order to minimise the costs of friction of distance.
2. Some activities are better able than others to bid for the most accessible central area sites and this gives rise to an orderly pattern of land use.
3. Site values decline according to distance from the market centre and land use becomes progressively less intensive.

4. The rent bid curve is derived from a range of factors additional to distance from the market centre.

*Factor analysis*

1. Factor analysis enables researchers to examine a large number of variables, which are in some way related to social characteristics within towns.
2. These are collapsed into a smaller range of significantly associated variables, which indicate underlying components of social characteristics. These principal components have been used to provide partial explanations of residential segregation.

*Structuralist interpretations*

1. Structuralists regard residential segregation as a symptom of the way in which society is organised.
2. Class conflict arises over competition for access to the 'rewards' of the capitalist system and this, in turn, leads to residential segregation as different classes use a mechanism of distancing to protect their positions in the class structure.
3. Neighbourhoods are affected by external economics or externalities which can be either favourable (positive) or unfavourable (negative).
4. The residential mosaic arises from individuals competing for space from unequal positions of income, status and power.

## Additional Activities

1. Burgess envisaged that towns grow by a process of invasion and succession. The process can still be seen in operation in districts of substantial Victorian villas and Georgian terraces adjacent to town centres. If there is such a district in your town you will be able to attempt some of the following suggestions to test Burgess's invasion-succession concept.
   *The original function.* Use street directories to determine when the villas were built and the occupation of the first head of household. If the villas were erected before 1871, refer to the census schedules (see page 55) for additional details of the composition of the entire household. Use early editions of large scale O.S. maps and plans in conjunction with the contemporary directories to construct a sequence of maps to show the changing functions of the buildings.
   *The conversion and replacement of villas.* Map the present-day functions of the villas using the following key. Record the information on an O.S. 1 : 2500 plan.

155

*Notation for conversion of villas*

| | | |
|---|---|---|
| Villas still maintained as a single dwelling | | V |
| Villas converted to flats and maisonettes (the number refers to the number of dwellings) | | F3, M4 |
| Villas converted to: | *hotel* | C1 |
| | *hospital/nursing home* | C2 |
| | *school* | C3 |
| | *shop* | C4 |
| | *medical surgeries* | C5 |
| | *public house* | C6 |
| | *(list other examples)* | |
| Vacant villa | | Va |
| Record also: | *conversion of outbuildings (e.g. stables into a dwelling)* | S/H |
| | *conversion of gardens (e.g. to provide parking space)* | G/P |
| Replacement and Infilling | *derelict villas* | De |
| | *vacant building plots* | P |
| | *inter-war houses* | Ih |
| | *bungalows* | Ib |
| | *flats* | If |
| | *post-war houses* | Ph |
| | *bungalows* | Pb |
| | *flats* | Pf |

*Notes for mapping.* It is often difficult to establish in the field which villas have been converted into flats. An exterior staircase, additional front doors, door bells and letter boxes provide a useful guide, but, in some cases, multiple occupancy of a villa can only be definitely established if the most recent electoral register is referred to. This lists each house and occupiers over eighteen years of age.

Try to discover how well maintained are the rear gardens of the villas and record if they are obviously neglected. The rear gardens are often quite extensive and could provide suitable building sites. If neglected, there is greater likelihood that the house-owner would be willing to sell a part of the garden as a building plot.

The results of your survey may be summarised on a bar graph showing the total original stock of villas and the proportion converted to different functions.

*Implications of building conversion*

(a) Revenue from the community charge will probably increase if villas

156

are converted into separate self-contained flats as there are likely to be more adults living in the building.

(b) The population of the district is likely to increase if many buildings have been converted. Electoral registers provide a useful indication of changes in population density. Select the registers for ten-year intervals and place an appropriate number of dots beside each building to represent the number of people residing there in each year. Remember, however, that you are only recording the adult population and that registers for 1970 and later include 18–21 year olds.

(c) The population structure of the district is likely to change. More families with young children may move into the area. If this is the case, are facilities such as schools, clinics and playgrounds still adequate? Such social considerations are difficult to evaluate other than by the use of sample interviews. Devise a suitable questionnaire which may be used in an area of villas to assess the implications of change.

2. Discuss the motives of individuals who deliberately choose less convenient locations (i.e. in relation to the CBD) than they can afford to pay for.
3. How far does the concentric zone model provide some understanding of the contemporary Western city?
4. How does the concept of economic rent account for the distribution of functional zones within a city?
5. Describe the structuralists' explanations of residential segregation and discuss how far these provide a satisfactory interpretation.

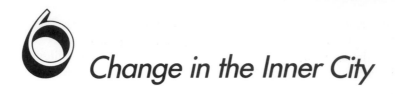

# 6 Change in the Inner City

## A. Introduction

Between the very centre of most cities, where the public buildings, parks and main shopping streets are, and the leafy suburbs where the car-owning commuters live, is an area that is mixed in function and character. Most of the buildings will be almost a century old, the roads congested, services in poor repair. Easily recognised, if not so easy to define, the *inner city* conjures up images of poverty, crime and depression. And yet the inner city was once the economic heart of most urban areas: the place where most people lived and worked. The inner city has suffered most of all urban zones from change, and especially from the loss of its former advantages of accessibility, industrial sites and high-density population (Horne, 1981).

The deterioration of the inner city, especially since the 1950s, is partly economic and partly social. In most urban locations, land values have risen as towns have grown. Once a building is erected upon a site, the use of that site is largely determined until the building becomes too old or inconvenient for its original purpose. Then it is either converted or replaced by a new structure. If the building has particular architectural merit or historic or cultural value, for example a castle, cathedral or a row of Tudor or Georgian houses, it may be preserved because of public *sentiment*: a concept to which we shall return later. But if the building is of poor quality or difficult to adapt and the site is not suitable for a new use, decay and neglect is more likely (Figure 6.1). Such areas of dilapidated or low-standard property are widespread, being the legacy of rapid, cheap, speculative development in the nineteenth century. Even when new, such housing areas catered for the least affluent, although with the passage of time better-quality housing has also become part of the deprived and run-down inner city, especially in the less prosperous regions of the country.

An early attempt at analysing the problems of poor housing and low income was made by Charles Booth in 1890. During the preceding century the British population quadrupled, and the proportion living in towns of over 20 000 people rose from 17% to 77%. Using information collected by the School Board Visitors, Booth calculated that at that time nearly one-

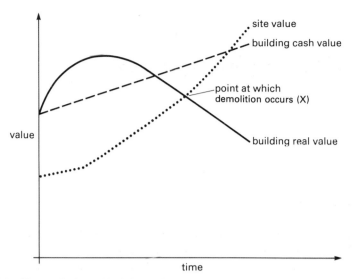

Figure 6.1  Changes in site and building value. Initially the value of a building will rise in line with demand for the service which it provides. However as time goes on the building becomes obsolete and a point is reached where the site value is worth more. At this point (X in the diagram) redevelopment occurs unless there is some special reason (or 'sentimental value') why the building should be preserved (for example, a historic monument).

third of London's population lived below the poverty line. His maps revealed, however, that the poor were not evenly distributed. Districts of severe poverty almost encircled the City of London and extended along the banks of the River Thames as far as the Isle of Dogs and East Greenwich. There were, in addition, outlying areas of extreme poverty in parts of Pimlico, Notting Dale, Paddington, Barnsbury, Holloway and Peckham (Shepherd, Westway & Lee, 1974) (Figure 6.2). At the time, the creation of large areas of cheap insanitary housing and grim warehouses and factories seemed a necessary price to pay for the economic prosperity which the industrial city brought to many of its occupants. However, since 1940, the population growth of most of Britain's major cities has stabilised or declined. Increased mobility of goods and people, the consequent decentralisation of jobs and the coincidental arrival of large numbers of immigrants seeking cheap accommodation have all contributed to the problems of the inner city by increasing the segregation of rich and poor (Loney, 1979).

The response of governments in the first thirty post-war years was generally to tear down the worst housing and replace it with new high-density estates, but this tended to weaken the sense of community which existed in many inner cities. In the remainder of this chapter we shall look at some attempts at identifying and solving the problems of the inner city and at preserving and re-establishing urban neighbourhoods. At this point it is worth pointing out that, although the idea of the inner city as a 'problem area' was generally associated with the old industrial conurbations in Britain

159

Figure 6.2   Degrees of poverty in London, 1889. (Source: after Shepherd, Westway & Lee, 1974, p. 26). Figures represent percentage of the population beneath the poverty line, the darkest shading representing areas of extreme poverty.

(inner London, Merseyside, Greater Manchester, West Midlands, West Yorkshire, Tyne-and-Wear, Clydeside) together with other old manufacturing centres such as Cardiff, Sheffield and Hull, until recently the more prosperous cities of the south, such as Bristol, were not included. Recent riots in such cities have pointed out the fact that significant areas of poverty and deprivation exist throughout Britain, and, indeed, because of the generally higher living costs in the south-east, problems may be especially severe in the 'prosperous areas' for those without work or decent housing. Identifying the areas of urban deprivation requires the development of a range of techniques which are considered below (Section E).

## B. Inner City Problems and Policies

### 1. The nature of the problem

Inner city problems are not new but were largely neglected in the 1950s and early 1960s when resources were concentrated on suburban expansion and

160

new town development. By the late 1960s, however, deteriorating inner city environments, coupled with a realisation of the seriousness of population losses and job losses, particularly in manufacturing industry, caused attention to be focused once again on the inner cities. In the period from 1979 to 1985, approximately 2 million jobs were lost in manufacturing industry with the greatest concentration of these being in the conurbations. This came on top of a 15.8% loss of jobs in the conurbations between 1971 and 1978 (Hall, 1985). The Urban Aid Programme was introduced by the Wilson government in 1968. This provided central government subsidies to those local authorities with inner city problems and also established a number of Community Development Projects which combined research on the causes of deprivation with an action programme to encourage self-help among inner city residents (Hudson & Williams, 1986). A further research programme, Inner Area Studies, was commissioned in 1972 by Peter Walker, then Secretary of State for the Environment, which examined the causes of inner city malaise in London, Liverpool and Birmingham. These research initiatives contributed to the influential White Paper, *Policy for the Inner Cities*, which was published in 1977.

The 1977 White Paper recognised that 'the decline in the economic fortunes of the inner areas often lies at the heart of the problem' (HMSO, 1977, p. 2). It is the relatively low wage levels of a predominantly unskilled labour force and the high rates of unemployment which provide inner city dwellers with a restricted choice in the housing market, health care, shopping provision and education, and force them to live in areas of poor environmental quality. They find themselves trapped in a cycle of poverty (see Figure 6.3) with low family income leading to poor-quality housing which in turn causes stress and contributes to relatively poor levels of health and under-achievement at school. The lack of recognised qualifications and marketable skills lowers employment prospects and gives most inner city dwellers little opportunity to escape from their impoverished environments.

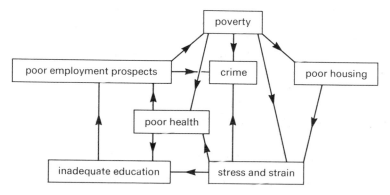

Figure 6.3   The cycle of poverty. (Source: Johnston, 1982, p. 257)

High crime rates add to the general malaise and may discourage new industry and other enterprises from locating in inner city areas (Johnston, 1982).

The 1981 inner city riots in Toxteth, Liverpool; Moss Side, Manchester; St Paul's, Bristol; Southall, Birmingham; and Brixton, London provided further evidence of the breakdown in social order in inner city areas. Following the Brixton riots, Lord Scarman was commissioned to enquire into policing and public order and the social and economic background to the riots. His report was published in November 1981 and in it he recognised that unemployment was a 'major factor in the complex pattern of conditions which lies at the root of the disorders in Brixton and elsewhere'. He also noted that the problems faced by many inner city dwellers are exacerbated by racial disadvantage. He concluded his report unequivocally:

> *The attack on racial disadvantage must be more direct than it has been. It must be co-ordinated by central government who, with local authorities must ensure that the funds made available are directed to specific areas of racial disadvantage.*

The Church of England's controversial report, *Faith in the City* (1985), concluded that conditions in the most deprived parts of Britain's inner cities were continuing to deteriorate.

> *It is our considered view that the nation is confronted by a grave and fundamental injustice in the Urban Priority Areas. The facts are officially recognised but the situation continues to deteriorate and requires urgent action. No adequate response is being made by government, nation or church.*

The violent and destructive riots in the Handsworth district of Birmingham and in Tottenham, north London, in 1985, provided further evidence of the very serious nature of the problem.

## 2. Policies for inner city regeneration

Since the problem of inner city areas was recognised in the late 1960s, there has been no shortage of reports about the nature and causes of the problems but no consensus over the best way to tackle them. We have already seen that the policies adopted depend on the prevailing ideology. The main debate revolves around to what extent the government can and should intervene in an attempt to break into the cycle of deprivation which characterises inner cities. The Labour Government, under the 1978 Inner Urban Areas Act, created partnerships with seven metropolitan authorities and counties to draw up agreed programmes of action to try to improve social, economic, and environmental conditions (Lawless, 1986). Glasgow was not included under the partnership arrangements as it already had its own special agency for inner-area development, the Glasgow Eastern Area Renewal (GEAR) Project, established in 1976. Since 1979, the Conservative administrations have continued with the partnership concept but have looked to a much greater involvement of the private sector. Michael Heseltine, when he was Secretary of State at the Department of the Environment in 1980, set out the aims of government policy for the inner cities as follows:

(a) to simplify existing partnership arrangements between local authorities and central government;
(b) to see the private sector playing a greater role;
(c) to see voluntary organisations maintaining their contributions;
(d) to attempt to make city communities more self-reliant.

Although direct expenditure under Urban Aid has increased, this has been more than offset by very substantial cuts in housing subsidies paid to local authorities and in contributions under the rate support grant (Dean, 1985). It is the government's contention that

> *It makes no sense to justify ill-focussed expenditure by the plea that it provides jobs. The inner cities will not be revived by putting up rates and taxes to provide more public sector jobs to offset job losses in the productive sector. Too many experiments in too many inner cities have provided proof of that (**Patten, 1987**).*

The government's aim is to bring about inner city regeneration through a partnership between the public and private sector, with the role of the public sector being essentially to act as catalyst for new initiatives, improving the infrastructure through road-building schemes, and other investments in communications, and through general environmental improvements. It is hoped that the private sector will fulfil the role of developer, building houses, offices, new industrial premises and so on. The Urban Development Grant scheme is one such public sector–private sector initiative which aims to attract private house developers to some of the most intractable inner city areas by providing an incentive of financial subsidies. The Urban Regeneration Grant, introduced in 1987, allows for grants to be paid directly by central government to a developer, without involving local authorities, to encourage them to redevelop rather larger sites (up to approximately 50 ha) than is possible under the Urban Development Grant scheme.

The Inner Cities Initiative has been introduced to try to stimulate job creation in eight sharply defined inner city areas. The scheme includes targeted help to black businesses and custom-designed training to meet local employment needs.

## C. The Urban Development Corporations

The most ambitious partnerships between central government and the private sector have been forged through the Urban Development Corporations (UDCs). The first two of these were designated in 1979 in the disused and derelict docklands of East London and Merseyside, and the legal framework for the UDCs was contained in the 1980 Local Government, Planning and Land Act. Each UDC was given the objective of securing 'the regeneration of its area, by bringing land and buildings into effective use, encouraging the development of existing and new industry and commerce...' (Local Government, Planning and Land Act, 1980, Section 136). The UDCs were given powers similar to those of the New Town Development Corporations. They are independent bodies with wide powers and are not subject to local authority controls but are directly answerable to central government. Because they stand outside the local government democratic process, they have been able to cut corners and galvanise action.

## 1. The London Docklands Development Corporation

The rate of change and regeneration in the London Docklands Development Corporation (LDDC) has been nothing short of remarkable with over £1500 million of private investment being attracted in the first seven years, approximately six times the level of public sector investment. Perhaps the main achievement of the LDDC was at the outset when it had to change the attitudes of private companies to the development potential of the dockland area.

*(a) The starting point*

The closure of the London Dock system in the 1960s and early 1970s had left the area devastated and demoralised. Areas such as the Isle of Dogs had been almost entirely dependent on the Port of London as a source of employment. Thus, when the docks closed, unemployment rates soared. Housing in the area was overwhelmingly public sector rented accommodation, with only just over 5% of the 14 881 households in the area being owner-occupiers. Much of the area had been subjected to large-scale urban renewal schemes in the 1950s and 1960s when maisonettes and high-rise blocks replaced the nineteenth-century terraces. There had been earlier attempts to redevelop the docklands area. In 1971, a report commissioned by the Heath Conservative Government had proposed that office developments and medium-income to high-income housing should be built in the disused docklands. The scheme met with severe opposition from the Labour-controlled local authorities and, after 1973, by the newly elected Labour-controlled Greater London Council. They preferred a scheme which would be more community based and provide jobs and better housing for the people who already lived in the area. The result was stalemate and by 1980 virtually no development had taken place.

## (b) The achievements of the LDDC

Since the establishment of the London Docklands Development Corporation in 1981, an enormous amount of development has taken place and the rate of change has increased year by year. Unlike the New Town Development Corporations, the LDDC did not start by drawing up a detailed plan of proposed developments. It preferred instead a much more flexible demand-led approach to planning. It saw its role as being 'limited to preparation and marketing of land for development and to helping to create the physical, social and economic environment likely to encourage future investment in housing and commerce' (Corporate Plan, Sept. 1984, para. 10.7.1). In other words to change potential developers' perceptions about the possibilities of the Docklands.

The enormous advantage that the London Docklands has is its proximity to the City of London, but, in spite of its physical closeness, in the past, communications from Docklands to the City have been notoriously bad. The LDDC, therefore, saw the *improvement of communications* as a priority. A light rapid transit rail system is being developed to give the Isle of Dogs and the Royal Docks direct access to the City (see Plate 6.1). The first phase was

Plate 6.1    A train on the Docklands Light Railway leaving Heron Quays Station and crossing the West India Docks. (Photograph: Docklands Light Railway Ltd)

165

operational in 1987 and includes a northward extension to Stratford (LDDC, 1986a). There is also considerable investment in road improvement schemes and plans to build a motorway connection from Docklands to the national motorway network via the M11. A new east London river crossing, to provide a link with the A2, the Kent coast ports and, eventually, the Channel Tunnel, is also under review. The potential of the River Thames as a routeway is being realised through the establishment of a frequent fast riverbus service running from Greenwich to Chelsea (Dineen, 1987). The operators are using highly manoeuvrable and high-speed catamarans. A new STOL (short take-off and landing) airport has been developed in the Royal Docks, with the cost of development being borne by a private sector consortium. The airport went from being an idea to being fully operational in the space of only six years. There are regular flights from the new airport to Amsterdam, Rotterdam, Brussels, Frankfurt and Paris as well as to a number of domestic airports within a 640 km radius (Evans, 1986). The airport is situated only 10 km from the very heart of the City of London, putting the City within less than 2 hours of Amsterdam. The LDDC has also been keen to ensure that firms moving to Docklands have high-speed computer links, and kilometres of new fibre optic cables have been laid (LDDC, 1985).

The LDDC has seen *the creation of a high-quality working and residential environment* as being very important to the attraction of new commercial developments. The water spaces provided by the docks have been used to

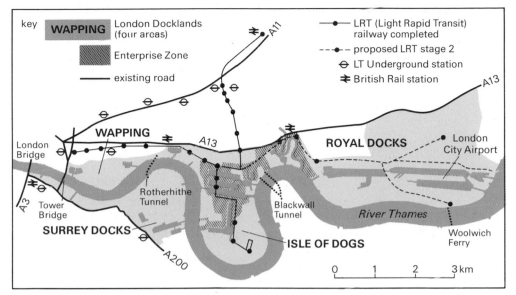

Figure 6.4 The area of the London Docklands Development Corporation which includes the Isle of Dogs Enterprise Zone. (Source: The London Docklands Development Corporation)

develop leisure facilities and to provide attractive water-edge sites for new buildings (see Plate 6.2). Urban conservation has been given a high profile and any existing buildings and artefacts of historic and/or architectural interest have been conserved and enhanced. High-quality street furniture has been used, and floorscapes, including road surfaces of varied colours and textures, add interest.

The LDDC has divided Docklands into four distinct areas: Wapping, the Surrey Docks, the Isle of Dogs and the Royal Docks (see Figure 6.4). The St Katharine's Dock, in Wapping, but close to the Tower of London and Tower Bridge, was where the regeneration began. Its old warehouses, dock buildings and other artefacts were restored and refurbished and the Dock has become a major tourist attraction, incorporating hotels, restaurants and up-market shops (see Plate 6.3). The importance of tourism in Docklands is reflected by the fact that there are currently 11 museums in varying stages of development. The development of *leisure and tourist facilities* is just one dimension of the changes that have taken place in Docklands. Wapping, the Surrey Docks and the Isle of Dogs are being developed as an extension eastwards of the concentration of *financial services* in the City of London. The headquarters of London's Commodity Exchange has moved to the St

◄ Plate 6.2 Housing at Lavender Quay in the Surrey Docks section of the London Docklands makes good use of the water edge site. (Photograph: London Docklands Development Corporation)

167

Plate 6.3  The restored St Katharine's Dock, where the regeneration of London's Dockland began and which has now become a major tourist attraction. (Photograph: London Docklands Development Corporation)

Katharine's Dock and collects under one roof dealings in sugar, cocoa, coffee, petroleum, vegetable oils and rubber (*The Times*, 19 February 1987). In the Surrey Docks area, London Bridge City, a 200 000 square metres commercial and residential development, has attracted the American Citibank, while the adjacent Butler's Wharf provides a further 90 000 square metres of mixed residential, commercial, retail and leisure space on a site overlooking the Thames. The Isle of Dogs has attracted the Stock Exchange's computer centre.

The biggest commercial development so far planned is the *Canary Wharf Scheme* on the Isle of Dogs (see Plate 6.4). The Isle of Dogs, 195 ha of land and enclosed water only 3 km from the City of London, was designated an Enterprise Zone in April 1982. Firms which have located there benefit from building grants of up to 50% and capital allowances of 100%. They are also exempt from rates up to 1992 and can take advantage of a greatly simplified planning regime which requires no planning permission provided they choose to locate in an area designated for that function. The proposed Canary Wharf Scheme is headed by a Canadian-based consortium and there are plans to invest £3 billion to construct a 1.1 million square metres financial

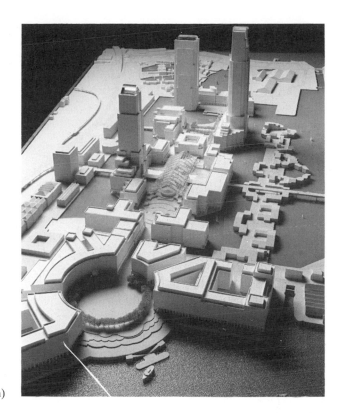

Plate 6.4 An architect's model of the proposed development at Canary Wharf in the Isle of Dogs Enterprise Zone, London Docklands. (Photograph: London Docklands Development Corporation)

centre on the 29 ha site. Approximately half of the floor space will be built in the first phase with over 900 000 square metres already committed to the international banks Morgan Stanley and Credit Suisse First Boston. The plans include a 240 metre high skyscraper which, if completed, will be the tallest building in London, 60 metres higher than the National Westminster tower (Barwick, 1988). When complete the financial centre could provide as many as 60 000 jobs and it is estimated that a further 23 000 jobs will be generated indirectly. The consortium has agreed a substantial 'planning gain' package with the LDDC and will invest in road improvements, the creation of a public open space and pay 50% of the cost of extending the Docklands light railway to Bank Station in the City.

London Docklands has also been successful in attracting the *publishing* houses of most of the nation's daily and Sunday newspapers, which have recently relocated from Fleet Street to new buildings which incorporate new technology. News International has moved to Wapping and Associated Newspapers, publishers of the *Daily Mail*, to the Surrey Docks. The *Daily Telegraph* and *Guardian* newspapers and Northern and Shell, international publishers, have relocated in the Isle of Dogs Enterprise Zone, while the *Financial Times* is moving to the East India Dock.

169

The London Docklands have also had some success in attracting *high-tech industries*, including British Telecom and Mercury. Small industries have not been overlooked and, for example, the refurbished Cannon Workshops in the Isle of Dogs provide premises for 130 small firms. In fact, of the 300 companies which moved to the Enterprise Zone between 1982 and 1987, 250 have 12 or fewer employees (Roland, 1987). There has also been some success in attracting *media industries*, most noticeably Limehouse Studios, to the Isle of Dogs (Plate 6.5).

In addition, much progress has been made in providing *residential accommodation* mainly for owner-occupation. This has taken the form of refurbishing disused warehouses, some of which overlook the Thames, as well as many new housing developments. Between 1982 and 1987, some 11 200 residential units were added to the housing stock on 133 separate sites and the rate of building has now reached 2500 homes per year (Hoppit, 1987).

*The Royal Docks* is the last of the four areas to be redeveloped. 'Their immense size and scope make them the most important redevelopment site in Europe' (Vesty, in 1987). Early developments have involved new housing in Beckton and North Woolwich, while the London City Airport opened in autumn 1987. The LDDC has bought some land, through compulsory

Plate 6.5   Limehouse Studios, Britain's biggest independent television production centre stands beside the West India Dock in the Isle of Dogs in London Docklands. (Photograph: London Docklands Development Corporation)

purchase, to assemble an uninterrupted site for development by three private sector consortia. The £2000 million proposals include: a vast exhibition complex; Londondome, a 25 000 seater arena; over 5000 new homes; office space; 'Festival Market', a new regional shopping centre; and leisure and community developments, including a water centre and over 9000 parking spaces. The whole complex is planned to generate 48 000 new jobs by 2001, 32 000 directly and a further 16 000 indirectly. The LDDC estimates that up to 50% of the labour force could be recruited from the local labour market, depending on the availability of skills (LDDC, 1987).

Urban redevelopment in London's Docklands has been swift and spectacular since the creation of the LDDC in 1981. It has been particularly successful in attracting private sector investment, £6.40 for every £1 spent by the LDDC (Gribben, 1987). One of its principal aims has been to extend the wealth of the City of London into London's traditionally disadvantaged East End. When agreement was reached with developers over the Canary Wharf project, Christopher Benson, the LDDC Chairman, stated: 'We are going to deliver through this development social benefits the like of which have not been given before from a development proposal' (*The Guardian*, 21 July 1987).

The Chief Executive, Reg Ward, was even more assertive: 'Its impact will bring the development axis in London back eastwards after 100 years' steady march westwards. It has already transformed all the development horizons in docklands beyond levels that even the most optimistic of us could have dreamed being real' (*The Guardian*, 21 July 1987).

One of the effects of 'bringing the development axis in London back eastwards' has been a dramatic increase in *land prices*. The LDDC has seen this increase as 'perhaps the most accurate barometer of physical and economic regeneration' (1984–5 Annual Report). But it has resulted in spiralling house prices, which, in spite of house builders being encouraged to provide some relatively low-cost units for local families, has kept owner-occupation beyond the reach of most local families.

*(c) Criticisms of the LDDC*

In spite of its record of achievement in attracting new investment to London's Docklands, the LDDC has come in for some severe criticism. Political conflict and local opposition have arisen partly for the following reasons.

1. The LDDC lies outside the process of democratically elected government and its policies have often been at variance with those of the adjacent London Boroughs that it replaced as a planning authority.

2. The LDDC is under no obligation to put the needs of the indigenous local community first. It has been tasked by government to secure the regeneration of the area through attracting new investment. It sees the

Docklands as being of Metropolitan, national and international importance and considers it inevitable that the national interest will sometimes be at variance with the interests of the local communities (Page, 1987).

The reasons for local opposition were summarised in an article in *The Times*:

> *Local people believe, with some justification, that their needs and wishes are being ignored, that they have little place in the new office buildings and high-tech industrial estates which are supplanting the old factories and warehouses and that they will be unable to compete in the housing market with the new generation of so-called yuppies and whizz-kids who are being offered company flats and huge low interest mortgages to enable them to live closer to the city (**The Times**, 19 February 1987).*

In 1985, the Docklands Consultative Committee, composed of the Greater London Council, the five Docklands Borough Councils and representatives of the local community, published a review of the first four years of the LDDC. Its main criticism of the work of the LDDC can be summarised as follows:

1. *Housing*. There have been too few houses built for rent and too few of the houses built for sale are at prices local people can afford.

2. *Employment*. Most of the jobs being created in the Docklands are for qualified and skilled labour and are not available to local people, the majority of whom are unskilled or semi-skilled. Furthermore, 'it has no policy for creating jobs for black people or ethnic minorities: nor has it policies for creating jobs for women or people with disabilities' (para. 3.47).

3. *Planning*. The LDDC has no firm plan for Docklands but is demand-led by the needs of big business. This inevitably means that local interests are sacrificed.

4. *Equality and equal opportunity*. The type of development that is moving into Docklands is in stark contrast to the council estates and working-class culture of the indigenous community. In a recent *Sunday Express* supplement, the social contrasts in the Isle of Dogs were vividly described. 'The Island has acquired a bewildering socio-economic geography. As you move through pockets of expensive new housing into the vast council estates...the frontiers are abrupt' (Green, 1987).

5. *Transport*. 'The whole of the LDDC's efforts to improve transport provision to, from and in Docklands are geared towards attracting private investment in development. New roads, new bus services and the Docklands Light Railway are routed primarily to serve new development areas as opposed to existing residents' (para. 6.13).

6. *Education and training*. The LDDC should co-operate with local authorities to increase education and training opportunities for local people.

Mary Honeyball, Chair of the Docklands Forum, an umbrella group set up in 1975 for 55 local organisations, summarised the priorities of local residents:

> *What everyone wants is firstly work training for locals at every stage of the development, then more public housing in each of the schemes, better bus services and measures to increase the local shops rather than let them be put out of business by the huge retail developments planned where residents won't be able to afford to shop (**Daily Telegraph**, 2 February 1987).*

One of the Docklands developments which has aroused most controversy has been the STOL Airport in the Royal Docks. This was the subject of a Public Inquiry in 1983, at which a local pressure group, the Newham Dockland Forum, put forward alternative proposals, *The People's Plan for the Royal Docks*. The People's Plan is summarised in Figure 6.5 and can be compared with the plans of the LDDC and the three consortia involved (Figure 6.6). It was drawn up after consultation with local residents and puts emphasis on public sector housing, dock-related industries and leisure and community facilities to serve local needs.

Another broad area of criticism of the LDDC is over the demand-led planning strategy it is choosing to adopt. David Hall, Director of the Town and Country Planning Association, considers that developments on the scale of Canary Wharf require a great deal of careful advanced planning. 'We need to know how much of the additional housing demand can realistically be met in the Docklands area, where any surplus housing demand is most likely to be felt, whether the existing capacity of the transport system could accommodate the consequential extra commuting, and if not what the costs would be of enlarging that capacity' (Hall, 1985). He doubts that the impact of the Canary Wharf scheme has been sufficiently thought through and goes on to argue that the LDDC should have a publicly agreed planning and development strategy for the area.

### (d) The LDDC's reply

The LDDC answers its critics by pointing to the national importance of the London Docklands area. London is one of the world's great financial centres and it can be argued that the prosperity of the UK is highly dependent on the well-being of the City of London. Recently, business in the City has been increasing rapidly. For example, between 1980 and 1986 foreign exchange trading doubled in London and share or equity trading greatly increased, with the rate of growth rising even more steeply since the deregulation of the London Stock Exchange in 1986. The physical limitations and the planning constraints imposed in the square mile of the City of London have made expansion there extremely expensive if not impossible.

174

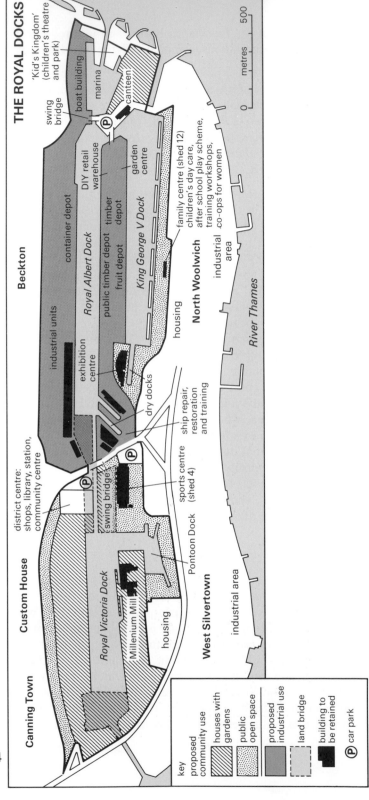

Figure 6.5  The People's Plan for the Royal Docks. (Source: The Newham Docklands Forum and the GLC Popular Planning Unit, 1983)

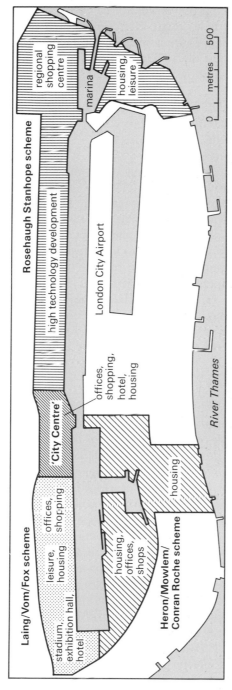

Figure 6.6   The Consortia development proposals for the Royal Docks. (LDDC, 1987)

'To provide the buildings which are needed, tinkering with ceiling heights and removing dividing partitions will not be enough. The office blocks need to be of a completely new design. Banks need high technology acceptance buildings' (Evans, 1986). There is space in the Docklands for such buildings and it is the overt aim of the LDDC that they should become the area into which the financial institutions and associated services of the City of London can expand.

The aim of the LDDC has been to generate a renewed confidence in the Docklands and to make the area more prosperous than it has ever been, so that the ultimate benefits will be widespread with a rapid growth of accompanying jobs in the service or tertiary sector, a great improvement in both road and public transport and a far greater choice in shopping, leisure and other service sector provision. The LDDC also claims that, even in the short term, local needs are not being disregarded. Subsidised housing schemes have helped some people resident in the area to become owner-occupiers by purchasing at below market values, and special schemes have been introduced to offer training opportunities to local residents to equip them to take up jobs in the expanding employment market. One of the proposals of the Canary Wharf developers is to establish a £2.5 million trust to help local people to acquire the skills they require if they are to find employment in the new financial centre. The LDDC also points to the short time scale within which the impressive range of developments have occurred, in contrast to the decade of relative inactivity preceding its formation.


ASSIGNMENT
*In their Four Year Review of the LDDC, the Docklands Consultative Committee (1985) claimed: 'Few would now accept that planning and redevelopment are neutral – the reality is too stark for that in Docklands' (para. 5.1). What do you consider to be the underpinning ideology of the LDDC? Does it reflect the philosophy of the radical New Right which considers that the role of planning is to create the conditions in which the market can operate with as little interference as possible? If so, how do you explain the incentives to new investors offered in the Isle of Dogs Enterprise Zone? How can the needs of local residents best be met, by transforming the entire socio-economic base of the Docklands or by providing more public sector housing and job opportunities appropriate to the skills of the existing workforce? Is the potential of the Docklands, with its unique location so close to the City of London, so important that, at times, national considerations must over-ride local considerations? Is the People's Plan for the Royal Docks a viable alternative or is it nostalgic, harking back to a dependence on the port which no longer exists and cannot be revived? Discuss these questions and others of your own in your group and try to clarify your own position on some of the important issues arising from the regeneration of London's Docklands.*

## 2. The Merseyside Development Corporation's strategy for urban regeneration

The approach adopted to urban regeneration by the Merseyside Development Corporation (MDC) is necessarily different from that of the London Docklands Development Corporation. The MDC was given the brief to regenerate the disused south Liverpool Docks, the Wirral Docks and an area of port hinterland in Bootle. It has found it much more difficult to attract private investment than has the LDDC and, in the financial year 1986–7, total investment by the private sector amounted to only £5.7 million compared with government grant aid of £25.8 million. There are a number of explanations for this difference including the fact that the London Docklands is part of the advantaged south-east while Merseyside is more peripheral to the UK's economic heartland. The confidence of the private sector in Merseyside was, however, significantly undermined by policies of the 1983–7 Labour Council, which was dominated by Militant Tendency supporters, 47 of whose members were disqualified from holding public office by the Courts in 1985 for delaying fixing a rate. That Council was ideologically opposed to the Merseyside Development Corporation and was unwilling to co-operate with it, unlike the Labour Council which replaced it, which has adopted a more pragmatic approach (Dunn, 1987).

At the time of designation 73% of the MDC's area was derelict. By 1987 this had been reduced to 22%, which has implications for the costs of preparing sites for development. This is recognised in the MDC's 1987 Annual Report which states: 'A major concern facing the Corporation remains the low capital values of completed developments, particularly in office and industrial development, compared with construction and other costs' (para 3.2). The report also refers to 'the very weak demand for industrial land in Merseyside' which led to the filled-in Herculaneum Dock site being reallocated from industrial use to a Retail Park (para 3.4). The designated area does include sites for industrial and office development, but the main thrust of the MDC so far has been to concentrate on leisure and tourist development, hoping to capitalise on the substantial growth in this sector of the economy. It is also hoped that the creation of high-quality leisure and tourist facilities close to the city centre will help to change Merseyside's tainted image and eventually attract a much higher proportion of private sector investment. The strategy of the MDC is modelled on similar strategies for regeneration which are being implemented, with some success, by a number of American cities such as Baltimore and Boston (see pages 187 to 192).

The MDC has been responsible for setting up and providing financial assistance for the Merseyside Tourism Board. The focus of tourist development has been the refurbished Albert Dock, which contains Britain's largest group of grade 1 buildings of architectural and historic interest and which, in

177

Plate 6.6 The refurbished Albert Dock, Liverpool, with its fine collection of grade 1 listed buildings (centre lower) now contains a variety of functions, including a Maritime Museum and the Tate Art Gallery. (Photograph: John Mills Photography Ltd/Merseyside Development Corporation)

1986, won for Merseyside the European Gold Medal for the Preservation of Historic Buildings. The restored warehouses have been adapted to house a Maritime Museum, the Tate Gallery, the Granada Television News Centre and an interesting complex of small shops and restaurants (Plate 6.6). Other plans for the south Liverpool docks are illustrated in Figure 6.7 and include a national aquarium, an ice rink, sports arena and a multi-screen cinema. The area includes 27.5 ha of water space which is to be used for displaying historic ships, water sports of all kinds and a 500 berth yacht haven. There are hopeful signs that the private sector is beginning to respond to the Development Corporation's initiatives. In 1987 a pressure group, Business Opportunities on Merseyside (BOOM), was formed which 'brings together representatives of the regional Chamber of Commerce, the CBI, the task force set up by the Government after the 1981 Toxteth riots and other investment bodies, professional organisations and major companies' (Halsall, 1987). There have been many previous attempts to market Merseyside

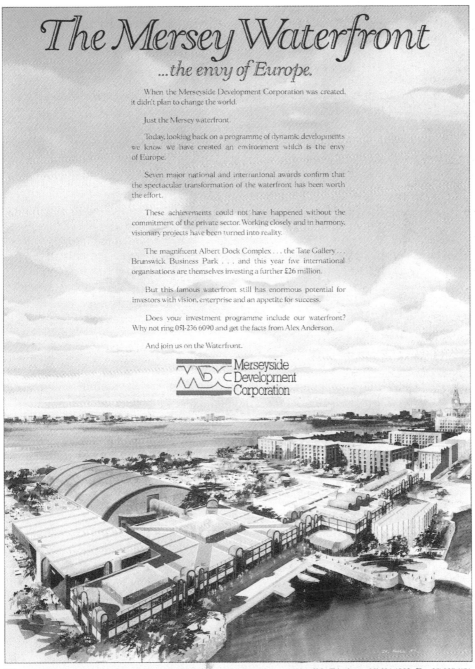

Figure 6.7    Plans of the Merseyside Development Corporation for the area to the south of the Albert Dock. The first phase will incorporate a major ice/sports arena, multi-screen cinema complex and shopping concourse. (Source: Merseyside Development Corporation, 1987)

which have received mixed receptions; it will be interesting to see if this private sector consortium is any more successful.

ASSIGNMENT

*What do you think of the Merseyside Development Corporation's strategy for urban regeneration? Is the tourist potential there? Who will benefit from the proposed developments? Will they help to change Merseyside's image and lead to further investment? How else might the grant aid have been spent? Is society progressing to a more leisured age?*

## 3. The designation of further Urban Development Corporations

The success of the London Docklands and Merseyside Development Corporations in spearheading new development has encouraged the government to designate, in 1987, further Urban Development Corporations in Tyne and Wear (Newcastle and Sunderland); Teeside; Trafford Park, Manchester and the Black Country (West Midlands). It is the Government's hope that these will act as catalysts for regeneration in some of the most depressed parts of Britain.

ASSIGNMENTS

1. *Read the following quotations by people living in or writing about the London Docklands. How far do you agree with each of the opinions expressed? What evidence can you draw on to justify your opinion?*

   *Prosperity coming to an area has to be good for everyone, there will eventually be better schools, better shops and the leisure facilities are already excellent (Lyn Holton, estate agent in Docklands,* Sunday Express, *2 August 1987).*

   *Apart from the improvement in housing for some of the people who've always lived there, the only benefits locals are going to get out of it are a few temporary gardeners' jobs on the landscaping schemes (Jack Dash, former dock workers' leader,* Daily Telegraph, *2 February 1987).*

   *We've no qualms about attracting the rich, though a lot of local people object. We want a mixed society. The rich help the area; use the shops, spend money. When we started, 95 per cent of the local housing stock was for rent. This was one of the troubles with the area in the old days. East Enders, like my family, who didn't want to live in a rented flat moved out. Of course it was the people with go who moved out, which was one reason for the decline (Ms. Trinnaman, LDDC employee,* The Observer, *1 September 1985).*

*The potential for a class war is there in Docklands. Even the houses being built by the Development Corporation, starting at £30 000 each, are believed to be beyond the means of three-quarters of East Enders; the private flats are just fantasy (M. Green,* Sunday Express, *2 August 1987).*

*The replacement jobs call for new skills. It is a shock awakening. It would be foolish to ignore the very real worries that people have. There is much to be done, but enthusiasm is generating investment. Much of it will stay and bring new life to the area (Christopher Benson, Chairman LDDC,* Daily Telegraph, *2 February 1987).*

*Ordinary people feel our localities are being taken away from us (Long-term Docklands' resident,* Daily Telegraph, *2 February 1987).*

*Traditional jobs and working class housing are what most local politicians demand. But the sons and daughters of the former dockers have a wider view. They want high-tech jobs, even if their parents do not (J. Petty,* Daily Telegraph, *2 February 1987).*

*The regeneration of London's Docklands will undoubtedly be seen as one of the greatest successes in urban renewal anywhere in London (*Times *leader, 19 February 1987).*

2. Compare the People's Plan for the Royal Docks with that of the LDDC. Which plan, in your opinion, provides a better solution for the regeneration of the Royal Docks? Give reasons to justify your choice.

## D. Power to the People?

### 1. Involving the residents: the role of community architecture

We have seen that the Government's schemes for inner city renewal have concentrated on partnerships between central government and the private sector. It is argued that the other elements which need to be taken into account are the aspirations of the local residents and the commitment and expertise of voluntary sector organisations. In Chapter 4 you saw how the Utopian schemes for urban renewal and new housing estates brought with them many problems in their implementation, and that many of the solutions put forward at that time, such as high-rise development, now stand discredited. It is suggested that one of the reasons for this is that these schemes were dreamt up and implemented by an uninvolved bureaucracy, experts who proposed housing solutions for others that they would not have tolerated for themselves (see Figure 4.2). In light of this, it is perhaps not surprising that many architects and planners have been re-assessing their roles and out of this has arisen the concept of community architecture which has been advocated by, among others, Rod Hackney. Although those practising community architecture will hold divergent views, most will subscribe to the following basic principles:

(a) The architect should act as an 'enabler', using his/her professional skills to help people who live in public housing to have what they want rather than imposing his/her solutions on them.

(b) The architect should be accessible: working and, if possible, even living in the neighbourhood so that he/she is able to discuss with individuals their particular requirements.

(c) The skills of people living in the area should be harnessed to implement schemes for housing and environmental improvement, and skill-training schemes should be introduced to help people acquire skills they may not possess. In that way, jobs for local people are made available through urban renewal schemes.

Community architects, like Rod Hackney, consider this to be most important, as they attribute high levels of unemployment, and the lack of direction and demoralisation which this causes, to be the root cause of the inner city malaise.

Community architecture initiatives have received considerable support and publicity from Prince Charles who has established a charitable trust, Inner City Aid, which aims to raise money and use it to provide financial support for inner city regeneration schemes based on community architecture principles (Marks, 1987).

## 2. Alternative perspectives on the nature of partnerships

Much of the debate surrounding policies for inner city regeneration is concerned with the nature of the partnerships that must be struck if significant progress is to be made. Some Labour-controlled authorities have looked essentially to solutions almost entirely dependent on public sector investment. For example, the Liverpool City Council of 1983–7 looked entirely to public sector finance to construct approximately 4500 semi-detached and town houses and to make good some of the mistakes that had been made in the housing developments of the 1950s and 1960s. Environmental and recreational improvements included the establishment of the 40 ha Everton Park, financed with the help of Urban Aid cash from central government, and the construction of a number of sports centres in conjunction with Task Force, the Department of the Environment partnership scheme set up after the 1981 Toxteth riots. When finance to sustain the housing programme was not forthcoming from central government, rather than abandon the scheme, the Labour councillors financed it with large loans received from foreign banks. The councillors were subsequently barred from holding public office because of their failure to set a rate for the city.

Other local authorities such as Sheffield and, before it was abolished, the Greater London Council, have set up local enterprise boards to try to generate new employment opportunities. Those authorities have seen themselves as pioneering a radical socialist economic strategy which embraces at least some of the following principles (Martin, 1987).

(i) An emphasis on supporting indigenous firms rather than trying to attract 'footloose' new investment.

(ii) Promoting more direct methods of intervention, including putting up capital and making available investment packages.

(iii) Assessing not just the commercial viability of firms but their social responsibility and accountability to the community.

(iv) Encouraging community-based actions, including specific schemes to help disadvantaged groups within the labour market.

Progress has been greatest where local authorities have forged partnerships with the private sector. This has been the case with the West Midlands and West Yorkshire Enterprise Boards and, more recently, in Sheffield which has attracted major new developments, including a major sports complex for the World Student Games.

## 3. The impact of gentrification

In American cities and some British cities where inner city regeneration has taken place, one of the consequences has been *gentrification* (see Plate 6.7). This is when houses have been improved by new, relatively high-income, families moving into a neighbourhood. Typically, these newcomers are well-educated young couples without children who both work in the city and look to the downtown area to provide them with a range of leisure facilities. Their joint incomes enable them to take out large mortgages and compete unequally with the established residents in the neighbourhood. Some of these latter families will become displaced, as they are effectively forced out, when rent and house prices escalate beyond their purchasing power (Short, 1984). Professor Bertsch, Professor of City and Regional Planning at Ohio State University, suggests that upgrading an inner city neighbourhood, while at the same time retaining at least a mix of income levels, is one of the great challenges facing those involved with inner city regeneration. It can be argued that to introduce a proportion of articulate, well-educated, middle-class families can help to bring about a general environmental improvement, which long-established residents can also enjoy. It becomes a cause for concern, however, if, over time, the social composition of the neighbourhood is totally transformed.

In Boston, Massachusetts, the process of gentrification has gradually pushed successive generations of blacks into the district of Roxburg. That area is now faced with the prospect of gentrification, and the Boston blacks for a time in 1986 flirted with the idea of *secession* – that is, becoming

Plate 6.7   A gentrified neighbourhood in Feynoord, Rotterdam. Families were rehoused in prefabricated temporary accommodation nearby while their properties were being renovated and modernised. (Author's photograph)

independent of the city authorities – as a means of resisting social and cultural change in their neighbourhood (Brummer, 1987b).

In Britain, some authorities have seen gentrification as a means of bringing about radical improvements to some of their most run-down council estates. Wandsworth Council has, for example, sold off some of its problem estates in Battersea to private developers who have totally rehabilitated them before putting the houses up for sale. The result has been, at a stroke, to eliminate an environmental problem but at the cost of displacing some of the families who lived there.

## 4. Some British case studies of inner city regeneration

### (a) Glasgow

The Glasgow Eastern Area Renewal (GEAR) Project, established in 1976, brought together a number of public sector agencies: the Glasgow City Council, the Scottish Development Agency, the Housing Corporation, the Greater Glasgow Health Board and the Manpower Services Commission. The population of the area had declined from 145 000 in 1951 to only 45 000 at the time of designation.

Between 1976 and 1986, about £470 million was channelled into the 1600 ha area, including about £300 million of public money. The regeneration

Plate 6.8   Examples of housing and environmental improvements achieved under the Glasgow Eastern Area Renewal Project.

(a) and (b) illustrate typical four-storey tenements before and after being sand blasted and comprehensively refurbished.

(c) and (d) illustrate typical maisonettes which were transformed from being vandalised and only partially occupied to being desirable residences, incorporating attractive balconies, and fronted by gardens with neat hedges. (Photographs: City of Glasgow Planning Department)

has been co-ordinated by the Scottish Development Agency, and the improvements have been considerable (see Plate 6.8). 15 000 houses have either been built or modernised, including 3000 new private houses, and 60% of those living in the area now have a better home. 250 new factories, workshops and offices have been built together with a large business development centre. Hundreds of hectares have been planted and new parks created. The Labour-controlled Glasgow City Council has adopted a pragmatic approach. Mrs Jean McFadden, the leader, stated in a recent *Guardian* article, 'We may have different political views to the people we co-operate with, but in many cases we put them aside if it is for the good of the city' (Hetherington, 1986).

### (b) Manchester

Manchester provides a good example of a British city tackling its problems of inner city decline through a vigorous partnership scheme. Population in the Inner City Partnership Area fell by 74% between 1951 and 1981. Job losses in manufacturing industry in the city amounted to 91 000, 56% of the total, with a disproportionate number being lost in the inner city area. Furthermore, unlike in many other UK cities, these job losses were not offset by an increase in jobs in the service sector. Between 1961 and 1981, Manchester suffered a net decline in service sector jobs of 1% compared with a national growth rate of 20%.

A study of the problems and potentials of business services in Inner Manchester was commissioned in 1981 and a number of initiatives have followed from this. Much attention has been paid to enhancing the physical environment and capitalising on the city's rich Victorian heritage. Pedestrian schemes have been extended and cleaning grants have begun to reveal the Victorian city centre at its finest. Housing schemes on a human scale, such as the St John's gardens scheme off Deangate, have been completed to attract a resident population back to the city centre and there are plans to convert some of the imposing vacant warehouses for residential use. The city's historic Castlefield area has become the focus of a number of major tourist initiatives, with the former City Exhibition Hall being converted to house an Air and Space Museum while, next door, the original terminus of the Liverpool to Manchester railway is being restored as a museum of science and technology. The excavations of Roman Manchester are being laid out as a public open space and the former Campfield Market Building has been refurbished as an urban studies and visitors' centre. There are also plans to develop the Bridgewater Canal basin and the extensive water areas of the Manchester Docks for recreational and leisure purposes. The first stage of riverside walkways along the River Irwell has been completed. The infrastructure of the city is also being improved. Work is well underway on renewing the antiquated sewers in central Manchester and a number of minor road improvements have gone some way to improving traffic congestion in the city centre. Congestion, however, remains a problem and there are plans to convert part of the suburban railway network for use by light rapid transit vehicles (Wright, 1985).

## 5. The American experience

Brummer, reporting on recent successes in regenerating inner city environments in the USA began his article thus:

> *From the gleaming towers of Cleveland on the grimy banks of Lake Erie, to the sundrenched skyscrapers of Los Angeles on the booming rim of the Pacific, America's inner cities are being re-shaped and revitalised with a flare and enthusiasm which would have seemed unthinkable even a decade ago when the flight to the suburbs was at its peak.*
>
> *This triumph of energy over despondency which has turned the industrial harbour of Baltimore into one of the nation's top tourist attractions and has converted Pittsburgh into one of the most liveable-in cities in the U.S., provides a shining example to Britain's urban planners struggling to come to terms with the desolation at Liverpool, the abandoned steel mills of Sheffield, and the blight at Bradford.*

To what does Brummer ascribe such a radical change of fortunes of the American inner cities? He sees partnership schemes, which cities and states have forged with the private sector, to be at the heart of it. The speed of regeneration has been facilitated by different forms of local government which give substantial powers to chief executive officers, who may be recruited from business and commerce, and who are encouraged to take decisions and initiate whatever action may be necessary. Financial incentives have also been instrumental in encouraging new investment. The most important of these is 'tax abatement', whereby a firm is exempted the payment of property taxes for a decade. Other incentives are available in designated Enterprise Zones. In Ohio, for example, the state offers credits in state taxes; training grants for each newly qualified employee; and help with costs of day-care provision for young children. In some cases, land in Enterprise Zones will be provided virtually free of charge, and plant and equipment may also attract various city, state and federal tax relief schemes (see Plate 6.9).

### (a) Baltimore

Baltimore is an example of a city which has been transformed in recent years from a city of social tension and physical deterioration to a city of

187

Plate 6.9   Urban renewal in Philadelphia's inner city. Contrast the housing and landscaping in the foreground with that in the middle distance. (Photograph: Philadelphia Convention & Visitors Bureau)

confidence and prosperity. 'Successive mayors have combined with 100 chief executive officers to rebuild a city just voted by its peers the 'most innovative' and the 'most successful' in the country' (Brummer, 1987b).

At the heart of the inner city's regeneration have been the Charles Centre, comprising a growth of prestige multi-storey office blocks and a conference and theatre complex, and Harbourplace, an imaginative development in and around the old harbour which has incorporated urban conservation measures to create an interesting mix of leisure and recreational facilities including an amazing array of ethnic and fast-food stalls, interesting small shops, an aquarium and naval exhibitions (see Plate 6.10). The Commercial Revitalisation Programme began in 1974 and has used a combination of public and private resources to establish a new economic basis for the city which has become self-sustaining. The public sector finance combined money raised through the city's own bond issue and Federal grants, Community Development Block Grants since 1975 and Urban Development Action Grants since 1978. The revitalisation programme was spearheaded by a partnership of the Department of Housing and Community Development and an association of local traders and residents. To be accepted, proposals for new commercial development must have local backing and the proposers must be able to demonstrate that there is a commitment to making improve-

188

Plate 6.10 Harbourplace, Baltimore, USA, which provided an important focus for the regeneration of the inner city. It incorporates a wide range of leisure and recreation facilities, including an aquarium and a great range of ethnic and fast food stalls. (Author's photograph)

ments in the neighbourhood. All proposals are assessed on strictly commercial criteria. If successful, the entrepreneurs will be given low-interest loans rather than grants. They also receive help with marketing, accountancy and other things necessary to get a new business off the ground or revitalise an existing one. Considerable attention has been paid to enhancing the built environment and there is a special shop front improvement loan scheme; special loans for refurbishment; and the department provides technical and architectural advice to the developers.

The rehabilitation of housing in the inner city has been spearheaded by a homesteading programme, through which houses are offered for a nominal $1 and the new owners are relieved of paying property taxes for one year (Martin, 1987).

### (b) Cleveland

The inner city of Cleveland has also experienced a marked change in its fortunes in recent years. Cleveland reached its ultimate low in the late 1970s. The population of the city had fallen from 914 808 in 1950 to 573 822 in 1980; pollution was a major problem and in June 1969 its main river, the Cuyahoga, which was polluted by oil and debris, burst into flames, virtually

189

destroying two railway bridges which crossed it. In 1978, Cleveland became the first US city to default when it failed to meet payments to six banks on some $15.5 million debts. Since 1979 the inner city area has undergone a notable transformation under the leadership of Republican mayor, George Vionovich. He brought in experts from the city's seven major accounting firms to proffer advice, and head-hunted business people to take over the major city departments. The mayor has worked in partnership with the city's chief executive officer and the managers of major local companies of transform the economic base of the city.

Cleveland had been a centre of heavy industry, in particular steel making, but had largely lost its traditional industrial base, through industrial contraction, in the 1960s and 1970s. The city has harnessed City revenue, Federal block grants, private sector finance and the resources of the Cleveland Foundation, a charitable trust set up by the Rockefellers to enhance the environment, improve the infrastructure and attract new enterprises. The downtown district has been transformed, with the conversion of existing buildings to new shops, restaurants and luxury hotels and a direct high-speed train link has been provided to the airport. The city has already had considerable success in attracting new enterprises and has gone a long way in diversifying its economic base.

An important start has also been made in improving some of the appalling inner city housing. The city's department of community development has rehabilitated some of the older property and overseen a new development, Lexington Village, in the black ghetto in the segregated East Side. The department developed the infrastructure and found a private developer to build the new houses.

Brummer concludes that 'the common thread running through all the initiatives aimed at restoring Cleveland to its former glory is the way in which public funds have been combined with private and foundation money to stem the outflow of people, capital and jobs' (Brummer, 1987a).

*(c)  An evaluation of American inner city policies*

Much of the regeneration of American inner cities arose from action initiated after the Watts district of Los Angeles riots of 1965 and the more serious and more widespread riots which affected a number of American cities, most notably Detroit, in the summer of 1967. The Johnson Administration set up a Commission under David Ginsberg to try to establish the cause of the riots and the Commission concluded that the most important single factor was racism which put black Americans at a grave disadvantage. The last 20 years has seen much progress in civil rights, and opportunities for America's black population have increased greatly. One indication of this is that in 1987 there were no fewer than 293 black mayors in the USA. Furthermore, city authorities have endeavoured to ensure, through 'contract compliance' arrangements, that any private sector construction company working for the city authorities employs at least 50% of its labour force locally. In addition, a proportion of local authority contracts must be placed with companies employing disadvantaged groups. Some would argue, however, that the highly capitalised city centre renewal schemes have provided few other benefits to inner city dwellers. For example, the brand new 73 storeys high Renaissance Centre (see Plate 6.11) in Detroit, which includes shops, offices, apartments and recreation and leisure facilities, is referred to by some of its critics as 'an island of renewal in a sea of decay'. Others see it as a catalyst for more widespread inner city renewal, and certainly some of the immediately adjacent neighbourhoods have benefited through a process of gentrification, with warehouses and other buildings being converted to apartments and ethnic eating places. Nevertheless, in Lower East Side, the soup kitchen, which was started as a temporary emergency

Plate 6.11 The 73 storeys high Renaissance Centre, Detroit, towers above the city. It was built through a partnership forged between the city administration and the private sector. It contains shops, offices, apartments, hotels and recreation and leisure facilities. (Photograph: Barnaby's)

measure in 1929, continues and is reported to be serving six times as many meals today as in 1967, the year of the riots.

## 6. Conclusion

Policies for tackling inner city problems have revolved around the establishment of partnerships but the precise nature of these partnerships depends on the prevailing ideology. There is no single panacea. Different inner city areas display different characteristics. This implies that policies must be flexible and imaginative if they are to be successful. Ideally they should have the resources of both local and central government, working in harmony to a set of agreed aims, and establish partnerships between the public and private sectors co-operating closely with local residents and community organisations who can ensure that what is done for their benefit is appropriate and in their interests. The 'solutions' must not be imposed from above by experts and bureaucrats but they must harness the energy and initiatives, and embrace the aspirations, of the people who live in the areas.

Parkinson & Wilks (1983) take a rather cynical, but perhaps realistic, view of the role successive governments in the UK have played in initiating and implementing policies for the inner cities:

> *national policy making for the inner city has been less an interactive process, as has sometimes been claimed by those involved, than it has been government by spasm. The inner city has been elevated or relegated in status on the political agenda and allocated resources according to a variety of criteria, frequently perceived political advantage, but rarely individual institutional need (p. 36).*

In spite of the progress that has been made in recent years in attracting new investment into inner city areas in both the UK and USA, there remains a hard core of underprivileged and disadvantaged people who have been little affected. Johnston (1982) has suggested that, to an increasing extent, a dual economy is operating in American and British cities (see Figure 6.8). The majority of urban dwellers are in employment and enjoy relatively high standards of living. They are part of what Johnston has described as the cycle of affluence. They have benefited from increased wage levels, which continue to outstrip rates of inflation. Their comfortable life styles are in marked contrast to those inner city dwellers trapped in a cycle of poverty and deprivation. Up to now, policies of successive governments have failed to make any significant impact on such people. The Church of England's (1985) report, *Faith in the City*, suggested that, as a nation, Britain has a moral responsibility for the disadvantaged. In a leading article, in response to this report, the *Financial Times* referred to the estimated 15% of Britain's population 'who are too far outside the mainstream of prosperity: not just the unemployed but the old, disabled and some members of minority

192

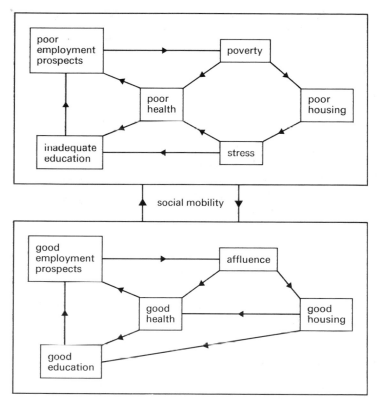

Figure 6.8   The dual economy: the cycle of poverty and the cycle of affluence. (Source: Johnston, 1982, p. 281)

communities'. The article went on to suggest that: 'The number is too high and is unacceptable in a civilised society. It is also low enough to be manageable and dealt with' (*Financial Times*, 24 December 1985). In the final analysis, one of the criteria for evaluating policies for inner city regeneration should be the impact they have had on those trapped in the cycle of poverty.

ASSIGNMENTS
1. *Immediately after the 1967 Detroit riots, President Johnson said 'We should attack these conditions not because we are frightened by conflict but because we are fired by conscience.' Discuss how far you think this is true for Britain today.*
2. *Do you think that racism is a major cause of inner city deprivation? In what ways is it manifest and how can it be counteracted?*
3. *What role, if any, do you think the public sector should have in inner city renewal?*

# E. Social Patterns: Techniques for Analysis

In order to formulate policies for inner city, or other, residential areas, it is necessary to be able to devise and apply criteria for determining where the areas are located and what their characteristics are. At first sight this may seem simple: we 'know' from the media that Toxteth, Sparkbrook, Camden and St Paul's are the inner city areas of Liverpool, Birmingham, London and Bristol respectively and that these are 'problem areas'. But if you live in one of these areas you may resent the implication that your address explains your status and behaviour. Similarly if you are a West Indian, Asian or Irish reader you may be angry with the common assumption on television or in the newspapers that your ethnicity is a major factor in determining how the rest of society views your employability or trustworthiness. In short, the kind of knowledge which enables people to pass judgement on areas of a town or its inhabitants is often mere prejudice. Clearly we need to refine our knowledge of the social areas of our cities if we are to plan for their efficient operation. The techniques available for us to do this are 'objective' or 'subjective'. Objective criteria, such as mapping areas of low property values or high unemployment, rely on the judgement of 'outsiders': statisticians, planners and other professionals. Subjective criteria involve the residents of an area determining their own perception of the neighbourhood under discussion.

## 1. Objective analysis

Factor analysis, which was discussed in the previous chapter, is one technique which has been used by geographers to try to tease out the social characteristics of small areas in towns. In Britain, data have been assembled for census enumeration districts, which each contain between about 250 and 750 people. The data, drawn from census material, combine standardised scores on such factors as the proportion of households lacking basic amenities such as hot and cold running water, inside toilet, the proportion of households which are overcrowded (that is, with more than 1.5 persons per room), and the proportion of heads of households who are unemployed. The combined scores provide some indication of the relative well-being of households within each enumeration district and these can be mapped to illustrate spatial contrasts within the town (see pages 146 to 150).

## 2. Subjective assessment

Earlier in this chapter the term 'sentiment' was used (p. 158) to describe the subjective cultural value which urban populations may place upon particular buildings or locations, often as a motive for their preservation. Some American geographers (Firey, 1945; Buttimer, 1975) observed that perceptions of the value of particular locations seemed to be an over-riding factor in determining their land use. Firey identified certain cultural and non-rational values operating in Boston which had exerted a considerable influence on the morphology of the town. For example, the district of Beacon Hill, situated close to the commercial core of Boston, should in theory have been invaded by commercial land uses, if ecological processes alone operated (see pages 117 to 123). Yet it had remained a high-class residential district. Firey suggested that this was because the district had acquired certain sentimental and symbolic associations which were collectively recognised and these had preserved it from commercial encroachment. In a rather different vein, cultural associations influenced the social composition of the population residing in North End, an area of dilapidated slum dwellings which would have been regarded by the classical ecologists as representing an area of minimum choice. This district had acted as a reception area for immigrant Italian families and retained certain sentimental associations for such families, even after they had improved their economic status and could have moved to better residential districts.

It is from pioneering works such as that of Firey that the concept of *social space* has developed. Social space may be defined as a synthesis of objective physical space and the perceived dimensions of space (Jones & Eyles, 1977). It embraces both activity space and awareness or perceptual space.

Social space

Activity space        Awareness space

*Activity space* describes the distribution of people (where they live), and the movement of people: to work, to shop and for social events (how people live within a spatial context). *Awareness space* describes the way people perceive their environment. An individual looks at the urban environment selectively, mentally organising what is seen and giving it meaning. Environmental images are influenced by personal values, aspirations and cultural traditions. These act as a kind of filter distorting what is seen and giving the objective dimensions of the environment subjective meaning. Images of the urban environment possessed by the individual thus form a link between reality and behaviour. J. Doherty's schematic representation of this link is shown in Figure 6.9.

Pocock & Hudson (1978) in their book *Images of the Urban Environment* include a series of mental maps of Durham, each compiled by different categories of people: the child, the student, working-class and middle-class residents, and tourists (see Figure 6.10). None conforms more than approximately to reality. The child's view (a) is egocentric – school and nearby house loom large – while the student's map (b) over-emphasises the district around the University with which he or she is most familiar. The mental

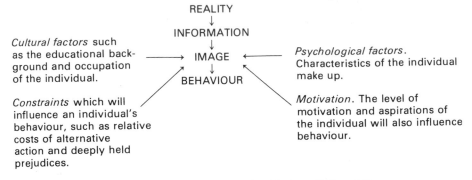

Figure 6.9   Reality-behaviour links. (Source: based on Herbert, 1972, p. 253)

map of the middle-class resident (d) is more accurate and detailed than that of the working-class resident (c). The tourists possess another distinctive viewpoint (e) (f). Their grasp of the structure of the town centre is limited and they concentrate on the aesthetic rather than the functional. The fact that we perceive places differently in turn influences the way we behave. The student, with a limited perception of Durham, is unlikely to use facilities in certain parts of the town which are unfamiliar, even if those facilities may be superior to the ones used frequently, and the tourists are unlikely to stray out of the city centre which they perceive to be surrounded by a somewhat hostile ring road.

Although each individual creates his or her own image there is a broad measure of image agreement among members of a social group, each member sharing common experiences and cultural traditions. A pilot study conducted by the Advance Planning Section of the Los Angeles City Planning Commission explored this concept, comparing the environmental imagery of five different samples. Each represented a distinctive social group drawn from contrasting locations in the city (Orleans, 1973). Figures 6.11 and 6.12 are the composite mental maps of Los Angeles as envisaged by two of these groups, one from Avalon, near Watts, a predominantly black sample located in a south-eastern district of the city, another from Westwood, a non-ethnic upper-class district adjacent to the University of California campus. The composite mental maps incorporated the following elements which had been identified previously by K. Lynch in his seminal work *The Image of the City* (1960).

(a) Paths: channels along which the observer moves.
(b) Districts: medium-to-large sections of the city perceived as having some common identity.
(c) Nodes or centres: strategic points such as route junctions and enclosed squares.

Figure 6.10   People's perceptions of Durham. (Source: Pocock & Hudson, 1978, p. 64)   ▶

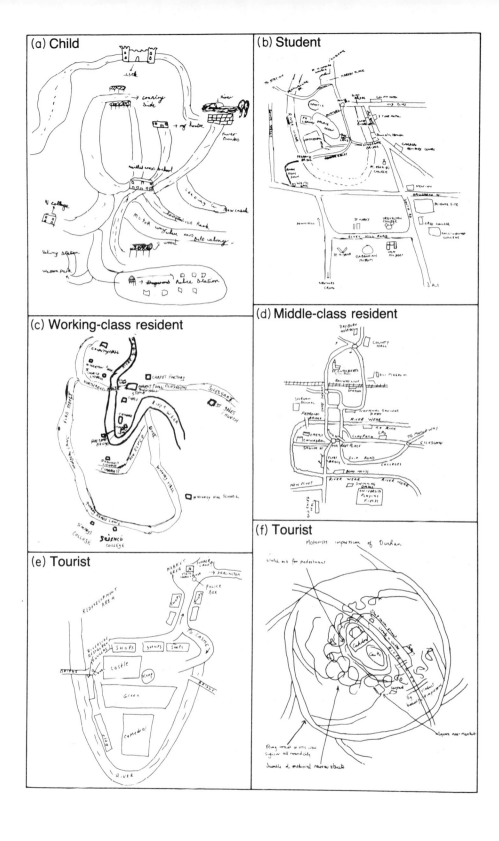

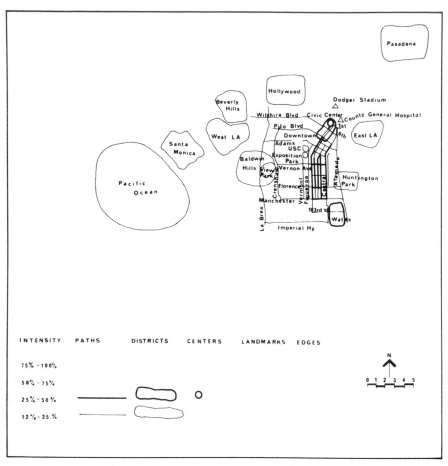

Figure 6.11   Images of Los Angeles: the residents of Avalon. (Source: Reprinted with permission from Downs & Stead, 1973)

(d)  Landmarks: distinctive features in the townscape.
(e)  Edges: linear elements comprising boundaries between districts and/or barriers to movement.

(The 'intensity' refers to the proportion of the sample that included the element in their mental map.)

These reveal that Avalon respondents had a rather restricted conception of the city. They primarily distinguished a number of parallel routes leading from Avalon to the city centre and several discrete and unconnected districts. In contrast, the perceptions of the Westwood respondents were well formed and detailed and indicated a good general knowledge of the entire city and its environs.

These variations in the degrees of awareness displayed by groups and individuals are fundamental to an understanding of the concept of social

198

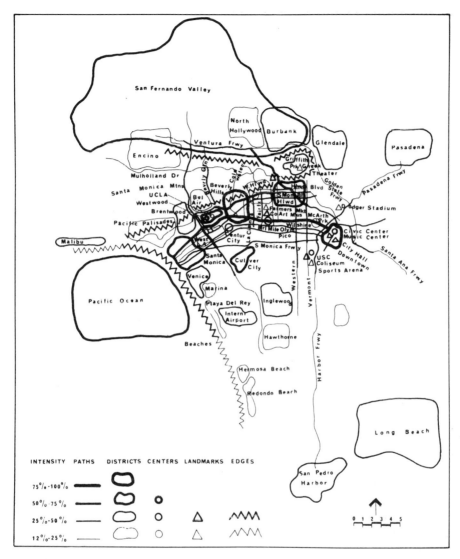

Figure 6.12   Images of Los Angeles: the residents of Westwood. (Source: Reprinted with permission from Downs & Stead, 1973)

space. For, as we have seen, social space involves the inter-relationship of both *awareness space* (the perceived dimensions of space) and the more objective and easily identifiable *activity space*. It provides some insight into 'how individuals and groups pattern space by their perceptions and activities' (Jones & Eyles, 1977). The concept of social space may be better understood by a study of the neighbourhood, the local area with which we are most familiar and with which we can often most readily identify.

# F. Neighbourhood and Community

## 1. Defining the neighbourhood

The neighbourhood is a territorial space which has both spatial attributes (area, location) and social ones (character, reputation, associations). The inter-relationship between the spatial and the social dimensions is not uniform and is perhaps best explored by using the notion of a continuum.

(a) At its simplest level, the neighbourhood is little more than an ill-defined territory lacking any sort of individual identity or social cohesion. The only feature which distinguishes such an *arbitrary neighbourhood* is one of *propinquity* or spatial proximity; that is, the people who reside in it all live relatively close to one another but have no real social or communal contact.

(b) The next stage in the continuum is the *physical neighbourhood* which is distinguished by distinct physical characteristics and clearly defined boundaries. For example, the houses may be of similar age and style and the neighbourhood may have boundaries formed by barriers such as a railway line, canal, major road, industrial estate, an extensive public open space, land liable to flood or steep slopes.

(c) The *homogeneous neighbourhood* possesses the attributes of the physical neighbourhood: a clearly defined territory with distinct physical characteristics. However, it has also acquired certain social characteristics and is occupied by a group of people with common social and cultural attributes, for example people of similar socio-economic status and/or members of an ethnic or racial minority group.

(d) The *functional neighbourhood* possesses all the characteristics of a homogeneous neighbourhood but within it additional activities such as shopping, education, church-going and recreation take place. In other words a local shopping centre, a primary school, a church and a branch library may act as foci within the neighbourhood, and their catchment areas will broadly coincide with the boundaries of the neighbourhood. Research by Glass in Middlesbrough led her to conclude that functional neighbourhoods can be most clearly defined as those parts of a town which are isolated and geographically separate entities, particularly if such areas also form the poorest parts of the town (Glass, 1948).

(e) At the most sophisticated level, the neighbourhood forms a distinct *community* in which people have 'developed a sense of togetherness and also tend to associate with each other more than outsiders' (Blowers, 1973). Obviously, such a sense of community develops gradually over a considerable period of time, and length of residence is clearly an important factor. Thus a neighbourhood will develop a sense of community only where there is stability and limited movement of families into and out of it. Other important factors in the development of

200

community are common social and demographic characteristics. For example, families may have reached a similar stage in the family cycle and have shared attitudes: there is a preponderance of families with young children, or old people.

Class is an important consideration in the development of distinctive homogeneous neighbourhoods with a sense of community. Long-established working-class neighbourhoods are likely to be more socially cohesive than their middle-class equivalents. In their study of Bethnal Green, a working-class district in the East End of London, Young & Willmott (1962) vividly describe the sense of community that existed there.

> *In Bethnal Green the person who says he 'knows everyone' is, of course, exaggerating, but pardonably so. He does, with various degrees of intimacy, know many people outside (but often through) his family, and it is this which makes it, in the view of many informants, a 'friendly place'. ... There is a sense of community, that is a feeling of solidarity between people who occupy the common territory which springs from the fact that people and their families have lived there a long time.*

In contrast, in Woodford, an established middle-class suburb on the fringes of London, the social ties are more loose-knit and the sense of community less well developed.

> *In Woodford there is not the same gregariousness as in Bethnal Green and parents and children often live at some distance from each other. Although they saw each other less frequently, contact with their families was maintained both by visiting and in many cases by car or telephone. Willmott and Young observed a distinct 'life cycle of kinship' with the generations living apart until the parents reached retirement age at which point they were often reunited with their children.*

## 2. Perception of the neighbourhood

It seems that one of the reasons why a sense of community would appear to be best developed in those parts of the city where the population is stable and well established is that an individual will often develop a unique relationship with his or her birthplace. This is because 'the immediate physical and social environment is, without doubt, crucially important in the early psychological and social development of the individual' (Pocock & Hudson, 1978).

Pocock and Hudson suggest that people have three basic psychological needs: identity, security and stimulation; and the local environment or neighbourhood is extremely important in contributing to the satisfaction of these needs. They conclude that people need to identify with a limited territorial space. Certainly studies of the way in which people perceive their neighbourhoods would seem to confirm this. For example there is a tendency among those who have lived in the same house for some time and who are very familiar with their local areas to 'better' them when describing them to others. If asked to draw a mental map of their neighbourhood they would tend to make it more uniform and attractive than it in fact is. Similarly, surveys of people's perception of neighbourhood facilities have indicated that they perceive the desirable elements, such as the school, library, park, post office, to be closer to their homes than they are in reality while the less desirable elements such as main trunk roads and heavy industrial plants may be perceived to be farther away.

## 3. Attempts to create new neighbourhoods

As we noted in Chapter 4, the post-war period has witnessed a phase of unprecedented urban renewal and growth. Vast slum clearance programmes in the inner cities have resulted in the destruction of established communities and many thousands of families have been uprooted and rehoused in sprawling suburban estates, new towns or comprehensively redeveloped parts of the city. It is hardly surprising, therefore, that one of the principal planning objectives in post-war Britain has been to recreate clearly defined neighbourhoods within the new housing developments. This has inevitably involved architects and planners in trying to establish what is the optimum neighbourhood design and, in this respect, consideration has been given to the following.

(a) *Layout.* Can housing estates be planned in such a way as to encourage social interaction and engender a sense of community? Probably the major single influence in this respect has been Clarence Perry's Radburn, New Jersey, scheme (Herbert, 1972). This incorporated traffic/pedestrian segregation and a network of footpaths designed, in theory, to make it more likely that people would meet and get to know each other. At the centre of each neighbourhood was a primary school, and shops and services were built in a cluster on the edge of the neighbourhood. Many of the neighbourhood designs incorporated in British new towns have been modifications of the Radburn layout.

(b) *The boundaries of neighbourhoods.* How clear cut should these be? Does spatial isolation enhance the development of functional and social interaction within a neighbourhood? In some British new towns attempts were made to isolate neighbourhoods by using wedges of open spaces to form their boundaries. Peterborough provides a good example of this. Both planned open spaces and the main road networks have been used to separate the new neighbourhoods which have been grafted onto the existing town (see Figure 6.13). Recent attempts at neighbour-

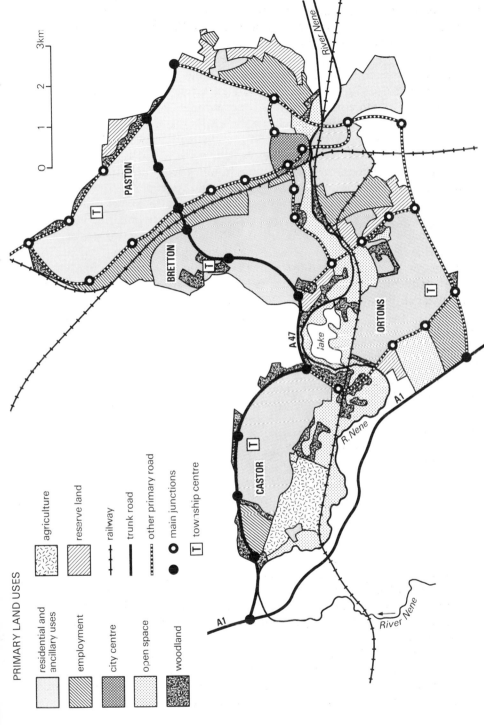

PRIMARY LAND USES

- residential and ancillary uses
- employment
- city centre
- open space
- woodland
- agriculture
- reserve land
- railway
- trunk road
- other primary road
- main junctions
- T township centre

Figure 6.13  Neighbourhoods in Peterborough. (Source: based on an original plan in *Greater Peterborough Master Plan*, Peterborough Development Corporation)

hood planning have, however, moved away from this policy, as it is recognised that physical isolation can be achieved only at the expense of convenience.

(c) *The degree of social homogeneity/heterogeneity.* In general within British new towns, planners have attempted to create socially heterogeneous neighbourhoods in which the social balance reflects that in Britain as a whole. The policy has, however, been modified in more recent developments and it is increasingly recognised that the pursuit of social balance may actively inhibit the development of a sense of community within a neighbourhood.

Unfortunately, attempts to create communities have been relatively unsuccessful and, partly as a result of this, the whole concept of the neighbourhood unit is increasingly being questioned. There are those who claim that the neighbourhood has less relevance as the urban population becomes more mobile and is less dependent on spatial proximity for social and functional interaction.

In contrast, others contend that an individual needs to be able to identify with a limited territorial space and failure to do so can create stress and psychological disorder.

ASSIGNMENTS

1. *Find out which districts in your town are perceived by your fellow students as displaying the greatest sense of community. Work through the distinguishing characteristics of neighbourhoods (page 200) and assess which of these characteristics apply to the community neighbourhoods in your town.*

2. *Conduct a questionnaire survey in your own neighbourhood to find out if there is image agreement over the boundaries of the neighbourhood, that is, if people living in the neighbourhood perceive it to have clearly defined boundaries. Test the hypothesis that local people have a clearer perception of the boundaries of old-established neighbourhoods than in neighbourhoods in new housing districts.*

## G. The Suburb: Ideal Home or Subtopia?

As has already been pointed out (page 83) the twin facilities of loan capital for house purchase and improved public transport enabled the aspiring middle class to separate their place of residence from their work place in the late nineteenth century. With the spread of bus services and private car ownership in the inter-war and post-war period the development of residential suburbs along and between the arterial roads linking major towns became a widespread feature of the urban landscape, especially in Britain and North America. Such areas became increasingly self-contained, with shops, schools and churches contributing to the development of social neighbourhoods which were nevertheless almost exclusively the preserve of middle-income groups.

Two main phases of suburban expansion can be identified in many towns. Firstly there was a period of growth between 1920 and 1935, characterised by the building of semi-detached three-bedroomed houses with small front garden and long back garden, in crescents and cul-de-sacs with little regard to local topography or architectural style. Estates of these houses are often served by small local shopping parades but have few other services. Although popular and originally quite cheap (costing about £400 per dwelling when built) they provide a rather inflexible environment, being designed for nuclear family occupation. The second phase of development took place in the late 1960s and early 1970s. A wider range of properties was constructed, including more large and individually designed houses, at lower residential densities (although, as land values rose, densities again increased towards the end of the decade). There was less emphasis on neighbourhood design, although to cope with the post-war 'baby boom' local authorities often had to provide schools, health and library facilities for these new housing areas. In some developments, maisonettes and small blocks of flats were included, though these were less popular on wholly private estates. No serious attempt was made to provide public transport; indeed as the real price of fuel fell it was assumed that increasing private car ownership would make local bus services unnecessary.

As urban land prices in the suburbs rose, reaching as much as £2.5 million per hectare in the south-east in the 1980s, developers preferred to redevelop inner city sites or to move to the smaller 'freestanding' market towns where land was cheaper, in their search for new locations. Moreover the suburbs were experiencing their own problems. The isolation of young mothers and the elderly, the lack of entertainment for teenagers, the high cost of journeys to work and the absence of local employment contributed to the boring and unattractive image of suburban life. Increasingly young couples postponed having children and 'settling down', partly because of the financial desirability of both partners continuing in full-time employment. Also the working population became more mobile, especially those in professional and managerial positions who are likely to travel more than 25 km to work each day, and to change their place of work (as a result of company strategy) quite often. For them, residence on the edge of a particular town may be less relevant than a location accessible to a number of towns within a 50–75 km radius.

As a result, the suburb has become less attractive, although the development of out-of-town shopping centres and the relocation of new and larger educational, hospital and industrial premises at the edge of towns has given a new lease of life to many, especially if a nearby bypass or motorway access point means rapid communication is possible with other centres. On the whole, however, the population, especially of the inner inter-war suburbs is ageing, and suburban expansion relies upon the increase in new households (as children leave home) rather than rapid population increase.

ASSIGNMENT
*Choose two areas of suburban housing in your own town, one from the inter-war period and the other from the post-war period. Compare (using the OS 1 : 2500 map if possible) the density of development, to identify districts with approximately the same number of dwelling units. Contrast the type, range and number of services (retail, social, recreational, etc.) available in each area. Sketch typical facades of houses in each area, noting the building materials and architectural features characteristic of each development. On the basis of these notes try to evaluate the positive and negative features of suburban housing areas and explain what processes appear to be going on there today. For example, you may be able to see clear trends in shopping, transport or property maintenance which will act as clues to the changing status of these areas.*

## H. Segregation and Mobility

Having discussed some of the techniques whereby social areas can be identified (the *pattern*) we can now turn our attention to the *processes* which help to bring these about. The two which will be discussed at some length are residential segregation and residential mobility.

As we have seen, not all segregation is discriminatory: some groups choose to preserve their own cultural identity by close residence. In other cases the otherwise attractive suburban housing estate may seem isolating to residents who have no car or whose social mores discourage interaction with neighbours. Moreover external cultural and economic factors may limit access to and enjoyment of housing in individual cases. For example, in the summer of 1987, *The Times* noted two instances of such factors. One was that Liverpudlians moving to the south coast were being dubbed 'Scousers' by other residents of Bournemouth and they claimed discrimination against them in the job and housing markets because of their accents. The other was a report that, because of the differential in housing and transport costs, a professional person in northern England earning around £16 000 per year would need between £5000 and £7000 more annually to sustain the same living standards if he or she moved to the south-east, while the actual salary differential was only £1200. This was blamed for the difficulty of attracting workers to the London region, despite higher unemployment levels in the north-west. Such examples remind us that the theoretical processes of segregation and mobility described below may be only part of the decision-making activity undertaken by individuals, and they underline the importance of subjective factors in spatial behaviour.

# 1. Residential segregation

Many studies using multivariate analysis have revealed racial and ethnic status as important variables in accounting for residential differentiation. The segregation of racial and ethnic minority groups into distinctive quarters of towns is not a new phenomenon. A feature of many medieval towns in Europe, the Near East and North Africa was an exclusive Jewish quarter or ghetto. This area was often walled and physically separate and had developed partly in response to the determination of the Orthodox Jews to retain intact their cultural identity (Jones & Eyles, 1977). In present-day cities the segregation is unlikely to be as extreme but will probably be most evident in multi-racial communities or where fundamental cultural differences exist.

## (a) Techniques

Studies of residential segregation within towns have demanded precise quantification, and a number of methods have been devised for measuring and mapping the distribution of minority groups. These include the *location quotient* and the *segregation index*.

The location quotient indicates the deviation of a minority population from what would be expected if its members were evenly distributed throughout the city.

$$\text{Location quotient} = \frac{\text{observed}}{\text{expected}}$$

Thus if 3% of the population of a city are Poles and they are evenly distributed, then each sub-division of the city will have 3% Poles. In this case the location quotient would be $3/3 = 1$. If on the other hand 10% of the population of a single ward were Poles, the location quotient would be $10/3 = 3.3$. Thus location quotients of more than 1 imply that the group in question is over-represented while figures below 1 indicate under-representation. The location quotients for each ward or enumeration district can be mapped to give an indication of the degree of clustering of the minority groups in the city. (For a fuller explanation of location quotients see Bale 1981). The segregation index is also a measure of the extent to which the distribution of a minority population group deviates from a random distribution (Boal, 1976). The index is applied to small areal divisions of the city such as census enumeration districts and extends from 0 to 1, where 0 represents an unsegregated population and 1 total segregation. Thus if 25% of a town's population are Asians, an enumeration district which also contained 25% Asians would have a segregation index of 0 whereas an enumeration district containing 100% Asians or no Asians would have a segregation index of 1. In enumeration districts in which the Asian population falls between 0 and 25% or 25 and 100% the segregation index will lie somewhere between 0 and 1.

Techniques such as these can be used to illustrate patterns of residential segregation. For example, studies of Asian households in Glasgow (Kearsley & Srivasteva, 1974) and the distribution of Commonwealth immigrants in Birmingham have both suggested a pattern of discontinuous clusters in the middle zone of each city. P. N. Jones (1970), in his Birmingham study, found that the distribution correlated closely with a broadly concentric ring of Victorian and Edwardian later by-law houses and modest villas (see Figure 6.14). The type of housing proved an important locating factor because much of the property in the 'zone in transition', which might be expected to be a reception area for newly arrived immigrant families (see page 135), was municipally owned and consequently not freely available to

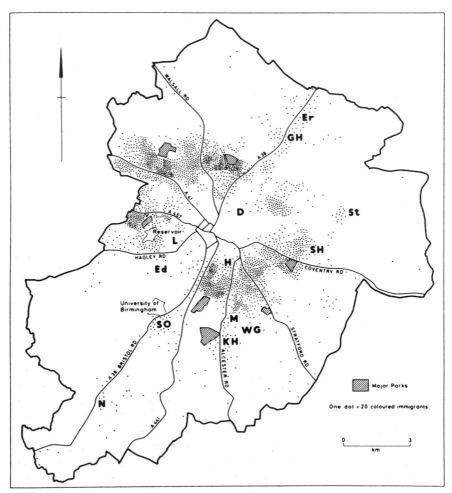

Figure 6.14   The distribution of Commonwealth immigrants in Birmingham, 1966. (Source: Jones, 1970)

208

immigrants. This made 'invasion' into the inner city largely impossible and had the effect of pushing it farther out into districts which contained substantial houses, often with short leases, which could be purchased.

In American cities, where the ethnic and racial minorities are of longer standing, sectoral segregation patterns have been observed. For example, Chicago's 'black belt' has migrated outwards in a wedge or sector within which there has been a degree of sifting based on socio-economic status. In other words the poorest families have been left behind near the city centre as the segregated sector has grown outwards (see Figure 5.22, page 150).

## (b) Functions of segregated areas

Population migration is the principal *raison d'être* for residential segregation based on race or ethnicity. When migrants first arrive in a town or city, they are usually easily distinguishable from the host group and, if it is possible, choose to live in closely knit socially and culturally distinct neighbourhoods. Increasing tension, and perhaps even conflict, between population groups can also lead to more exaggerated residential segregation. This has been the case in Belfast since the onset of the most recent civil disturbances. Housing areas have become more and more homogeneous as Protestants have moved from predominantly Roman Catholic areas and vice versa (see Figure 6.16).

F. W. Boal (1976) identifies a number of distinct functions that ethnically segregated residential areas fulfil. These are:

(i)   *defensive functions*, the area providing for the migrant, in a strange 'land', psychological security and a secure haven in which language and customs are familiar;
(ii)  *avoidance functions*, allowing migrants a period of adjustment during which they can become gradually more familiar with the customs of the host group;
(iii) *preservation functions*, permitting the cultural heritage of the minority immigrant group to be preserved more easily;
(iv)  *'attack' functions*, providing a basis for political strength and facilitating joint action by the minority group members.

The segregated residential area may be a transitory feature of the city which breaks up gradually as the second and third generation migrants are assimilated and disperse, or it may become more permanent, developing into an enclave or ghetto. Boal suggests that the degree of permanence of the residentially segregated area depends to a large extent on the degree of racial and cultural distinctiveness of the immigrant group from the host group. The range of possible spatial outcomes of migration are summarised in Figure 6.15. In cases where the ethnic group differs little from the host society, the minority group is assimilated relatively quickly. On the other hand, where contrasts are very pronounced, a permanent enclave or ghetto

209

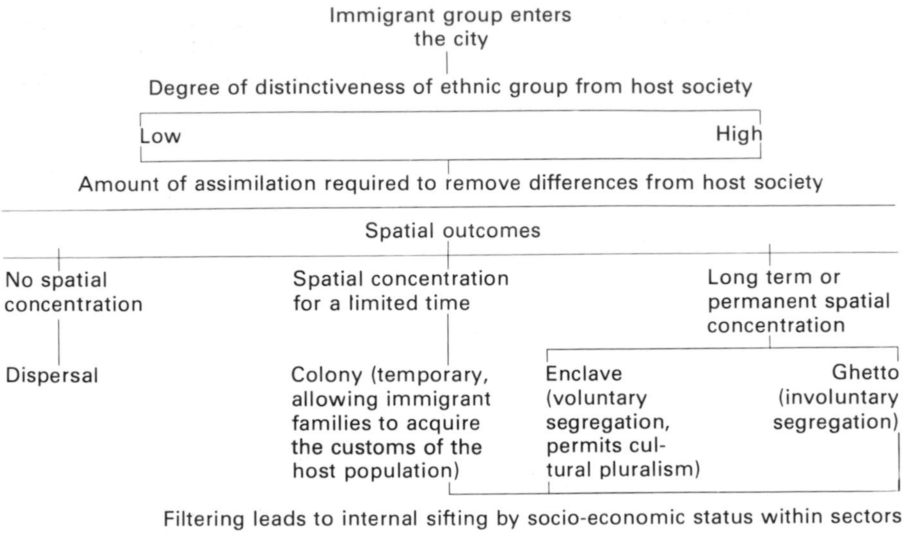

Immigrant group enters
the city
|
Degree of distinctiveness of ethnic group from host society

| Low | High |
| --- | --- |

Amount of assimilation required to remove differences from host society

Spatial outcomes

| No spatial concentration | Spatial concentration for a limited time | Long term or permanent spatial concentration |
| --- | --- | --- |
| Dispersal | Colony (temporary, allowing immigrant families to acquire the customs of the host population) | Enclave (voluntary segregation, permits cultural pluralism) | Ghetto (involuntary segregation) |

Filtering leads to internal sifting by socio-economic status within sectors

Figure 6.15 The possible spatial outcomes of immigrant ethnic minority groups moving into a city. (After F. W. Boal)

may develop. The diagram also envisages an intermediate stage where a temporary 'colony' is formed allowing the immigrant families gradually to acquire the customs or patterns of generally accepted behaviour before they are assimilated.

### (c)  Residential segregation in Belfast

In his study of residential patterns in Belfast, Boal found that, in common with other Western cities, there is an increase in average socio-economic status and decrease in population densities with distance from the city centre (Boal, 1970a). Superimposed on this are sectors of high and low status. A further differentiation in the western low-status sector arises from religious differences. In this sector divisions between the Protestant and Roman Catholic housing areas are very sharp and are often marked by non-residential land uses such as factory sites or railway lines. Where this is not possible the transition occurs within the width of a single street. Boal, conducting his research before the outbreak of civil disturbance, analysed site characteristics to define two culturally distinct residential areas: Clonard, in which 98% of the population was Roman Catholic, and Shankill (I) in which 99% of the population was Protestant (Boal, 1970b). The two areas meet in a very narrow band restricted to a single street, Cupar Street (see Figure 6.16).

Boal then proceeded to examine the activity patterns of the two clearly segregated groups and found these to be extremely territorial. He discovered that 89% of those living in Shankill (I) went to Shankill Road to catch a bus

210

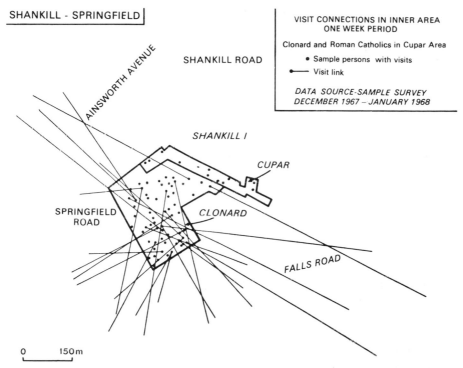

SHANKILL ROAD

AINSWORTH AVENUE

SHANKILL I

CUPAR

SPRINGFIELD
ROAD

CLONARD

FALLS ROAD

VISIT CONNECTIONS IN INNER AREA
ONE WEEK PERIOD

Clonard and Roman Catholics in Cupar Area

• Sample persons with visits

•——— Visit link

*DATA SOURCE-SAMPLE SURVEY
DECEMBER 1967 – JANUARY 1968*

0    150m

Figure 6.16    An indication of territoriality in Belfast based on local area names in the Shankill–Springfield district. 94% of those in Clonard called the area Clonard, Springfield or Falls and none used the term Shankill. In Shankill I no one used Clonard, Springfield or Falls and 77% used Shankill. In the transitional Cupar St., 37% used Clonard, Springfield or Falls and 26% Shankill. (Source: Boal, 1970a)

to take them to the city centre, while 93% living in Clonard went to the Falls or Springfield Road, not all minimising the distance. He also found that shopping trips were strongly focused on each area's 'own' spine road and that visitor connections revealed mutually exclusive networks (see Figure 6.17). In other words there was practically no spatial interaction between the two groups. Each group identified with a clearly defined territorial space which gave it security and a sense of belonging. Thus in Belfast cultural and religious differences have caused the Roman Catholics and Protestants to become increasingly segregated and, in effect, enclaves have developed.

## 2. Residential mobility

Studies which concentrate on the demand side of the housing market must inevitably be concerned with decisions made on an individual single-family basis, for it is at this level that a decision to move house is taken. Each year

211

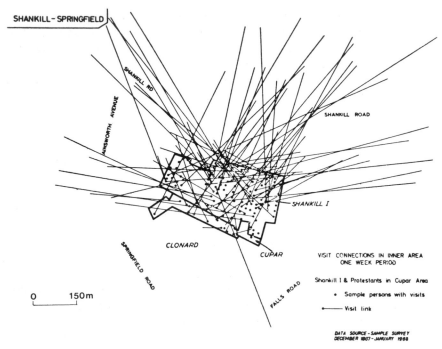

Figure 6.17 Territoriality in Belfast, visitor connections of Catholics and Protestants in the Shankill–Springfield district. (Source: Boal, 1970a)

approximately one in ten households in Britain moves house. In the USA residential mobility is even higher and approximately 18% of the households change residence in the course of a year (Adams & Gilder, 1976).

### (a) Why people move house

The reasons why people choose to move are varied. The principal motivators have been identified as

(i) *changes in the family size related to the life cycle*, for example, a person is likely to move house on marriage and may move to more spacious accommodation to bring up children, then to a smaller property after the children leave home or on retirement;

(ii) *career changes*, which account for most of the longer distance moves and involve, in particular, members of the higher socio-economic groups, who constitute a mobile elite;

(iii) *a reassessment of how the family sees itself*, that is brought about through income changes, social aspirations and so on, which may lead the family to consider the house and neighbourhood no longer suitable;

(iv) *the neighbourhood may change in character* and undergo social change through a process of invasion and succession (Backler, 1974). This may

212

lead on the one hand to an area being downgraded as it is 'invaded' by families of lower socio-economic status and population densities increase as substantial houses are divided for multiple occupancy. On the other hand, there is the possibility of upgrading as homes of artisans are acquired by more affluent middle-class families who make substantial improvement to their properties ('gentrification').

## (b) The relocation process

Once the decision to move house has been taken, the relocation process involves three distinct phases:
(i)   establishing the criteria for a different house;
(ii)  the search procedure during which the original criteria may be modified;
(iii) the actual purchase or rental agreement.
When establishing the criteria of choice for a different house, the family will take into account the physical accommodation required (number of bedrooms, whether there is a garden, garage, etc.), the quality of the built environment and the availability of essential services such as schools, shops and public transport. Behavioural factors will also play a significant role at this stage for each family makes an estimate of its social standing and will eliminate districts of the town which it regards as unsuitable or unattainable. These criteria of choice will be constrained by such factors as income, socio-economic status and, in Britain in particular, type of tenure. For in Britain there is a dual housing market, private and public. Once a household moves into either sector it rarely moves out, but rather moves within its own tenure (Robson, 1975). However the opportunity for council tenants to buy their homes has begun to erode this established pattern.

## (c) Effects of relocation constraints

(i)   These constraints give rise to *opportunity space*, and this is obviously much more extensive for a high-status high-income family than for a low-paid wage earner who lacks job security. This is why the most wealthy families have a wide choice and can afford to live almost anywhere in a city and its surroundings. It also helps to explain why the inner city is characterised by poverty and contains many of the socially and financially most disadvantaged families: the unemployed, single-parent families, recently arrived and migrant families, the elderly, who fail to move out as the area undergoes social change. The opportunity space of such families is very restricted and thus they have little alternative but to reside in the socially and environmentally poorest parts of the city.
(ii)  Once the criteria for a different house have been established the family

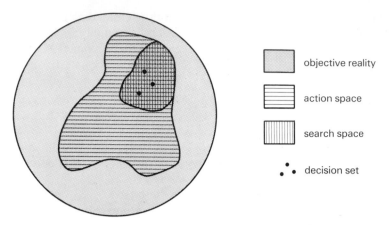

Figure 6.18  The spatial context in which residential decisions are made. (Source: after Backler, 1974, p. 49)

is in a position to start house hunting. The family defines a *search space* in which to look. This constitutes a subset of the family's *awareness space* which will include parts of the town directly familiar to them and other parts of which they have no direct experience but only images which have been derived from the mass media or conveyed to them by friends and acquaintances (see Figure 6.18).

When they start their search, their awareness space may be extremely restricted. For example a commuter may have a dumb-bell shaped awareness of his or her town, being familiar only with the restricted areas surrounding home and workplace and the linear routes which connect them. As we have seen, the work of Lynch and Orleans has demonstrated that, in general, middle-class professional people have more wide-ranging and more accurate mental images of their towns than manual workers. In other words, their awareness space is more extensive. Of course when searching for a different house, a family is likely to extend its awareness space by seeking information from such formal channels as local newspapers and estate agents or simply by either walking or driving round parts of the town unfamiliar to them. The information so acquired may cause them to redefine their search space. Studies by D. T. Herbert and others have demonstrated that formal channels of information are relatively unimportant to families moving to low-cost areas as they are far more likely to rely on casual channels such as information passed on by friends.

In the light of the above comments it is, perhaps, hardly surprising that the average distance of move of the least advantaged families will be short as such families are constrained by limited *opportunity space* and are likely to possess a very restricted *awareness space*.

(iii) A number of studies have also been conducted to establish where

214

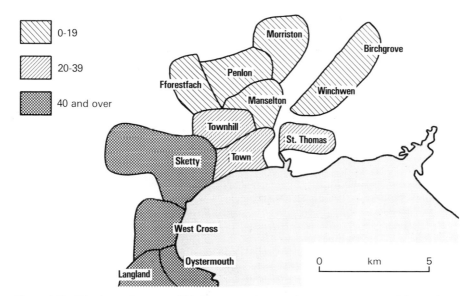

Figure 6.19    District preferences within Swansea. The map shows the percentage of the total sample placing a district in the first three choices. (Source: after Herbert, 1972)

people would choose to live if they had the chance; in other words their *preference space*. A survey by D. T. Herbert (1972) in Swansea (Figure 6.19) indicated that the high-status western resort districts, Sketty, West Cross, Langland and Oystermouth, were the most sought after and each of these districts was placed in the first three choices of over 40% of the total sample. The survey also revealed, however, that a high level of desirability was attached by the respondents to their existing neighbourhoods so that districts such as Morriston which appeared less desirable to the total sample were often still preferred by the people residing there.

ASSIGNMENTS
1. *Explore the inter-relationships of opportunity space, awareness space and search space in the context of someone who is looking for a new house.*
2. *By what means may an individual extend his/her awareness space?*

# I. Conclusion

In this chapter we have looked at the changes which the inner city has experienced since the Second World War. In Britain's inner cities, decline has been followed, in some areas, by regeneration and the return of a resident population. However, the community now occupying inner city areas is quite different from that in pre-war days. The loss of working-class housing and jobs has caused some resentment and the advice to 'mug-a-yuppie' can be found sprayed on walls in docklands. Although successive governments have collected information and devised initiatives, the 'inner city problem' remains. Creating new communities in and attracting new industries to former wastelands has proved a difficult task and one which, increasingly, governments prefer to leave to private rather than public investors. Critics of the new Enterprise Zones and recreation centres doubt the long-term viability of such schemes to provide jobs or social foci for the urban population. The basic problem, of a decline in urban manufacturing employment despite a growth in national economic prosperity, is not confined to inner cities or peripheral regions but it is felt most strongly there, and exacerbates a difficult situation.

## Key Ideas

*A. Introduction*

1. The inner city was formerly the economic heart of most urban areas but has declined greatly.
2. The inner city has lost its former advantage of accessibility and has experienced population loss and a massive decline in its manufacturing industrial base.
3. Buildings are subject to a continuous cycle of decay and renewal unless conserved for reasons of sentiment.
4. Socially segregated residential areas were established in the nineteenth century and have been perpetuated.
5. Pockets of deprivation are to be found in all large cities, including those situated in more prosperous parts of the country.

*B. Inner City Problems and Policies*

1. Inner city problems were exacerbated by 1950s and·1960s policies which concentrated investment in the suburbs and the new and expanded towns.
2. Many inner city dwellers are trapped in a cycle of poverty.
3. Racism and racial discrimination further disadvantage racial and ethnic minorities concentrated in inner city areas.
4. There is no consensus on the best way to tackle inner city problems. Policies reflect the prevailing ideology.
5. Present policies aim to regenerate inner cities through private and public sector partnerships and to encourage inner city communities to be more self-reliant.

## C. The Urban Development Corporations

1. A number of Urban Development Corporations have been established to try to secure new investment for certain inner city areas. They have been given powers similar to those of New Town Development Corporations.
2. The London Docklands Development Corporation has spearheaded swift and spectacular development in Docklands.
3. The LDDC has been criticised for allegedly not paying sufficient attention to the needs of the indigenous Docklands' communities and for adopting a demand-led planning strategy.

## D. Power to the People?

1. Community architects see their role as interpreting people's housing needs and aspirations and designing housing schemes which incorporate these.
2. They also consider it important that the skills of local people are harnessed to implement the schemes.
3. Some Labour-controlled local authorities, such as Sheffield, have adopted alternative strategies for inner city regeneration based on socialist principles. These aim to support indigenous firms and enterprises which are important to the local community and to provide specific help for disadvantaged groups.
4. Some inner city neighbourhoods have been regenerated through an influx of upwardly mobile middle-class families who have purchased and renovated houses there.
5. This process alters the social composition of a neighbourhood and is known as gentrification.

## E. Social Patterns: Techniques for Analysis

1. Both objective and subjective criteria can be used to increase our knowledge and understanding of inner city areas.
2. Culture and tradition exert powerful influences and certain parts of a town may acquire sentimental and symbolic connotations which may counteract the forces of competition.
3. Social space is a synthesis of objective physical space and the perceived dimensions of space.
4. Social space includes both activity space and awareness space.
5. A person's activity space is the area in which he or she lives and moves.
6. Awareness space is the perception that an individual or group has of its environment.
7. Groups and individuals acquire mental images of their environment which are influenced by their values, aspirations and cultural traditions.

217

8. An individual's images of the urban environment form a link between reality and behaviour.

## F. Neighbourhood and Community

1. A neighbourhood is the local area with which a group is most familiar and with which its members can most readily identify.
2. It is a form of territorial space with both spatial (physical) and social attributes.
3. The balance between spatial and social attributes varies between neighbourhoods.
4. At the simplest level of definition, propinquity or nearness is the only distinguishing characteristic of the neighbourhood.
5. At the most sophisticated level, the neighbourhood forms a distinct cohesive community in which there is much social interaction.
6. Neighbourhoods with social attributes tend to have clearly defined boundaries.
7. Length of residence, class and, possibly, physical isolation contribute to the development of community neighbourhoods.
8. One of the prime planning objectives in post-war Britain has been the establishment of neighbourhoods in new housing areas.
9. In the initial stages, the layout of housing estates may influence the development of a sense of community.
10. Homogeneous neighbourhoods are more likely to develop a sense of community than heterogeneous neighbourhoods.

## G. The Suburb: Ideal Home or Subtopia?

1. Urbanisation in the inter-war and post-war periods was largely accommodated by residential growth at the current urban margin.
2. Service provision remained concentrated in the inner city until the 1970s when new retail and industrial estates were also built at the edge of towns.
3. The respectable middle-class life style associated with suburbs in the immediate post-war period has not proved sufficiently attractive to retain the more affluent in these areas.

## H. Segregation and Mobility

### Residential segregation
1. Residential segregation fulfils a number of functions: defensive, avoidance, preservation, and 'attack', facilitating joint action.
2. The extent to which ethnic and racial minorities will be assimilated in the host community depends partly on the degree of distinctiveness of the ethnic group from the host community.

218

*Residential mobility*

3. A person selecting a new housing area must work within the constraints of opportunity space. This is most limited for certain sections of society such as the low paid and unemployed.
4. A person's search for a new house is further restricted by his/her limited awareness of the town in which he/she is moving.
5. The search space is a subset of a person's awareness space.

## Additional Activities

1. Examine the problems of inner cities and critically evaluate policies which aim to bring about inner city regeneration.
2. In a 1970s study of people's perception of Hull, two groups were chosen: one local with first-hand experience of Hull, and the other consisting of people from other parts of Britain whose mental images of Hull had been derived indirectly (for example, through what they watch on television or read in their newspapers). Each group was asked to select ten terms from a list of 48 which best described Hull. Table 6.1 summarises the results of the survey and indicates the percentage from each group which listed the various terms. Describe how the local and non-local groups perceived Hull and try to account for differences in the responses.
3. If you live in a town which attracts tourists, you could attempt a similar exercise by comparing the perceptions that local people have of the town with those of tourists.
4. If you live in a new housing area, conduct a questionnaire survey to try to discover if the layout of houses exerts an influence on the development of a sense of community. Are there contrasts in the degree of social

Table 6.1  Leading characteristic attributes of Hull as perceived by inhabitants and outsiders

| Inhabitants | % | Outsiders | % |
|---|---|---|---|
| Good shopping centre | 85 | Docks | 90 |
| Working-class city | 84 | Working-class city | 85 |
| Docks | 81 | Ships | 79 |
| Large council estates | 75 | Fishy | 75 |
| Friendly | 74 | Heavy industry | 67 |
| Trees, parks | 74 | Slums | 63 |
| Ships | 65 | Large council estates | 59 |
| Low wages | 61 | Unemployment | 57 |
| Fishy | 58 | Cold | 56 |
| Congested traffic | 57 | Smoke | 53 |
| Tower block flats | 56 | Congested traffic | 50 |
| Redevelopment | 55 | Drabness | 49 |

Responses in percentages. There were 180 people in each group.

Source: E. W. Burgess in Pocock & Hudson, 1978

interaction in streets of differing layout? You can test this by constructing restricted surveys in (a) a cul-de-sac, (b) part of a main road, (c) a pedestrianised housing district and (d) a minor road which also takes through-traffic. In each of these find how many of their neighbours each person can name, or how many neighbours' houses they have visited. The data can be presented on sociograms as illustrated in Figure 6.20.

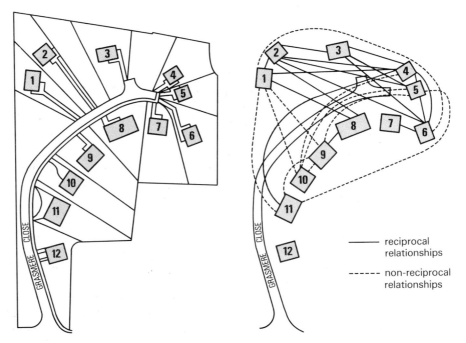

Figure 6.20  Sociogram of visiting relationships on an estate in the North Midlands. (Source: Carey & Mapes, 1972)

220

# 7 The Central Business District

The one feature common to all the models of city structure discussed in Chapter 5 was a central business district (CBD) where commercial activities such as specialised shops and offices are dominant. The CBD is at the very heart of the urban system, the commercial hub about which the rest of the city is structured (Carter, 1976). In its most pronounced form it is essentially a twentieth-century phenomenon. Developments in construction technology have led to the erection of multi-storey buildings, and in transport technology have meant that people can reach shops, offices and places of entertainment relatively swiftly. These factors combined to make the centralisation of activities feasible.

The CBD has traditionally been *the most accessible part of the urban system*, at the focal point of the transport network. It is accessible not only to those living in the built-up area but also to those residing within the town's urban field. It is often ringed by bus termini, suburban railway stations and extensive off-street car parks. Its position at the centre of the urban and regional communications network greatly influences the type of development located there. As we saw in Chapter 5, commercial activities compete with one another for the most accessible sites located within the relatively confined space of the town centre. The competition for space pushes up land rent and property values so that they are at their highest within the CBD, reaching their maximum at what is described as the *peak land value intersection (PLVI)*, and declining fairly rapidly with distance from that point (Murphy, 1972). This is because, within the town centre, most movement must necessarily be on foot and walking distance from the PLVI is, therefore, a critical factor. Pedestrian densities are extremely high at and near to the PLVI. If the area has not been pedestrianised, the pavements are often very wide so that they can accommodate the many shoppers and office workers who use them. Pedestrian densities decline rapidly with distance from the PLVI and are reflected in a parallel decline in property values.

Not only is the CBD the most accessible part of the urban system but it also provides commercial enterprises with unique linkages with other businesses and the public (Rannells, 1956). Shops benefit from *cumulative attraction* if their potential customers are concentrated into a limited area. A number of similar retail outlets confined to a specialised area can each expect to attract more customers than an equivalent number of isolated stores. The customers also benefit from such a concentration because this makes comparison shopping easier: that is, the possibility of inspecting the quality and price of similar goods being offered in several shops. Offices benefit because the CBD, more than anywhere else in the urban system, offers the possibility of rapid personal contact with ancillary services such as legal advisers, advertising agencies and accountants, as well as banks, stockbrokers and the Stock Exchange.

It is the combination of maximum accessibility and the unique linkage it offers for commercial activities that gives rise to the distinctive characteristics of the CBD. We shall now discuss these in greater detail.

## A. The Characteristics of the CBD

### 1. Concentration of department stores, variety goods stores and specialist retail outlets

The accessibility of the CBD attracts retail outlets that provide goods and services which have a wide range and a high threshold population (see page 266) and, therefore, depend upon customers being drawn from a very extensive catchment area (Carter, 1976). This accounts for the specialised nature of retailing. Department stores and variety goods stores such as Marks and Spencer, British Home Stores and Woolworth are likely to be located at the 'node' of the CBD occupying the most desirable sites at the intersection of the busiest thoroughfares (see Plate 7.1), while specialist shops such as book shops and jewellers will occupy less expensive sites. There will also be a number of shops and retail services which cater specifically for the many people who work in the CBD. These will include men's and women's clothes shops, office stationers and cafés and will be located mainly among the offices (see Plate 7.2). The extensive catchment area enables the specialist shop to carry a wide range of goods, including high-quality expensive items.

### 2. Concentration of offices

In a large city the offices in the CBD will include the principal regional, or even head, offices of a number of companies which must be accessible to as many potential clients as possible (see Plate 7.4). A central location also makes it easier for offices to assemble their labour force, drawn from middle-class workers who often live in peripheral suburban locations.

Plate 7.1  Department stores, Oxford Street, London. (Photograph: J. Allan Cash)

Plate 7.2  Shops and retail services on the ground floors of office blocks in Fleet Street, London, which cater for the needs of office workers. (Photograph: J. Allan Cash)

223

## 3. Absence of manufacturing industry

Although in general there is no manufacturing industry in the CBD, there are, however, a few specialised manufacturing activities such as the *publication of periodicals and newspapers* which, at least until recently, have found it desirable to locate some of their processes here. In the publication of periodicals and daily newspapers speed in production is crucial. Immediate access to contributors, illustrators, photographic agencies and other relevant services is vital. Likewise speed of despatch is essential, particularly with morning newspapers which need to be sent out nationally during the previous night. However, the introduction of new technology to the printing industry has led to some decentralisation even of the publication of some national daily newspapers (see page 169).

## 4. Functional zoning

Similar activities tend to be concentrated into distinct areas and it is often possible to distinguish concentrations of offices, places of entertainment and one or more shopping districts. In addition, there is often a certain degree of specialisation within these functional zones. For example, in the office zone

it is often possible to delimit a financial quarter where there is a concentration of banks and stockbrokers. In a similar way, insurance company offices and legal firms may well be grouped together in different parts of the office zone; while within the retail shopping zone the department and variety goods stores are often close together and it is sometimes possible to distinguish a street dominated by more expensive specialist shops. Regent Street, in London, provides a good example of this. At a more detailed level of specialisation, certain streets or parts of streets become renowned for a particular activity. Many city centres include an 'automobile row' where car dealers are concentrated or a street where medical specialists are clustered (see Plate 7.3).

## 5. Multi-storey development

The high values of land and rent in the town centre encourage multi-storey development, and multi-storey buildings will often occupy the most expensive sites, giving the CBD a three-dimensional quality (see Plate 7.4). In this way the effective floor space in the CBD can be greatly increased and is generally much greater than the ground space. Thus the 'real area' of the CBD is often considerably larger than it appears on a map; it might, in fact, be four or five times greater than the ground space (see Figure 7.1).

## 6. Vertical zoning

Within the multi-storey blocks in the CBD the same use is generally not made of each floor. Those activities which need maximum contact with the public such as retail shops and services, building societies and banks tend to occupy the lower more-accessible floors where the rents are higher. Other users who need a central location, but do not require sites which will attract passing trade, such as solicitors, architects and advertising agencies, are often found on the higher less-expensive floors (see Figure 7.2).

## 7. A low residential population

The high land values within the CBD dictate that commercial enterprises dominate to the virtual exclusion of certain other functions. In particular, the CBD tends to be characterised by a low residential population. Some dwellings may survive around the fringe of the CBD and it is possible that a few blocks of luxury flats may recently have been built in the city centre itself, but generally the residential population of the CBD is very small. This

Plate 7.3   Harley Street, London, renowned for its concentration of medical specialists. (Author's photograph)

226

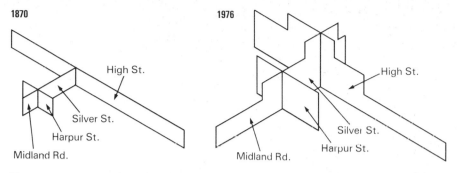

Figure 7.1 The increasing three-dimensional quality of Bedford's CBD. (Source: R. Hardaker)

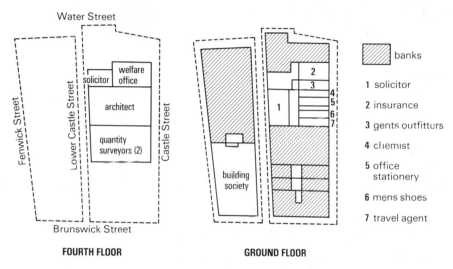

Figure 7.2 Vertical zoning in an office block. (Source: Cross & Daniel, 1968, p. 53)

has encouraged some geographers to describe the CBD as the 'dead heart' of the city (Johnson, 1972) but such a description applies only at night-time. During each working day, the CBD becomes the focus of an intense concentration of people.

ASSIGNMENTS

1. *List the features characteristic of a CBD as illustrated in Plate 7.5.*
2. *Explain the distribution of offices in the office block illustrated in Figure 7.2.*

Plate 7.4 Multi-storey development; the City of London. (Photograph: Aerofilms)

Plate 7.5  Liverpool's
CBD (Author's
photographs)

## B. The Delimitation of the CBD

Many of the earliest studies of the CBD by geographers were concerned with attempts at areal definition: that is, to delimit the precise extent of a town's CBD. Such studies have been justified in that they make possible comparisons between the CBDs of a number of towns. These, in turn, permit generalisations to be made about the CBD as a concept of universal application at least within the Western city (Carter, 1976). Precise definition also facilitates studies of the processes of change and evolution through time within a single CBD.

Within American cities the CBD might well end abruptly in what has been described as a 'cliff-line' which marks a sharp break between the distribution of commercial and non-commercial activities. In most Western European cities, however, the edge of the CBD is not so distinct. It tends to be gradational and fragmented, more of a zone than a line, and any attempts at areal definition must take this into account.

## 1. Some techniques of delimitation

### (a) Pedestrian flows

During the working day, pedestrian densities tend to be greatest at the peak land value intersection (PLVI) and, very roughly, decline with distance from it. It is thus possible to use pedestrian density data, collected at intervals throughout the central area, to gain some idea of the extent of a town's CBD. The pedestrian counts should, of course, be made at judicial times of the day, such as mid-morning or mid-afternoon when few non-central business pedestrians, such as school children returning home, will be included. The recorded values can each be converted into percentages of the highest pedestrian count and an isopleth map constructed to distinguish surfaces of varying degrees of pedestrian intensity.

### (b) Restricted parking zones

Traffic congestion in city centres has for long posed a problem and traffic management schemes and parking restrictions have been in operation for many years. In some British towns the extent of the parking meter zone or parking disc zone (where drivers must display discs indicating their time of arrival) provides a useful indication of the extent of the CBD. In some instances restrictions of traffic in town centres are even more acute. For example, central Göteborg, Sweden, is divided into five separate traffic zones which are surrounded by a circular route from which there are special entrances to each zone. To travel from one zone to another it is usual to use the circular route (see Figure 7.3). Within these zones parking spaces are limited and generally restricted to short-stay parking (as little as 15 minutes

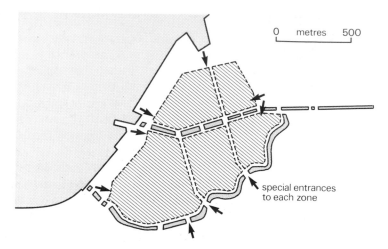

Figure 7.3  Traffic zones in central Göteborg

in some cases). For longer-stay parking there are extensive car parks beyond the circular route. The extent of the traffic zones provides a useful indication of the extent of Göteborg's CBD.

### (c)  The rate index

Rates, which contribute towards local finances, are payable on all properties in England and Wales. Gross rateable values reflect the rent at which the properties might reasonably be let and, therefore, provide a good indication of the considered commercial advantages of a particular site. A number of studies have used rateable values in attempts to define a 'hard' commercial core within a CBD. These have generally taken into account variations in total floor space of different premises by standardising the data through the application of a rate index (Murphy, 1972).

$$\text{Rate index (RI)} = \frac{\text{gross rateable value (in £s)}}{\text{ground floor space (in square metres)}}$$

The RI is expressed in £ per square metre of ground floor space.

The information thus obtained can be mapped (see Figure 7.4) using somewhat arbitrarily defined categories or by the use of isopleths which join points of an equivalent rate index (see Figure 7.5). From April 1989 in Scotland domestic rates are replaced by the community charge, and this is likely to happen in the rest of the UK at some time in the future.

### (d)  The central business index (CBI)

This is a technique of CBD delimitation devised by Murphy & Vance (1954)

| | | |
|---|---|---|
| ■ 32 and over | ▨ 8 - 15 | |
| ▓ 24 - 31 | ▨ 5 - 7 | |
| ▒ 16 - 23 | ⋯ 4 and under | |

0        metres        300

Figure 7.4    Rate index scores, Hanley, Staffs. (Source: Herbert, 1972, p. 82)

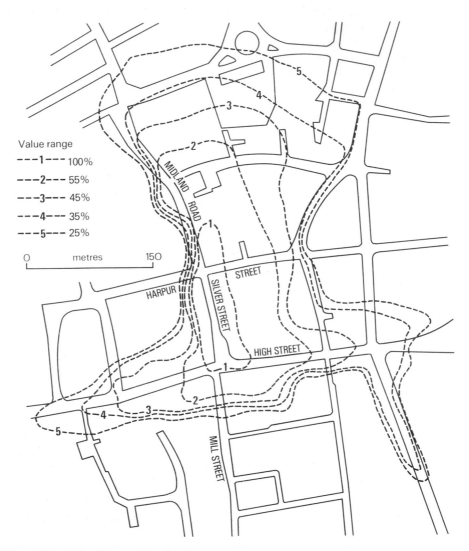

Value range
--- 1 --- 100%
--- 2 --- 55%
--- 3 --- 45%
--- 4 --- 35%
--- 5 --- 25%

0    metres    150

MIDLAND ROAD

HARPUR    SILVER STREET    STREET

HIGH STREET

MILL STREET

Figure 7.5   An isopleth map showing shop values in the central area of Bedford. (Source: after *The Bedford Study: Central Area Shopping*, Beds. County Planning Office, 1967, p. 26)

in the 1950s. The technique involves determining for blocks and premises within the central area of a town the proportion of floor space which is in central business use.

To apply the CBI, the following steps must be taken:
(i)   On a large-scale plan of the whole of the central area record central business (C) and non-central business (X) functions for each floor of

232

each building. Murphy and Vance distinguish the following non-central business functions:

- permanent residences
- government and public buildings and open spaces (including civic buildings, schools and parks)
- organisational establishments (churches, colleges, etc.)
- wholesaling and commercial storage
- vacant premises and building sites
- railway lincs and yards

Other functions, such as shops, offices and other commercial activities, are distinguished as central business functions.

(ii) For each block of buildings within the central area calculate the proportion of the total floor space in central business (C) and non-central business (X) uses. (This method is more easily applied in North American cities which are invariably planned on a grid basis.)

(iii) By applying the following formulas the central business height index (CBHI) and the central business intensity index (CBII) can then be calculated for each block.

$$\text{CBHI} = \frac{\text{total C floor space}}{\text{ground floor space}}$$

Thus a CBHI of 1 indicates a complete ground floor or equivalent coverage in commercial or central business uses.

$$\text{CBII} = \frac{\text{total C floor space}}{\text{total floor space}} \times \frac{100}{1}$$

The CBII measures the proportion of the total available floor space within the block which is in commercial or central business uses. Thus if a block has a CBII of 50%, central business uses occupy at least half the total floor space of all storeys (see Figure 7.6).

(iv) Murphy and Vance suggest that, in order to be included within the CBD, a block must have a CBHI of at least 1 and a CBII of at least 50% (see Figure 7.6).

The central business index has been criticised because of the subjective nature of the non-central business functions listed by Murphy and Vance. Certain functions, such as garages and hotels, do not fit easily into either central or non-central business categories. A second criticism concerns the apparent degree of subjectivity used in determining the limiting values that qualify a block for inclusion within the CBD, although Murphy does claim that they are based upon reasoning and empirical research (Murphy, 1972).

One of the great virtues of the CBI is that, in common with pedestrian densities and rateable indices, it can be used to distinguish, within a town's CBD, a commercial 'hard core' from the 'frame'. D. H. Davies, in his study

central business height
index of 1 or more

central business intensity
index of 50 or more

central business height
index of 1 or more, and
central business intensity
index of 50 or more

······ CBD boundary

● PLVI

0    metres    300

Figure 7.6   The CBD of Worcester, Massachusetts, USA, delimited by applying the central business height and intensity indices. (Source: after Murphy & Vance, 1954, Fig. 6)

of land use in central Cape Town, adopted a CBHI of 4 and a CBII of 80% in his delimitation of the 'hard core' of the CBD of Cape Town (Davies, 1960) (see Figure 7.7).

234

Figure 7.7 The 'hard core' of Cape Town's CBD. (Source: after Hywel Davies, 1960)

## 2. The CBD core–frame model

The methods described above by which the CBD may be delimited have been selected because they can be adapted to distinguish a highly concentrated central area within a CBD, the 'core', from its bordering area, the 'frame'. The 'core–frame' model of CBD structure was proposed by Horwood and Boyce in 1959 (see Figure 7.8). The core is the area with the greatest concentration of daytime population and most intensive land use. Land values are at their highest and multi-storey buildings dominate. Within the core it may be possible to distinguish districts where particular activities are concentrated and which form sub-functional zones. The frame is less intensively developed; land values are lower and functions more varied. There are, however, clusters of functions derived from linkages and the model

235

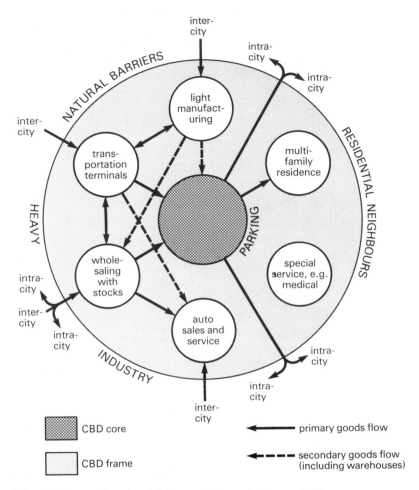

Figure 7.8   A CBD core–frame model. (Source: Horwood & Boyce, 1959)

identifies such sub-zones as car sales and services and specialist medical facilities. As conceived by Horwood and Boyce, the frame comprises peripheral districts of the CBD but overlaps into Burgess's 'zone in transition'.

## 3.  The CBD and the zone in transition

Once the notion of a clearly defined CBD is relaxed and replaced by a core–frame concept, it is pertinent to reconsider the surrounding zone in transition. This is essentially an area of conflict and adjustment which aptly demonstrates the dynamic qualities of the modern city. As city centres expand, CBD functions may be extended into this transitional zone. This

236

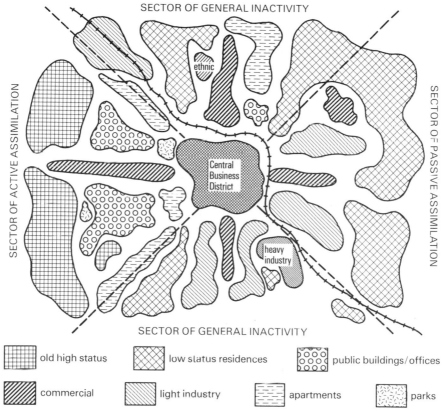

ethnic

SECTOR OF ACTIVE ASSIMILATION

SECTOR OF PASSIVE ASSIMILATION

Central
Business
District

heavy
industry

SECTOR OF GENERAL INACTIVITY

old high status    low status residences    public buildings/offices

commercial    light industry    apartments    parks

Figure 7.9   A schematic pattern of land use in the zone of transition for the American city.
(Source: after Griffin & Preston, 1966)

process has been referred to as 'invasion-succession' (see page 119) and has been summarised in a model developed by Griffin & Preston (1966) which recognises the interaction of the CBD and the zone in transition (see Figure 7.9).

Thus, within the zone in transition, Griffin and Preston distinguished sectors of:

(a) *active assimilation* where new CBD functions are in the process of development, such as an extension of the shopping floor space.

(b) *passive assimilation* where there is less new development and this tends to be of a non-CBD character, such as warehousing.

(c) *general inactivity* where there is little change.

## 4.  The perception of the city centre

We have seen in the previous chapter that individuals form images of their urban environments and it can be argued that in many respects people's

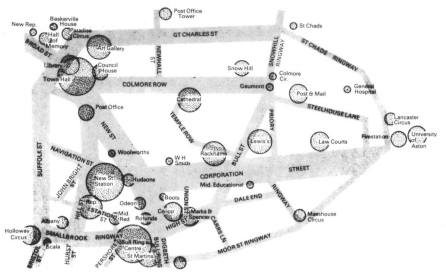

Figure 7.10   A composite map of people's perceptions of central Birmingham. The width of the roads and the size of the circles indicate the relative number of respondents who referred to each road/building. The named features are the only ones referred to on their maps. (Source: Gould & White, 1974, p. 29)

perception of the CBD is of more relevance than attempts at objective definition and delimitation. A town's residents will have their own mental images of what comprises the commercial core of the CBD. Brian Goodey's study (1971), investigating Birmingham residents' perception of their city centre, recognises this (see Figure 7.10). Readers of the *Birmingham Post* were asked to send in sketch maps, compiled without reference to accurate street maps, that conveyed their broad impressions of the city centre. The sketch maps summarised the images that people carried in their heads and which they used to find their way about on visits to the city centre. The individual responses were combined to build up a composite map illustrating people's preferences for features in Birmingham's centre. Perhaps not surprisingly, the responses demonstrated a clear preference for developments on a small and more personal scale. Some of the tall skyline features were far less prominent than might have been expected. Such a map provides useful information to planners whose role it is to influence the nature of central area redevelopment.

ASSIGNMENTS

1. *Using the evidence presented in Figure 7.5, try to distinguish a 'hard' commercial core within Bedford's CBD. Why is it difficult to delimit the CBD definitively?*

2. *Compare the core–frame concept outlined by Horwood and Boyce with the CBD and zone in transition envisaged by Burgess.*

238

3. *Work in groups. Each person in the group should use their knowledge of the local town to:*
   *(a)  delimit a CBD;*
   *(b)  distinguish a hard commercial core within the CBD;*
   *(c)  locate the PLVI within the CBD.*
   *(An estate agent's map might be used as a base map.)*
   *Use these individual mental maps to compile a composite map to illustrate the group's perception of the extent of the CBD.*
4. *Use the CBHI and CBII to delimit the CBD of your local town. Use the criteria suggested by D. H. Davies to distinguish a 'hard core'. Compare this map with the mental map and attempt to account for any discrepancies.*

## C. Analysing the Internal Structure of the CBD

In order to gain some insight into the internal structure of the CBD of a city it is necessary to identify and delimit functional districts, and determine the degree of clustering of different shop and office types. It has long been recognised that certain types of shops and offices such as shoe shops and stockbrokers tend to cluster while others such as newsagents and travel agents are usually more widely distributed. A number of techniques have been devised which quantify the degree of clustering of CBD functions, and the *centre of gravity* and *index of dispersion* are among the most useful of these. The centre of gravity, as the term suggests, defines the most central point of the distribution of a particular functional type, while the index of dispersion measures the degree of clustering within the distribution. They are derived as follows.

(a) Draw horizontal ($x$ axis) and vertical ($y$ axis) lines to contain the distribution in question, representing each unit of floor space by a point plotted at its centre.

(b) Measure the shortest distance from each point to the $x$ and $y$ axes.

(c) Work out the mean of the distance to the $x$ and $y$ axes (i.e. total the distances to the $x$ and $y$ axes respectively, and divide by the number of points in the distribution).

(d) The centre of gravity of the distribution occurs where the two means intersect. To obtain a more accurate result, a weighting factor should be introduced to take into account variations in floor space; that is, some shops will be bigger than others.

(e) The index of dispersion is obtained by measuring the distance from each point to the centre of gravity and determining the mean of all the distances.

(f) Some indications of the boundary of the cluster may be gained if a circle is drawn from the centre of gravity, of radius equal to the mean of all the distances from each point to the centre of gravity.

From Figure 7.11 the centres of gravity and indices of dispersion have

y axis

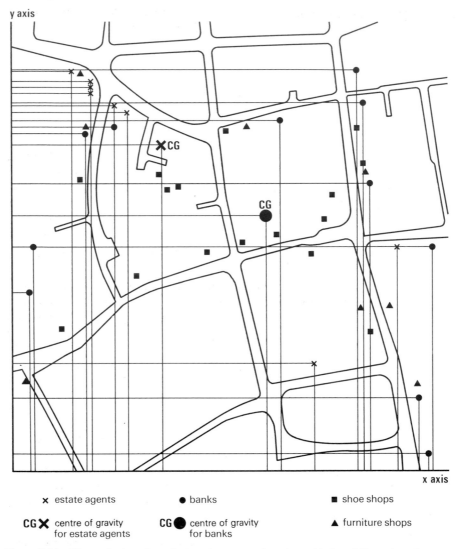

x axis

| ✗ estate agents | ● banks | ■ shoe shops |
|---|---|---|
| **CG ✗** centre of gravity for estate agents | **CG ●** centre of gravity for banks | ▲ furniture shops |

Figure 7.11 The method used to calculate the centre of gravity and index of dispersion of estate agents and banks in a given urban area.

been worked out for banks and estate agents in central Bedford. They are as follows:

> Banks: *Centre of gravity* is at the intersection of the mean distance from the *y* axis (6.7 cm) and the mean distance from the *x* axis (6.7 cm).
>
> *Index of dispersion* is the mean distance from the centre of gravity for the distribution of banks = 4.9.

Estate agents: *Centre of gravity* is at the intersection of the mean distance from the $y$ axis (3.9 cm) and the mean distance from the $x$ axis (8.7 cm).

*Index of dispersion* is the mean distance from the centre of gravity for the distribution of estate agents = 3.3.

Note that it is the relative figures, rather than the absolute ones, which are important.

The indices of dispersion indicate that estate agents demonstrate a greater degree of clustering than do banks. Why do you think this might be?

This is a somewhat crude method of determining the location and extent of the cluster boundary. Far more sophisticated techniques of cluster analysis have been adopted by researchers such as D. H. Davies (1960) in his study of Cape Town's CBD.

It is possible to study trends in spatial patterns within the CBD if changes in the centre of gravity and size and shape of clusters are monitored. This may be done with the help of earlier editions of street directories and large-scale Ordnance Survey plans.

A number of recent studies of the internal structure of the CBD have suggested that it is necessary to go beyond the delimitation of land use patterns in the CBD to gain some understanding of the processes which bring these about; in other words, to identify and analyse the related linkages and activity patterns. In this respect, however, data can be difficult to collect and appropriate research techniques are still being developed.

ASSIGNMENTS

1. *Suggest reasons for the variations in the indices of dispersion for functions in central Manchester summarised in Table 7.1.*

2. *Work out the centres of gravity and indices of dispersion for the distributions of furniture shops and shoe shops in central Bedford (see Figure 7.11) and compare them with those for banks and estate agents. Try to account for any differences.*

Table 7.1 The degree of scatter of selected activities in Central Manchester. Note that the lower the figure the greater the degree of clustering.

| Type of establishment | Index of dispersion |
|---|---|
| Stock and share brokers | 1.77 |
| Barristers | 2.33 |
| Building societies | 3.24 |
| Insurance offices | 3.28 |
| Solicitors | 3.36 |
| Estate agents | 4.03 |
| Travel agents | 5.95 |

Source: after Varley, unpublished thesis (1968), reproduced in Carter, 1976, p. 224

# D. Change within the CBD

## 1. The redevelopment of central areas

### (a) Comprehensive redevelopment schemes

The 1960s 'Utopian solutions' for housing, which resulted in vast council estates and tower blocks, were paralleled in redevelopment schemes for the central areas of towns. Many of Britain's towns and cities went in for comprehensive redevelopment schemes in the 1960s and 1970s. In many cases, the historic core of the city was ripped out and replaced by a glass and concrete complex of gargantuan proportions. Rents, rates and other overheads in the new shopping centres rose steeply, often squeezing out the small local independent shopkeepers and replacing them with the ubiquitous chain stores. Many of these new shopping developments had a depressing uniformity, with branches of the same stores, with similar house-style shop fronts, cropping up in virtually all of them. At the same time, office developments were entirely functional, lacking interesting design features or varied building materials (see Plate 7.6a,b).

In most town centres, the motor car reigned supreme and every attempt was made to accommodate it. Inner ring roads were built on routes which invariably cut great swathes through inner city areas, leaving adjacent streets blighted and affected by noise pollution. Car parking was a perennial problem, partially solved by the construction of multi-storey car parks, sometimes in inappropriate and obtrusive sites.

Every attempt was made to separate functions through the implementation of rigid zoning policies. The central area of the town was considered to be the preserve of commercial functions and all other activities were actively discouraged, with some, such as small workshops and craft industries, being relocated through compulsory purchase orders when necessary. The residential population, which had been declining in the inter-war period, dwindled even further, so that, at night, the central areas became the dead heart of the city.

### (b) Urban conservation

It was during the late 1960s that the first expressions of concern began to be made about the undesirable consequences of comprehensive central area redevelopment. Utopian solutions, which were reflected in modern architectural designs, began to be challenged and, even, discredited. Gradually, there was a movement into a period of post-modernism, characterised by a return to more vernacular styles of architecture: traditional building materials, at least for the facades of buildings, and developments on a smaller

Plate 7.6 a,b Examples of 1960s redevelopment in Bedford's town centre (Author's photographs)
(a) The Howard Rooms, next to the Victorian Corn Exchange building situated on the north side of St Paul's Square, show little regard for the visual importance of the site.
(b) The Moat House Hotel, situated on the prime site adjacent to Town Bridge and overlooking the River Great Ouse, is a glass and concrete multi-storey block quite out of scale with its surroundings.

Plate 7.6 c–e Examples of urban conservation in Bedford's town centre. (Author's photographs)
(c) The facade of the former Bedford Modern School, designed by Edward Blore and built between 1831 and 1834, has been preserved and incorporated into a modern shopping precinct.
(d) The Bedford Museum occupies a refurbished building that started life as a brewery.
(e) The small shops in Clare Court surround an enclosed and intimate space which was formerly an auctioneer's yard.

and more humane scale, incorporating intimate enclosed spaces in which people can feel comfortable. One of the features of post-modernism has been the much greater attention that has been paid to *urban conservation* (see Plate 7.6c–e). The 1967 Civic Amenities Act encouraged local authorities to designate as conservation areas those 'areas of special architectural or historic interest, the character or appearance of which it is desirable to preserve and enhance'. Conservation area status gives some protection to the whole of the townscape through demolition control of all buildings and control over tree felling. Local authorities were quick to embrace the conservation area concept and, by 1984, 5500 conservation areas had been designated in settlements of vastly differing sizes. Further protection is provided to towns of outstanding architectural interest through historic town schemes. These arose out of recommendations of the four Historic Town Reports (Buchanan, 1968; Burrows, 1968; Insall, 1968; Esher, 1968), detailed case studies conducted in Bath, Chichester, Chester and York that had focused attention on particular issues affecting historic areas, including the importance of providing further grant aid for historic buildings, the difficulties of finding appropriate uses for them and the design difficulties in adapting them. It was the identification of these pressing problems which led the Preservation Policy Group to recommend that local authorities should be permitted to designate a new type of general conservation scheme, the town scheme, 'designed to deal with the repair of groups of buildings which are important as a whole but not of outstanding or special importance individually' (Dobby, 1978). Under these arrangements, 50% of the cost of repairs is financed by the owners; 25% by the local authority and 25% by the Department of the Environment. There are now over 60 such schemes operating in England, the most heavily financed being those in Chester, Bath and York (see Plate 7.7).

The renewed interest in urban conservation has had a profound effect on the sort of developments now being carried out in many of our towns and cities. Every attempt is likely to be made to retain those buildings which, over the years, have proved to be demonstrably successful. Sometimes this may mean preserving the integrity of a streetscape through retaining only the facade of a building and constructing a new development behind it. Where redevelopment occurs, it is far more likely to be of an appropriate scale with buildings designed so that they are in harmony with their context. There has also been renewed interest in environmental enhancement schemes, which may incorporate quality street furniture, interesting floor scapes, tree planting and pedestrianisation (see Plate 7.8).

The desirability of rigid functional zoning is also being challenged. Many towns are now trying to attract back a residential population to their centres. Some planning authorities have seen the conversion of buildings of historic or architectural interest, such as the disused warehouses of the

Plate 7.7  Gamul House, a Jacobean hall with later brick facade and a grade II listed building, in Lower Bridge Street, Chester, was restored by the Chester City Council under the Town Scheme arrangements. (a) shows the building as it was in 1967, vacant, derelict and in danger of collapse. The roof leaked and crude repairs had disfigured the building's facade. (b) shows the building fully restored and now in use as a restaurant. The restoration won a Civic Trust European Architectural Heritage Year Award in 1975. (Photographs: Chester City Council)

Albert Dock, Liverpool or St Katharine's Dock, London as spearheading a change of attitude towards the desirability of town centre living. Many towns with a rich Victorian heritage, such as Bradford, have been particularly innovative in this respect. After years of neglect, the Old Town of Edinburgh is being revitalised. The population of the Old Town had declined from 60 000 in the 1860s, when it was overcrowded and deteriorating, to only 4000 by the mid 1980s. An Enterprise Trust has now been established which is co-operating with the City Council to renovate the Old Town and increase substantially its residential population (Stead, 1986). Where new houses are being built in city centres, they are likely to be two

Plate 7.8    A fine example of urban conservation in Southsea, Portsmouth. It is part of the King Street Area which was designated a Conservation Area in 1969 and a General Improvement Area in 1973. Note the careful restoration of the buildings and the environmental enhancement which has resulted from a combination of tree planting, quality street furniture and interesting floorscape. This was previously a through-road to traffic. (Photograph: Portsmouth City Council)

or, at most, three storeys, arranged around squares or open courts, which include high-quality street furniture and trees and shrubs, to add interest (see Plate 7.9). New housing schemes built within the walls of the City of York provide good examples of this sort of development, which is entirely sensitive to the existing townscape (see Plate 7.10).

Large-scale central area redevelopment schemes are also likely to be on a humane scale, incorporating existing townscape features of interest and mixed building and land use. The redevelopment of Covent Garden, in London, provides a good example of this sort of central area redevelopment

Plate 7.9  As recently as the late 1970s, much of the Old Town of Edinburgh was neglected and deteriorating rapidly. The cycle of decay was reversed with the establishment of an Enterprise Trust which has co-operated with the city council to restore the townscape. The photographs illustrate parts of the Old Town before and after regeneration. (Photographs: Edinburgh Old Town Conservation Committee)

246

Plate 7.10   A high-density inner city housing scheme built as part of the Aldwark urban renewal project within the walls of the city of York. The two- and three-storey houses are arranged around mews courts, paved with York stone. Clay pantiled roofs, carefully selected bricks and traditional cast iron gutters and drain pipes all help to integrate the development with its historic neighbours. The development won a premier national Housing Design Award in 1981. (Photograph: Shepherd Homes Ltd)

(Spence, 1985). There were proposals to 'modernise' the area when the old fruit and vegetable market was relocated to Vauxhall in 1974. Fortunately, however, pressures for comprehensive redevelopment were resisted and the Covent Garden Action Area Plan was approved in 1978. Under this Plan, the Central Market was restored and adapted to incorporate a number of small shops, market stalls and restaurants (see Plate 7.11). The residential population was to increase from 2800 to 6000 with associated community facilities being provided. Large developments, particularly offices, were not included. Rather, new development was to be for multiple usage and in the form of sensitive infill, which conformed to the existing street design. The refurbished Central Market was opened in 1980 and within five years had become, after the Tower of London, the second most visited place in London by tourists. There are now plans to relocate Spitalfields Market in 1988 and there is a good chance that a similar conservation-conscious redevelopment scheme will be adopted here also. Spitalfields has been described as that 'depressed, dirty, confused and yet marvellous survival of

248

Plate 7.11   The interior of Covent Garden which incorporates restaurants, high-quality shops, craft stalls and street entertainment. It was opened in 1980 in imaginatively restored buildings which had previously contained London's main fruit, vegetable and flower market. The central Arcade Market was designed by Fowler in 1830. (Photograph: Topham)

Georgian London' (Stamp, 1986). Architect Leon Krier's plan for its re-development is on a humane scale and promotes a vital mix of urban functions in which 'new streets respect the pattern and alignments of old streets and converge in small, irregular urban spaces' (Stamp, 1986).

Where modern architectural solutions are still being proposed for con-servation areas, they are likely to be closely examined and publicly debated. Prince Charles has been an outspoken critic of the insensitive qualities of much modern architecture. In a speech to the Royal Institute of British Architects in 1984, he was particularly scathing about the Mies van der Rohe 296-foot glass tower proposed for Mansion House Square, describing it as 'yet another glass stump better suited to downtown Chicago than to the City of London'. He also challenged the appropriateness of a proposed extension to the National Gallery in Trafalgar Square, describing it as 'a vast municipal fire station' and 'a monstrous carbuncle on the face of a much loved and elegant friend' (30 May 1984). In a leading article in the *Observer*, Stephen Gardiner (1984) described the speech as 'the voice of the public speaking, outraged by the architectural disasters which have overwhelmed towns and cities up and down the country over the past 30 years'. The van der Rohe glass tower was subsequently replaced by a design of James Stirling on a smaller scale which did not dwarf the existing buildings (Pawley, 1986). The National Gallery extension was also rejected and replaced by a proposal which continues the classical lines of William Wilkins' 1838 building (Pawley, 1987).

*(c) Opposition to urban conservation*

The renewed emphasis on urban conservation is not without its critics. Some, like Berthold Lubetkin, regard the urban conservation movement as a form of unhealthy nostalgia. 'The "gentlemen" of the Press, the senile young men and aged adolescents, best-preserved conservationists, antiquarianists and retrogrades of all sorts seek refuge in an idealised past. They wallow in a mass of nostalgia, ignoring the rhythm of today' (Lubetkin, 1985). Martin Pawley is concerned about the implications urban conservation has for the future of architecture and regrets that 'architects are being employed to make the outsides of their buildings look as though they were designed in the heyday of the hansom cab. They are not being employed simply as stylists but as something even more limited than that. Architects today have come perilously close to being aesthetic consultants working only on the outer skin of their buildings. Cosmeticians, in fact, denied even the right to carry out plastic surgery' (Pawley, 1986). He is also concerned that urban conservation policies, rigorously implemented, can severely restrict commercial development.

> *City planners may boast that their restrictive policies actively disperse the wealth and job-creating power that are concentrated in the Square Mile – by driving stockbrokers to Hackney, or insurance companies to Whitechapel – but they should have a care that their forced decentralisation does not turn into a migration that would not stop until Brussels, New York or Tokyo (**Pawley, 1985**).*

A further area of criticism is that conservationists pay little regard to the cost of conserving old buildings. This led Michael Manser, in a letter to the *Guardian* (24 May 1985), to claim: 'The obvious and major architectural and historical treasures must be preserved, but no one should doubt the cost. It is extremely expensive and can only be justified by absolute merit. In this area only the very best can be supported by public funds.'

ASSIGNMENTS
*1. What do you think about the impact of urban conservation on town centre*

*developments? Are town planners, architects and developers beginning to provide the sort of town centre schemes favoured by the majority of people? Is urban conservation a luxury we cannot afford? Is it anything more than mere nostalgia, trying to recreate an idealised image of the past? Compare any 1960s and 1980s town centre developments that have oc-curred in your area. Which do you prefer and why?*

2. *Refer to Plate 7.6 and evaluate how far the 1960s developments illustrated pay regard to the context in which they have been set. Establish criteria to help your evaluation. The mosaic of photographs also illustrates examples of conservation in practice. Discuss how far they succeed and whether it might not have been better to have redeveloped the sites with purpose-built shops and a new museum.*

## 2. The decentralisation of CBD functions

### (a) Retailing

The process of the decentralisation of commercial functions is one common to all Western developed countries but it started much earlier, and has proceeded much further, in the USA than elsewhere. The process was triggered off by massive shifts of population to the flourishing suburbs in the 1950s and 1960s, accompanied by much greater personal mobility arising from an increase in car ownership. In many instances edge-of-town and out-of-town purpose-built shopping centres challenged the supremacy of retailing in the CBD, often resulting in the city centre being just one of a number of retail centres within the urban system. In Detroit, for example, the central area no longer contains a single department store while, in Atlanta, the city centre ranks as only the sixth most important shopping centre in the metropolitan area (Lord, 1987). The lack of planning restraints meant that market forces were unbridled and the major retailers chose locations which could best serve the predominantly white middle-class population which had the greater spending power. The outcome of this process of change is what Berry, Simmons & Tennant (1963) described as 'spatial anarchy'.

In the UK, until relatively recently, government policy at both national and local levels has been to protect city centre retailing and strongly resist retail decentralisation. The costs and benefits of retail decentralisation are not, however, clear cut. They have been summarised by Davies (1984) under the headings economic, environmental and social considerations.

### (i) Economic considerations

*Benefit:* The retailer benefits from lower overheads as, for example, land and rateable values will be lower than in the CBD. These can be passed on to the consumer in the form of lower prices and/or better services.

*Cost:* It is possible that this price differential might be eroded or disappear if and when the retailer gains a spatial monopoly by putting competitors out of business, although there is little research evidence to suggest that this happens (Davies, 1984).

*Benefit:* Hypermarkets and superstores generate between 100 and 500 jobs when they are first opened, although many of these are only part-time.

*Cost:* It is unclear what effect the opening of a new hypermarket or superstore has on employment in shops elsewhere, and there is likely to be some job loss as a result of the competition.

*Benefit:* Stores in suburban locations may fill a 'trade vacuum', making shopping more convenient for people living in the vicinity.

*Cost:* Because the new stores have extensive catchment areas, existing local shopping centres and even town centre shops may be adversely affected. Small supermarkets in local shopping centres might be particularly hard hit. These shops often act as 'anchor stores' in the local centres and their decline may have serious implications for the other shops located there.

### (ii) Environmental considerations

*Benefit:* Hypermarkets and superstores will be built on very extensive sites which means ample free car parking spaces can be provided for shoppers, and cars and delivery vehicles can be kept separate.

*Cost:* Stores built beyond the built-up area can contribute to urban sprawl, or may in some cases make incursions into the Green Belt. They may also deflect development from vacant sites in the inner cities. Some of the buildings may be purely functional and visually obtrusive, although planners can demand certain requirements such as landscaping and a high-quality facade on new buildings.

*Benefit:* Edge-of-town and out-of-town shopping centres will deflect some traffic from town centres, thereby easing traffic congestion.

*Cost:* Service roads to the shopping centres will have been built for local traffic only and be inadequate for the extra traffic generated by the new shops. The mixing of local traffic, that is, shoppers visiting the out-of-town centre, and through-traffic on, for example, ring roads, may cause congestion and increase the risk of traffic accidents.

### (iii) Social considerations

*Benefit:* The opening of an edge-of-town or out-of-town shopping centre, incorporating a hypermarket or superstore, increases shoppers' choice, providing them with an alternative to town centre and local shops. The hypermarkets and superstores will have extended opening hours enabling late-night shopping. They make bulk purchasing easier and customers can shop less frequently.

*Cost:* Such centres are more likely to be used by the younger, more affluent and more mobile sections of society and may be more difficult to reach by the carless, older and less well off.

*Benefit:* The large purpose-built shopping centres will be on a single storey and make provision for the disabled. The wider aisles and check-out points in the stores also make it easier for people in wheelchairs and shoppers with young children. Some centres provide crèches and play areas.

In the face of consumer demand for more convenient forms of shopping, many local authorities have been reconsidering their total opposition to any form of retail decentralisation. This has led some of them to accept that a degree of decentralisation is inevitable and that it is better that this is planned rather than it being allowed to arise haphazardly. There is an increasing acceptance that a strong argument can be made for the decentralisation of certain retail functions such as food retailing, do-it-yourself merchandise and self-assembly furniture. This is the policy now being pursued pragmatically by the North Bedfordshire Borough Council, which is still endeavouring to uphold the County Structure Plan Policy 17 which states that 'planning permissions for out-of-town, out-of-centre shopping developments (apart from local facilities) are not normally granted'. The Borough Council, having fought unsuccessfully a number of appeals to resist any decentralisation of retailing, has now bowed to the inevitable and has designated a site for a new superstore in a new development area on the eastern edge of the town which will serve shoppers living north of the River Great Ouse. This will complement a superstore already opened in the south-west of the town. The city centre is now ringed by a number of purpose-built do-it-yourself stores, each providing extensive free parking spaces (see Figure 7.12). Superstores provide between 2325 and 4650 square metres of retail floor space, at least two-thirds of which is likely to be devoted to food retailing (Herbert & Thomas, 1982). They do not, therefore, pose a threat to the town centre shops specialising in consumer durables. In contrast, hypermarkets provide over 4650 square metres of retail floor space, two-thirds of which is likely to be devoted to non-food retailing. They, therefore, pose much more of a perceived threat to existing town centre shops, and have been more vigorously resisted. There are still relatively few hypermarkets in the UK. The Carrefour hypermarket at Caerphilly was Britain's first. An impact study conducted by Lee and Kent concluded that 'there is no evidence to suggest that the hypermarket has had a widespread adverse impact upon the established hierarchy . . . there have been substantial

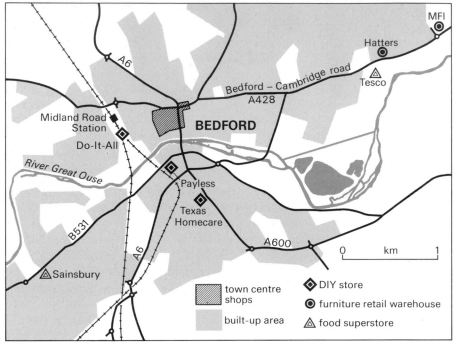

Figure 7.12　Bedford's central shopping area and the superstores, DIY and furniture stores which have been developed recently on sites away from the town centre.

changes . . . yet these relate more closely to the normal evolution of centres'. In spite of such research findings, there remains an entrenched resistance to hypermarket expansion in the UK. This has not been the case in France, where many and, in some cases, very large hypermarkets have been built over the last decade or so (see Plate 7.12).

The other form of retail decentralisation which has also been resisted in the UK is the new large regional centre. The Metro Centre, Gateshead, is one of the few examples of such a development in the UK (see Plate 7.13). Its impact on retailers in central Newcastle and other towns within its catchment area has been carefully monitored. The interim findings have shown that different groups of shoppers are attracted to the Metro Centre than to the city centre of Newcastle. With those using the Metro Centre there is an under-representation of young people, and a domination of car owners, to such an extent that, in spite of the extensive car parks which have been provided, parking is already being identified as something of a problem. Shoppers are prepared to travel considerable distances to the new centre, with 41% travelling over 15 kilometres, and the average amount each shopper spends is relatively high. One of the more interesting consequences of the development of the Metro Centre is that it has encouraged

254

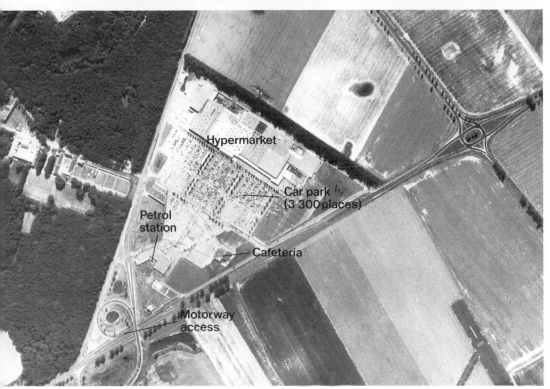

Plate 7.12   Carrefour hypermarket at Villiers-en-Bière near Fontainebleau in northern France, just off the N7 motorway. (Photograph: Carrefour)

Plate 7.13   Part of the interior of the Metro Centre, Gateshead, a new regional shopping centre in the north-east of England, which has added a leisure dimension to shopping. The Centre includes landscaped areas where shoppers can sit and relax, children's play areas and even a fairground. (Photograph: Metro Centre Management Offices)

255

the Newcastle city centre to respond to the competition it poses. Retailers and other interested parties have combined to market the city centre and have succeeded in getting it cleaned up, cutting parking charges and persuading more shops to stay open for late-night shopping (Reynolds, 1987). Another regional centre, the Sprucefield Centre, has been proposed in an area south of Belfast, but it remains to be seen what impact this centre would have on shops in Belfast city centre. In North America, of course, a number of large purpose-built regional centres have been developed and one of these, West Edmonton, is described on pages 287 to 289.

Ironically, at a time when the UK is coming to terms with an element of decentralised retailing, there is evidence of the beginnings of a reverse trend in the USA. Some downtown areas, which had slipped down the shopping hierarchy and served essentially inner city catchment areas, are being revived partly in response to a reversal of population trends which have seen young, more affluent, families moving to gentrified inner city areas. Cities such as Milwaukee, Chicago and Philadelphia, whose city centres were being written off only a few years ago, have benefited from very substantial investment and urban renewal programmes (see Plate 7.14). Lord (1987), however, warns us to treat with circumspection some of the hyped-up reports of central area revitalisation and reinvestment, which he claims are sometimes exaggerated.

Plate 7.14  Philadelphia's revitalised city centre. (Photograph: Philadelphia Convention and Visitors Bureau)

*(iv)  Conclusion*

The American experience of very rapid and far-reaching retail decentralisation which occurred in the 1950s and 1960s badly affected city centre retailing, resulting in severe contraction and diminished quality. This has been avoided in the UK because planning controls in Britain are stronger and more effective. Nevertheless, there are those who have argued that absolute resistance to any form of retail decentralisation has not been in the best interests of the consumer. Davies has been particularly aware of some of the shortcomings of retail provision in the UK.

> *The bulk of the population remains heavily constrained in its choice of shopping facilities. Prices of goods remain high because of the difficulty of achieving scale economies in small separate shop units; the variety and range of goods remains equally limited, often with too much duplication; goods have to be hauled around without the use of trolleys or store buggies; there remains the discomfort of shopping in bad weather conditions (except in the case of enclosed shopping centres); untidiness and vandalism are difficult to control when the upkeep falls to the local authority; the main visual impact on the shopper is one of concrete and bricks rather than of the internal decor of the actual shops (**Davies, 1978**).*

In the decade which has intervened since Davies wrote this passage, consumer pressure for more convenient patterns of retailing has caused many planning authorities to adopt a more flexible approach to applications from retailers for out-of-town and edge-of-town shopping centres.

*(b)  Offices*

Offices are concerned essentially with *information handling*. A distinction can be made between the *producer services*, that is finance, insurance, property and other private sector activities, and *non-profit services and government* (Hall, 1985). In the UK and Western Europe there has been a strong resistance to decentralising producer services. In France, for example, 90% of the headquarters of major national companies are located in Paris (Alexander, 1979) while, in the UK, London's domination of the office sector is equally strong. There are many factors which have encouraged a continued concentration of offices in major cities, including the importance of a prestige address, a contact-rich environment and the need to assemble a diversified, and mainly skilled, white-collar workforce. Furthermore, the savings that can be made in moving to a suburban location are limited. It has been estimated that the cost of labour accounts for between 84% and 86% of expenditure of offices and for this there is little variation between the city centre and the suburbs (Herbert & Thomas, 1982). Suburban locations may also have little effect in reducing the length of journeys-to-work, while at the same time increasing the likelihood that office workers will use private cars rather than public transport.

In the UK, any pressure to decentralise office functions has arisen from an awareness of the diseconomies of scale arising from increased concentration and the attendant congestion. In 1964, the Labour Government introduced Office Development Permits in London, which applied to all office developments over 270 square metres. The aim was to channel new office development to locations beyond an 80-kilometre radius of central London and the Location of Offices Bureau was established to help this process. Policies changed with the incoming Conservative Government in 1979 and restrictions on further office development in central London were relaxed.

In the USA many offices moved from city centre to suburban locations in the 1950s and 1960s, and by 1960 49% of New York's office floor space was located in the suburbs (Manners, 1974). There is some evidence that a reversal of this trend has occurred in recent years and cities such as Chicago and Baltimore have seen much new office development.

It can be argued that it is mainly inertia that keeps offices so concentrated in London and other major cities of Western Europe. Developments in the application of information technology make it increasingly possible for office workers to be based in smaller decentralised offices near their homes, or even to work from home and communicate via telephone links to mainframe computers. It is possible that in the future the *raison d'être* of the CBD will be undermined further but the American city has demonstrated that city centres are very resilient and have a propensity to survive, with modified functions, long after they have been written off.


ASSIGNMENTS

1. *Do you think more out-of-town and edge-of-town shopping centres should be allowed? What is the balance of costs and benefits? What form should any permitted retail decentralisation take? How can the town centre shops be protected? Does it matter if town centres decline? How can the retail interests of disadvantaged groups, such as the elderly, the carless and the less well off, be looked after? Discuss these issues and others arising from the decentralisation of retailing.*
2. *The battle over the Mansion House Square site has been one of the most fiercely fought planning controversies of recent times. It has been suggested that it was modern architecture that was on trial at the Planning Inquiry. Read the following two commentaries on the Secretary of State for the Environment's decision to reject Mies van der Rohe's building and look at the artist's impression of the development (see Figure 7.13). Do you think the decision was the right one? Give reasons to support your opinion.*

258

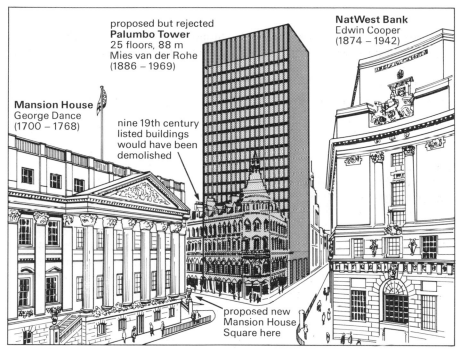

Figure 7.13 Mies van der Rohe's 290 foot tower superimposed on Mansion House Square. The tower was strongly opposed by conservationists and was not built.

Editorial in the *Guardian*, 22 May 1985

# The Tower Tumbles

The Government's rejection of the proposed 290 feet high Palumbo Tower in Mansion House Square (expected to be confirmed today in Parliament) may well set the tone for inner city planning for the rest of the century. The decision was not an easy one, especially for a government dedicated to laissez-faire. The tower, a good building of its kind, designed 20 years ago by Mies van der Rohe, the high priest of modernism, would have stood proud in place of any of the vast majority of barren glass blocks erected in the misbegotten high rise fashion of the sixties and seventies.

The case against is not just the known (now) shortcomings of tall glass buildings, the "greenhouse" effect inside, the wind vortexes at the bottom. Nor the misplaced argument that the City "needs" another tall office block close to the Bank of England (a stone's throw away) when, patently, it doesn't. The advances of information technology have cut the umbilical cord between banks and the square mile. You can be part of the market as well in Hammersmith as Threadneedle Street. Even the Governor of the Bank of England is said to be against Mr Peter Palumbo's 20-year-old grand design.

The main objection is that the tower is totally out of character with the 18th and 19th century complex of streets and buildings in medieval surround. To have planted a mausoleum of modernism in such a place would have been to have learned nothing from inherited mistakes. This is not to say that there should be no redevelopment at Mansion House Square. What is needed now is something which starts from the evolving present rather than the faded dreams of the past, and something that arrives in a good deal less than twenty years.

259

An extract from Martin Pawley's leading article in the *Guardian* on the same day. Martin Pawley is the *Guardian*'s architectural correspondent.

The Secretary of State for the Environment has decided to refuse permission for Peter Palumbo's Mansion House Square project:

As a result London has lost £100 million worth of private sector construction in ultra modern bank building, an enclosed shopping centre, and a public square flanked by works of undisputed architectural genius. But to the City of London, the GLC Historic Buildings division, the Royal Fine Arts Commission, the Victorian Society, and the other organisations and individuals that have won a famous victory, this price will not seem excessive.

The battlefield itself, with its scaffolded and boarded-up buildings, crumbling remnants of long-lost imperial merchant power, now lies like so much of the rest of Britain, purposeless and exhausted.

What will become of the energy that went into the assembly of Peter Palumbo's 25-year dream? The site that was so painstakingly assembled into a state of possibility must now be split up – re-let, or compulsorily purchased. Whatever replaces Mansion House Square can only be less than it might have been – and that is the true victory of conservation over creative architecture.

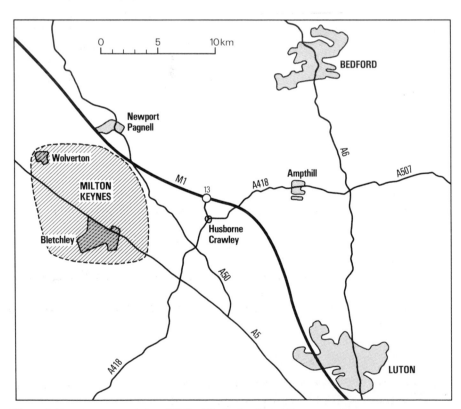

Figure 7.14    The proposed site of Helicol Parks development.

3. *Helicol Parks Ltd applied for planning permission to develop a large hypermarket in the Bedfordshire village of Husborne Crawley.*
   *(a) Examine Figure 7.14 and summarise the advantages of the situation for the proposed development.*
   *(b) A planning committee has been invited to consider whether the proposed development should receive planning permission. The committee consists of the following individuals:*
   *(i) an unemployed young person residing in Husborne Crawley;*
   *(ii) a retired military gentleman who has recently moved to Husborne Crawley and would like to see the village conserved;*
   *(iii) a working woman with three children living in Milton Keynes New Town (the family owns two cars);*
   *(iv) the manager of a supermarket in the centre of Bedford;*
   *(v) a young executive representing the developers;*
   *(vi) an old age pensioner, without a car, living in Luton.*
   *Write role profiles for each of the committee members and give each one a brief or an indication of the interests he or she represents. The role profiles and briefs can then be given to members of your group who will become a simulated planning committee. The committee members should each in turn put their case and the committee eventually arrive at a consensus of opinion which should be reported back to the rest of the class. If you have a large enough class it will be interesting for more than one committee to discuss the planning application. The groups can then compare decisions and the processes by which they were reached.*

# Key Ideas

*Introduction*

1. The CBD develops at the most accessible part of the urban system.
2. Competition for CBD sites results in high site values, higher than in any other part of the urban system.
3. These high land values dictate that commercial enterprises dominate to the virtual exclusion of other functions.
4. The CBD provides commercial enterprises with unique linkages with other businesses and the public.
5. Shops and other commercial activities benefit from cumulative attraction within the CBD.

*A. The Characteristics of the CBD*

1. Certain types of retail outlets, such as department stores and variety goods stores, which have a wide range and high threshold population, are likely to occupy the most central space.

2. Offices may occupy rather more peripheral sites within the CBD.
3. There is a marked absence of manufacturing industry within the CBD.
4. The potential linkages with other business and the public which a CBD site provides encourages the development of distinctive functional zones such as shops and offices. Within these broad functional zones marked sub-sections can often be identified, for example a financial quarter within the office zone.
5. High site values within the CBD encourage multi-storey development.
6. Within individual office blocks, activities which need maximum contact with the public usually occupy the lower floors.
7. Within the CBD there is a low residential population.

## B. The Delimitation of the CBD

1. The boundary of the CBD is generally gradational rather than clear cut.
2. In general, pedestrian densities and rateable values decline with distance from the CBD.
3. An examination of parking restrictions within the town centre may provide some indication of the extent of the CBD.
4. It is often possible to distinguish a 'hard core' of commercial activity within a town's CBD.
5. The core–frame model distinguishes a core, a district of intensive land use where land values are highest, from a less intensively developed frame.
6. CBD functions may be extended into the zone in transition where it may be possible to distinguish sectors of active and passive assimilation and general inactivity.
7. Individuals will have their own mental images of what comprises the commercial core of a town. A composite map of these will provide an indication of the perceived extent of the CBD.
8. Individuals' mental maps of town centres would seem to indicate a preference for developments on a small and more personal scale.

## C. Analysing the Internal Structure of the CBD

1. Certain types of shops and offices, such as shoe shops and stockbrokers, have a propensity to cluster while others, such as newsagents and travel agents, are usually more widely distributed.
2. The centre of gravity and index of dispersion can be employed to analyse the internal structure of a CBD.

## D. Change within the CBD

1. During the 1960s many towns went in for insensitive comprehensive central-area redevelopment schemes.

2. There has been a reaction against functional modern architecture, and urban conservation has become very popular.
3. Comprehensive redevelopment has been replaced by sensitive urban-renewal schemes, which conserve what is best of the existing townscape.
4. Critics of urban conservation claim that it is no more than nostalgia, harking back to an idealised past which cannot be re-instated.
5. Free market forces and a lack of planning controls have resulted in retailing in the USA being decentralised.
6. There are economic, environmental and social costs and benefits arising from retail decentralisation.
7. In the UK, consumer demand is causing planners to re-think their policies for retailing and permit the decentralisation of certain functions such as do-it-yourself merchandise and convenience foodstuffs.
8. In the UK, offices remain strongly centralised, although developments in information technology may make this less essential in future.

## Additional Activities

1. Describe the features which distinguish the CBD of a large city.
2. Critically examine the techniques you would adopt to:
   (a) delimit the CBD of a large town,
   (b) analyse the internal structure of a town's CBD.
3. Write an essay on 'The CBD in twenty years' time', incorporating a reasoned account of the changes you envisage taking place.

# 8 Central Place Theory

## A. Economic Factors: Supply, Demand and Choice

### 1. The need to choose

Suppose that you decide, while reading this section, to have a cup of coffee, only to discover that there is none in the kitchen. Assuming that you have some money and that the shops are still open you could either (a) go out and buy some coffee, come home and make a cup or (b) if it's late, or you live in a large enough town, go and buy a cup of coffee at a coffee bar. These choices assume the *availability* of what you want, if you are prepared to travel to get it. Our reluctance to travel is an aspect of *friction of distance*. Alternatively you could stay at home and make a cup of tea or open a bottle of coke, in other words accept *substitutes* for what you want. Thirdly you could forget the whole idea and carry on with your reading.

Which of these alternatives appeals to you will depend in part upon your personality, but it will also be conditioned by how strong your desire is to obtain the commodity in question and by the means available to satisfy it. The variety of choices available each time we want something illustrates fundamental concepts of supply and demand which become more apparent if we explore further. The need or *demand* for coffee is only one of a whole group of needs which are satisfied by the *supply* of some item or service. How much effort we are prepared to expend upon satisfying the need will depend upon how important it seems to be, relative to all the others. Generally speaking, the keenness of our *demand* for goods or services declines with a rise in its cost. This cost may be the actual price we are charged, but it also includes the cost of time and effort expended in satisfying the need. If this cost is too high we may turn to a substitute or abandon the demand altogether. Diagrammatically this may be represented as in Figure 8.1 where the $D$–$D_1$ demand curve indicates an increase in quantity with a decrease in price, indicating that we are prepared to buy more goods if prices are reduced. The steepness of the demand, and indeed the supply, curve indicates how much more or less people will buy or sell as prices change. This steepness is referred to as the *elasticity* of demand. A

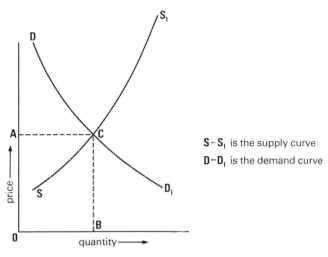

Figure 8.1 A supply and demand curve. At price A, quantity B will be supplied, and the intersection point C is the equilibrium point. If the price falls, the excess demand will force it back up and if it rises the decline in demand will force the price down again.

steep curve is said to be elastic, and a shallow curve, indicating little change in quantity with price, is said to be inelastic. Goods for which there are easily available substitutes will have very *elastic* demand.

## 2. How do we choose?

A manufacturer is likely to be more willing to supply goods when the price obtained for them is high, and when a greater profit is made. The coffee bar will make a greater profit if it is either selling a lot of coffees, or charging a high price for them; because overheads such as staff, wear and tear on equipment, rental and so on will remain fairly constant so the marginal return on each extra item sold is greater to the owner. The compromise position will be reached in something of the manner of the diagram, where the public are prepared to pay price $P$ and consume quantity $Q$ of a given commodity at that price (see Figure 8.1).

This analysis of supply and demand is, of course, over-simplified. In reality the price of goods is also conditioned by manufacturing costs (for raw materials, transport, power, etc.). At the same time the public's willingness to pay is influenced by their ability to change from one commodity to another: that is, to substitute satisfiers. In some circumstances we can change fairly easily if the price becomes too high: from potatoes to rice, butter to margarine, coffee to tea. However, with more specialised services such transfer is less possible and, consequently, the most essential of these are generally run as legalised monopolies in the form of public utilities: hospitals, schools, postal service. Clearly in understanding the working of

265

the interactions of supply and demand in the urban landscape we must take account of the urgency and frequency of specific needs. It should also be remembered that suppliers may not be able to change their levels of output easily. Supply may also be inelastic and shortages or gluts can thus occur, because of the time lag in manufacturers' reaction to changes in demand. From what has been said so far, it seems evident that there are various categories of goods which we use frequently and expect to find conveniently near. On the other hand, we are prepared to travel farther to obtain the goods which we purchase rarely, especially if they are expensive. Also we like to have a greater choice with important purchases: this may help to explain the grouping of particular shops into districts. Obviously we do not expect small shops or groups of shops to stock every item we might require. They could not afford to do so and they would make only a very small profit on items that were rarely asked for. The underlying idea that there are different *orders* of goods is basic to an understanding of how a hierarchy of shopping centres or settlements develops.

## 3. The application of supply and demand in the landscape

If we can now generalise about how far people are likely to travel to obtain goods or services of different orders, we can see why 'urban fields' are of different dimensions. This average distance from which people will come to use a particular service or purchase a particular good is more briefly defined as the *range* of that good or service.

So far we have looked at the business of trading only from the viewpoint of ourselves as consumers. From the suppliers' point of view, a minimum number of purchasers is necessary before it is worth while setting up a supply outlet. The less frequent the average purchase of the good or service, the greater the 'market population' needed in order to ensure that the supplier receives an adequate level of demand to remain in business. The 'minimum level of demand necessary to sustain a service' is referred to as the demand *threshold*, above which a particular facility will be profitable and thus come into existence.

Major supermarket chains such as Tesco and Sainsbury's now need a threshold population of around 80 000 to 90 000 people to make opening a new store worth while, and firms such as John Lewis need over 100 000 potential customers to support a department store. However, medium-sized towns of 40 000 to 50 000 population may attract 'food only' supermarkets such as Waitrose, especially if the town is clearly expanding as are many along the 'silicon ridge' from Peterborough to Bristol, where new hi-tech industries are attracting young well-paid families to settle.

In the remoter parts of Britain, the *catchment area* from which stores draw customers may be much wider than the confines of the town in which they are located. Thus Inverness, with an urban population of only about

36 000, has another 20 000 people living within the local government boundary and a further 100 000 resident in the Highland region. It can consequently support major stores such as Marks and Spencer, because people are prepared to travel further in northern Scotland to use these facilities than they might be in the more densely settled parts of England and Wales.

We can begin to see that some towns will provide smaller or greater varieties of services than others on the basis of the threshold population available to utilise them. That there may be a statistical relationship between the size of a settlement and the amount of trade it attracts is an idea which we shall examine in Chapter 9. If centres are reasonably close together and transport is fairly cheap, it is likely that people will 'shop around' for the best value in a particular commodity. Hence the range of a particular service from an urban centre is limited by competition from other places supplying the same or similar services. The range of a service is controlled at the lower level by the minimum threshold population necessary to sustain it.

As a result of the interaction of threshold and range it can be shown that a hierarchy of places supplying goods of different orders will emerge. Although an individual service such as a shoe shop may have a unique threshold and range it will be located in an urban centre where it benefits from the proximity of other similar shops. Indeed as most of the 'high street names' in the footwear and clothing trade are now branches of major conglomerates such as the British Shoe Corporation or the Burton Group, the apparent choice between brands in different shops may be a spurious one.

Distinctive groups of services will develop in settlements which provide the right threshold for their survival within the range of urban field appropriate to them. As we have already surmised a ranking of settlements in order of the number of services they offer demonstrates that small centres (villages) provide a limited number of facilities accessible locally. The majority of the population requiring greater choice or higher order goods may have to travel considerable distances to larger centres to obtain them. This has implications for the land values in the more favoured centres. These larger centres serving extensive urban fields are commonly called *central places*.

ASSIGNMENTS

1. *Using a local map, preferably at 1 : 250 000 scale, and a tracing overlay, plot the distribution of settlements of different sizes, using the style of typeface of the place names as a guide to their relative importance. Graph the relative numbers of each type. By reference to the Yellow Pages of the local Telephone Directory, plot the number of facilities (e.g. banks, estate agents, public houses) and compare the ranking of settlement size and range of services. The maps of Lincolnshire at a scale of 1 : 100 000 and*

*1 : 250 000 would provide a suitable case study area in which to try this exercise, but a more detailed survey could be undertaken using larger-scale maps and population figures from the Bureau of Population and Census Reports. If a large number of settlements is studied it is worth ranking them in order and applying a correlation coefficient test to the two rankings. The simplest formula to apply is Spearman's rank:*

$$r = 1 - \frac{6\Sigma d^2}{(n^3 - n)}$$

where $r$ is the coefficient of correlation,
$\quad\quad$ $d$ is the difference in ranking, and
$\quad\quad$ $n$ is the number of cases ranked: in this case settlements.
*(See Table 8.1.)*

Table 8.1

| Town | Population | Population rank | Number of facilities | Facilities ranked | $d$ | $d^2$ |
|---|---|---|---|---|---|---|
| a | 25 000 | 8 | 45 | 7 | 1 | 1 |
| b | 35 000 | 7 | 27 | 10 | 3 | 9 |
| c | 130 000 | 3 | 200 | 3 | 0 | 0 |
| d | 23 000 | 9 | 35 | 8 | 1 | 1 |
| e | 22 000 | 10 | 30 | 9 | 1 | 1 |
| f | 250 000 | 2 | 400 | 2 | 0 | 0 |
| g | 75 000 | 4 | 92 | 4 | 0 | 0 |
| h | 320 000 | 1 | 420 | 1 | 0 | 0 |
| i | 65 000 | 6 | 78 | 5 | 1 | 1 |
| j | 68 000 | 5 | 68 | 6 | 1 | 1 |

**$n = 10$** $\quad\quad\quad\quad\quad\quad\quad\quad\quad\quad\quad\quad\quad\quad\quad\quad\quad\quad\quad\quad$ $\Sigma d^2 = 14$

**Substi**tuting in the formula:

$r = 1 - \dfrac{6 \times 14}{1000 - 10} = 0.92$

*If we compare the figure obtained for* r *with Table 8.2 we find that in over 99 cases out of 100 such a correlation is likely to be the result of factors other than chance; in other words one variable is likely to vary with the other. This does not mean that one variable, in this case population size, actually*

Table 8.2 Statistical significance and confidence levels for Spearman rank correlation coefficient

| Number of items | Values of r at confidence levels | |
|---|---|---|
| | 95% | 99% |
| 10 | 0.564 | 0.746 |
| 15 | 0.440 | 0.620 |
| 20 | 0.377 | 0.534 |
| 25 | 0.336 | 0.475 |
| 30 | 0.306 | 0.432 |

causes *the other, but we can claim that the relationship between the two is of* statistical significance. *This statistical significance at particular levels (or percentage of cases) is a convenient method of measuring how far two quite different characteristics are related, because the test does not rely upon their being measured in the same units. The frequency with which this is likely to prove a correlation is termed the 'confidence level' and normally geographers aim at confidence levels of 95% or 99%. (See Table 8.2.)*

2. *Which of the following products do you think will have 'elastic' demand and which 'inelastic' demand: salt, butter, cornflakes, fuel oil, coffee, frozen peas, newsprint, disposable nappies? Give reasons for your answers, bearing in mind that the substitutability and the relative proportion of our average expenditure which these items comprise will be important factors.*

3. *Which of the following services and goods do you think will have elastic and which inelastic supply: beef production, dishwashers, new houses, motor cars, package holidays, soap powder? Bear in mind that the capacity for suppliers to change output at short notice will be important. Will any other factors affect supply levels (e.g. advantages of large-scale production, government restrictions on production)?*

4. *A special offer of 40% reduction is advertised on one of the following items at a store 30 kilometres from your home. Which item would you feel most anxious to obtain in order to take advantage of this offer, and why: radio-cassette recorders, current Top Ten LP records, tights (packs of two dozen only), shoes, your favourite range of perfume or aftershave?*

## B. Central Places: the Christaller Model

As we saw in Chapter 2 there tends to be a pattern of declining intensity of land use around rural settlements. This can also be noted as one moves away from lines of communication, and is attributable in part to increased problems of accessibility of land and thus its relative unattractiveness for development. These ideas, originally applied to the changing value of agricultural land as one moved outwards from a market centre, were put forward in the eighteenth century by Ricardo and Von Thünen. An extension of this thinking was put forward in 1933 by Walter Christaller, who noted the relationship of threshold and range of settlements of different orders in southern Germany. In order to express his ideas he simplified the landscape which he was describing: hence the rather formal and unrealistic nature of the diagrams, which are not intended to be maps (Christaller, 1933).

## 1. The underlying assumptions

Christaller realised that it is possible not only to view the rural landscape as serving its local centre with produce but also to see the area around each

Table 8.3 Urban areas of Great Britain

| Settlement size | Number of settlements | Type | Examples |
|---|---|---|---|
| Above 5 million | 1 | Capital | London |
| Above 1 million | 1 | Conurbation | Birmingham |
| 400 000–1 million | 4 | Provincial centres | Liverpool, Manchester |
| 250 000–400 000 | 10 | Regional centres | Bristol, Cardiff |
| 150 000–250 000 | 18 | Large manufacturing towns | Newcastle, Hull |
| 100 000–150 000 | 25 | Manufacturing and retailing towns | Peterborough, Reading |
| 70 000–100 000 | 38 | Commercial and market towns | Bedford |
| 40 000– 70 000 | 130 | Market towns | Taunton |
| 20 000– 40 000 | 185 | Small market towns | St Neots |
| 10 000– 20 000 | 220 | Small towns | St Ives |
| 2 000– 10 000 | 300 + | Large villages | Wymondham |

Source: *Geographical Digest*, 1986

town as the recipient of services produced in the town. However, these tributary areas or urban fields were not uniform in size, nor were the settlements, and the comparative growth of some at the expense or stagnation of others demanded explanation. The comparable settlement orders in Britain to those identified by Christaller in Germany are shown in Table 8.3. In order to explain the variations in settlement size and importance in the area about which he was writing Christaller envisaged a homogenous plain, sometimes referred to as an *isotropic surface*, upon which early settlement was evenly distributed in the form of small nucleated hamlets. If it is assumed that the landscape quality is everywhere similar and that each settlement has the same number of farming families gaining their livelihood from the land, then a regular distribution of hamlets may be expected. The spacing in his model is at 2-mile intervals (3.2 km) approximately similar to that in some areas of Saxon lowland occupance, but inferior or superior conditions of terrain and productivity would alter this distancing. After some time, as technology and road transport improve, specialisation of production is able to develop, and trade between the towns increases. If 3 km or thereabouts is as far as a village farmer is willing to walk to market, some farmers will have a choice of places to go to, while the residents of those villages which have a market will presumably trade there. Christaller suggested that villages with markets would also draw a proportion of the trade from up to six surrounding centres, but that other market villages would also share this trade. If the whole region is covered in 'market areas', a pattern of hexagonal networks may grow up (see Figure 8.2a) with each

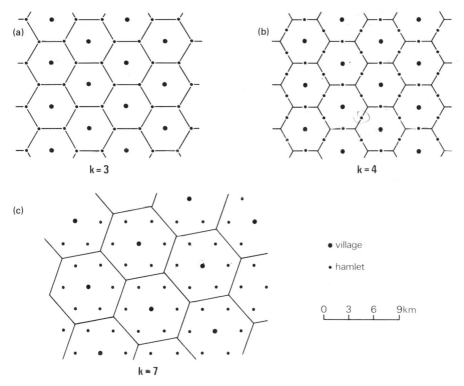

Figure 8.2　The pattern of $k = 3$, $k = 4$ and $k = 7$ hierarchies applied to a landscape of regularly spaced settlements.

central market village receiving the trade generated by up to three times its own population. The surrounding villages each contribute one-third of the population because there are three central villages to which each outer village has access (see Figure 8.2a). This total trade allegiance which a market centre received from surrounding hamlets Christaller expressed as its $k$ value. He then went on to consider alternative ways in which small settlements might depend upon larger ones, and to devise $k$ values to describe these relationships as well.

## 2. The determining of $k$ values

Christaller went on to suggest that if the business of marketing goods was the most important determinant of landscape organisation in a region then the $k = 3$ hierarchy would operate at all levels of settlement. There would be a fixed ratio of towns in one size group to settlements in the next (for example, one large city, three regional centres, nine large towns, etc.). However, other possible organising principles existed. One of these, based

271

on the most effective transport network to serve a region, would generate a k ratio of 4 to 1 (see Figure 8.2b). If a settlement is located between two or more central places it is likely that its inhabitants will be divided in their allegiance, so that the k value will be composed of the 'fractions' of six outer village populations. Such 'sharing' is more likely for purposes of trade than for purposes of transport. Christaller also envisaged a pattern of settlement networks where the k value is 7 (see Figure 8.2c). This he called his defensive or administrative principle, implying that a town responsible for acting as the military focus of surrounding territories would not share that control with another town but rather keep control entirely within its own hands. Once the principle by which the ratio between towns of different levels of importance or orders was established, Christaller argued, then the whole range of settlements in that area would relate to each other in accordance with that ratio as the settlements grew. In time a hierarchy of settlements would develop based upon the ratio, and these he believed could be identified in various parts of Western Europe.

The pattern has been shown to have validity in a number of other rural areas, especially in China (Skinner, 1964), and it was adopted as the principle upon which planned settlements in the Dutch polderlands were based in the 1950s (Figure 8.3), but improvements in transport and especial-ly in private car ownership have meant that fixed k values are obsolete for most landscapes today. In suitable terrain, the regular pattern of settlement arrangement may be demonstrated in Britain, especially in pre-industrial landscapes such as those of eastern England in the nineteenth century (Figure 8.4).

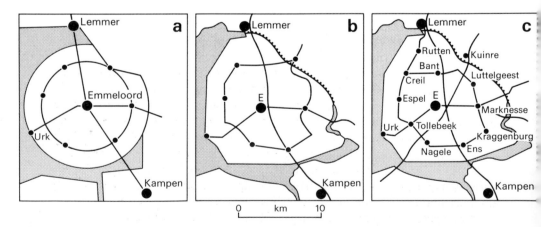

Figure 8.3 'Christaller' planning of settlements in the North East Polder: (a) geometrical diagram of the settlement pattern, (b) plan with five new villages, (c) the revised plan as carried out. (Source: IDG, Utrecht)

272

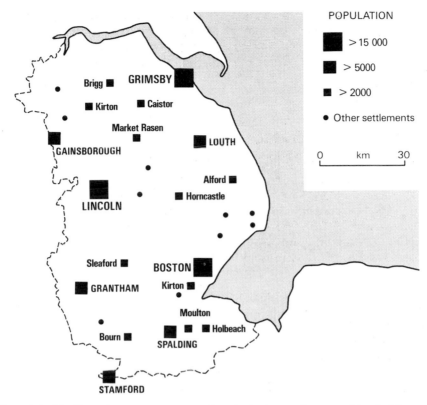

**POPULATION**

■ > 15 000

■ > 5000

■ > 2000

● Other settlements

0        km        30

Brigg ■     GRIMSBY ■

■ Kirton     ■ Caistor

Market Rasen ■

■ LOUTH

■ GAINSBOROUGH

Alford ■

■ Horncastle

■ LINCOLN

Sleaford ■     BOSTON ■

■ GRANTHAM     Kirton ■

Moulton

■ ■ ■ Holbeach

Bourn ■     SPALDING

■ STAMFORD

Figure 8.4   The hierarchy of settlements based on size in nineteenth-century Lincolnshire.

## C. Development of the Theory

### 1. Making the theory more flexible

It is obvious that, although the different orders of settlement which Christaller identified may well exist in many areas, it is unlikely that they will
relate to each other in the neat inflexible ratios of fixed $k$ values. Before
criticising the theory on these grounds it is perhaps valuable to consider the
work of another German writer, some twenty years later. August Lösch
(1954) used the same hexagonal networks or *lattices* for his theoretical
landscape. He took Christaller's model and developed a more sophisticated
form by superimposing all the various hexagonal systems so far mentioned,
and many others. By superimposing all the lattices on one point and rotating
them he achieved a pattern of sectors. You can do this yourself if you trace
the $k = 3$, $k = 4$, and $k = 7$ hierarchies onto transparent film or thin tracing
paper and then rotate them keeping the centre point uniform. Six of these
sectors have many relatively high-order settlements – these he called *city-*

273

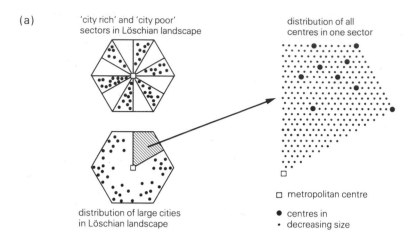

(a) 'city rich' and 'city poor' sectors in Löschian landscape

distribution of all centres in one sector

distribution of large cities in Löschian landscape

□ metropolitan centre

● centres in
· decreasing size

Figure 8.5   Löschian landscape developed by the rotation of a number of *k* system hexagons, developing 'city-rich' and 'city-poor' sectors.

*rich* sectors – and six were relatively sparsely settled or *city-poor* (see Figure 8.5). Hence we should not dismiss the application of central place theory if we find that a particular area is lacking in the 'correct' number of subsidiary settlements; at least not until we have examined adjacent regions, for these may compensate for the sparsity of settlement that we have found.

Under this system of a variable *k* hierarchy the pattern of settlements appears much more 'realistic' with a continuum of settlement size, rather than distinct tiers or orders as in the earlier model. This is true not only of the population size but also the functional variety of the settlements in terms of services supplied there. There has been considerable discussion by geographers as to whether Lösch's 'continuum' or Christaller's 'tiered' system of urban centres is more closely approximate to reality.

ASSIGNMENTS

1. *(a) Using the OS map and the overlay that you prepared for Assignment 1 on p. 267, measure the average distance between settlements of the same size or order.*

   *(b) Taking this distance as the diameter, draw circles with their centres based upon these settlements.*

   *(c) Attempt to explain areas of overlap, or where there are gaps between the circle boundaries. You should refer to both physical and human map evidence in your explanation.*

2. *Rank in order how frequently you obtain or visit the following:*

   *a pair of shoes*          *a part for*          *a pair of jeans,*
   *a packet of sweets*     *car, bicycle*       *aftershave or*
   *an LP record*              *or moped*           *perfume*

| a library | a soft drink | a football match |
| a restaurant | a new coat | a bus pass |
| a magazine or paper | a cinema | a present for |
| | | someone else. |

(a) Try to explain any correlation you notice between the price of these goods or services and the frequency with which you replace them or make a return visit.

(b) Indicate whether there is any relationship between these two factors and the distance you are prepared to travel.

3. With reference to the map of Lincolnshire (Figure 8.4) draw boundaries around the higher-order settlements to take in the ones of the order immediately below. Does the resultant pattern bear any relationship to Christaller's model?

## 2. Limits to central place theory

There are obvious simplifications in the basic theory of Christaller which he did not intend to be overlooked. *Distortion* of the hexagonal pattern of lattices due to irregular terrain, and variations in distances and direction as a result of landscape configuration and differences in soil fertility and of mineral deposits, are ones that will immediately come to mind. In addition there is the factor of *temporal change*. Settlements once founded do not disappear but rather stagnate or decline when their role is challenged by later technology. For example a change in transport technology may make them more, or less, effective service centres. But it would be unreasonable to dismiss Christaller's theory on the basis of simplifying real world situations, for those simplifications are necessary to develop a theory. In other words, we try to remove the background 'noise' which prevents us from seeing the plain ideas of the theory. This method of eliminating the distracting 'noise' in a model theory is quite valid, as long as we are careful to reintroduce the 'noise' gradually to see how the model stands up to real world situations. However, a serious criticism of the theory so far discussed is that not all towns came into existence as, or indeed presently function as, service centres for the surrounding rural area. As well as market towns with dependent villages linked to them by public transport services, there are many examples of ports, mining towns and oddly or badly sited settlements which do not approximate to the service centre pattern. If we leave out of consideration deliberately planned towns we can recognise with Johnson (1969) three groups of factors responsible for settlement siting which are not dealt with by central place theory:

(1) those cities or towns that have grown because of a location that links an area to the outside world or with certain types of manufacturing;

(2) the availability of highly localised physical resources;

(3) the chance element or 'human whim' in urban location and develop-

275

ment, a factor which is often overlooked because it is so difficult to assess.

These factors give rise to important exceptions to Christaller's theory which will be considered in the following section.

ASSIGNMENT

*Figure 8.6 illustrates the settlement pattern of villages in an imaginary landscape. What effect will the following events have upon the pattern?*
*(a)  The granting of a Charter in 1500 for a market to be held weekly at A.*
*(b)  Discovery of coal in 1700 in small quantities at B.*
*(c)  Building of a canal along the line indicated in 1785.*
*(d)  Coming of the railway along the route indicated in 1856.*
*(e)  Establishment of a trading estate at C in 1955.*
*(f)  Closure of the railway in 1964.*
*(g)  Opening of the motorway in 1970 along the route indicated, with access at P.*
*(h)  Scheduling of upland area as Green Belt in 1975.*
*It is suggested that you redraw lines of communications and relative sizes of settlements (A, B, C, D, and E) at each period.*

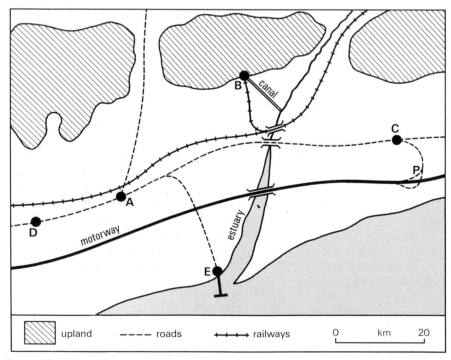

Figure 8.6   The settlement pattern of villages in an imaginary landscape.

# D. Exceptions to the Theory

## 1. Transport centres

Many towns developed either as staging points or stations on road or rail routes. The existence of 'way traffic' as it is called helps generate demand for retail services, accommodation and some employment as in the case of railway workshops or transport depots. Similarly, break of bulk points, where cargo is transhipped from one form of transport to another, are often nodes for settlement development. Examples of such centres can be found in most industrialised countries, and their relative importance changes with shifts in transport technology. A city such as Chicago where 21 rail lines terminate at the Great Lakes railhead is a good example. It is also a city which has kept pace with transport innovations, now possessing the internationally important O'Hare airport. In Britain we can find examples of settlements created by transport: the railway towns of Crewe and Swindon, and the more recent container port of Felixstowe. The important factor, however, is not the number of routes which focus upon a centre but the amount of interchanging of goods and passengers that takes place there. Transport centres are of several types, depending on the amount of traffic and the trade they generate:

(a) small wayside centres which service transport or act as collecting points in otherwise empty areas, for example elevator and service station points on trunk routes across the Canadian Prairies;
(b) break of bulk points where refining or distribution is concentrated, as at major ports;
(c) major redistribution centres, where goods are stored and where wholesaling is an important commercial function.

Often settlements which owe their origin and growth to forms of transport also suffer if that medium is superseded. In its location, plan and history, Winnipeg fits this pattern very well. Originally sited by the Hudsons Bay Company, the town attracted two rival railways and grew up between their respective stockyards and hotels. In the late nineteenth century it was the fastest growing city in Canada; now it is among the slowest, as the 'frontier' has passed it by. Its role as a centre for immigrants has largely been superseded, the streets around the railway lines are rundown and the station hotels dilapidated. Grain and fur traffic still flows through the city but the new wealth of western Canada is to be found north and west of the prairies in the tar sands of northern Alberta. The new growth cities of the Canadian west are Edmonton and Calgary (Plate 8.1) which provide the financial and technical services for exploiting these new resources.

Plate 8.1 The CBD of Edmonton, Alberta, Canada. (Author's photograph)

## 2. Towns located in relation to physical resources

Frequently urban clusters grow around some physical resource, where *manufacturing* is the dominant occupation. In England the textile towns of Lancashire and Yorkshire are examples of this, where coal has been the major locating factor. Of the numerous towns on the Lancashire coalfield only one, the glass manufacturing centre of St Helens, failed to develop a textile industry, and almost all the textile towns are coalfield based. In Germany the process has developed further: the Ruhr coalfield led to the development of steel-producing centres, these in turn led to textile machinery and cloth, thence to dyestuffs, and eventually perfume and cosmetics, all utilising coal by-products. But physical resources do not necessarily generate manufacturing enterprise. Holiday resorts utilising the attractions of sandy beaches, spa water, or a combination of transport links and dramatic scenery have been equally significant in causing a new settlement pattern to emerge in the last two centuries. The street pattern of nineteenth-century holiday resorts is highly individual; and is related to the growing promenade or sea front, backed by shops and boarding houses (see Plate 8.2). A municipal park and railway station are often important elements too and these are located near the centre of the town. This was possible because there was frequently little growth of these settlements before the advent of cheap rail travel. A few more isolated settlements have endeavoured to capitalise on their lack of development in more recent years, by exploiting their unspoilt image.

278

Plate 8.2   Southend in the nineteenth century. (Source: Callcut & Beavis, *32 Views of Southend-on-Sea and District*, supplied by Southend Central Library)

The distribution of physical resources may be important in locating a cluster of settlements, while not affecting their subsequent growth or specialisation. Industrial concentrations in areas like the Potteries, or the metal manufacturing towns of Birmingham, may well be due to agglomerative factors more adequately explained by Weber's theory than by central place concepts (Bale, 1981). As Pred (1977) has argued, the very existence of specialist towns encourages their further development. Local industries become increasingly enmeshed by the system of linkages that develops between them, and this makes the prospect of relocation unattractive, while new firms join those already there because of the locational advantages of existing services and allied activities. Over time the region becomes the accepted centre of a particular group of trades, even after the initial advantages of the site have disappeared.

This pattern of self-sustaining urban concentration has led to our recognition of urban clusters around large metropolitan centres, resulting in city regions. This process may culminate in a 'megalopolitan' situation as in the north-eastern USA where an interconnecting group of towns and their attendant suburban satellites stretches along the coast. If deliberately planned, the process may produce a combination of established, new and expanded towns located in an economically favoured situation, as in south-eastern England. Here the economic potential of location close to London

279

and the EEC leads to a competition for space which has only partially been overcome by planned dispersal of settlement and employment farther afield. Hence we find a variety of groups of industrial centres:

(a) those related to a mineral or power resource which in turn have attracted related industrial enterprises to the initial site;

(b) groups of towns, each of which specialises in a particular aspect of a trade, as is often the case in textile-producing areas;

(c) planned industrial estates, designed to reduce congestion in old centres and to encourage relocation of firms to sites designated by government or the local authority;

(d) declining industrial complexes which, despite the gradual slipping away of their initial site advantages, remain because of the cost of re-establishment elsewhere. Such agglomerations often seek to retain their importance by pricing agreements on their products which safeguard their position, or by obtaining government aid. The 'phantom freight' system operated by the Pittsburgh steel makers in the USA before the Second World War is a famous example.

Whatever the reason for the continued existence of industrial urban concentrations such as these, it is clear that they provide exceptions to a pattern of market centres based on spatial principles such as those contained in Christaller's model. In such cases the *interrelationship* of the individual settlements, and their reliance on interconnecting transport links and high levels of mobility on the part of their populations have enabled specialisation of functions: for example, 'dormitories', 'shopping centres', 'light industry' on a large scale. A special case is the deliberately planned retail centre, often located outside established urban areas, which acts as a focus for the car-owning shopper (Plate 8.3).

## 3. Towns established by whim or chance

It is likely that the original choice of almost all early settlements had a strong element of personal decision, as nomadic or invading groups would have limited knowledge of their new terrain. (This point has been discussed in Chapter 2.) In later times and with improved knowledge and techniques of decision making, the choice of sites for industry, or even whole settlements on a large scale, is likely to be at once more informed and more serious in its consequences. Despite the gradual improvements in our ability to determine good settlement locations, and the operation of economic forces to 'weed out' the settlements that are unlikely to survive, examples of 'historical accidents' in settlement development based upon whim or local initiative occur: for example, Morris at Oxford, and Boeing at Seattle. Also the decision to choose a new centre for settlement may in fact be almost a chance one.

Plate 8.3   Rheinpark hypermarket, St Margerethen, eastern Switzerland. Opened in 1974 at the side of the Rhine and affording easy access along the valley and from across the border with Austria, this site prospered because almost half the customers came from across the river to take advantage of cheaper Swiss prices. Since then the change in currency exchange rates has meant that fewer find the visit worth while. The colonisation of areas of land at motorway intersections by such hypermarkets is relatively new to Europe although the process has been going on for many years in North America.

*Madison, Wisconsin, provides an interesting example of the actual factors which influenced the founding of an individual city. At first sight the location of this city, on what now seems an accessible and attractive site, seems a good instance of the role of the physical environment; but the history of the choice of site reveals that other forces were at work. ... The decision to locate the capital on its present site was taken by 15 votes to 11, and this decision owed more to intrigue by the most subtle of the speculators than to any careful assessment of site and situation. (**Johnson, 1969**)*

It is worth remembering that few totally unsuitable sites survive even when local invention had made them famous; thus no planes are now built in Dayton, Ohio despite the Wright Brothers' epoch-making flight.

281

It might seem likely that in looking at actual settlement distribution there is considerable deviation from the theoretical distribution, as envisaged by Christaller and Lösch. However, the models do isolate some of the factors involved in this distribution. We can refine our understanding of settlement pattern by considering the individual circumstances conditioning the location of specific towns.

## 4. Planning and urban functions in the post-war period

Perhaps the two most important influences on the urban hierarchy of Britain in the post-war period have been the emergence of *interventionist* planning and the divergence in economic behaviour of *different kinds of towns*.

Throughout Europe and the Soviet Union, as well as in Britain, the influence of central government in planning the activities of individual cities by regulating their growth, offering subsidies in some areas and controlling development in others, has meant that the urban hierarchy which developed in pre-industrial times and in the Victorian period when capital was able to move fairly freely and the site constraints of available energy were gradually being reduced, is now no longer uncontrolled. Many writers have pointed out the impact which state planning has had, especially in Britain and Germany and lately in France and the USA, in stimulating urban growth in some areas, bolstering up declining industries and restraining building expansion elsewhere. The desire to adjust regional economic imbalances, often for social and political rather than economic ends, has modified the urban landscape greatly (Johnston, 1984; Clark, 1982). Moreover it has become clear that some types of urban economy have prospered more than others. For example, an urban classification by Armen (1972) of 100 cities in England and Wales outside London, identified six major classes of town. *Market centres* are distributed fairly evenly throughout Britain, but *industrial cities* and *conurbations* are largely concentrated in the north and Midlands, and *new towns* have a strong orientation to the prosperous south-east. The *'freestanding' towns* of the M4/M25/Mll corridors illustrate the important point that good communications, especially to the economic core of Europe, are more significant than raw materials or site factors in determining the present and likely future zones of urban prosperity. More recent work on 154 British towns by Donnison & Soto (1980) confirms the economic strength of the expanding small towns of the south-east (e.g. Chertsey, Walton on Thames), the new industrial suburbs (e.g. Pudsey, Worcester) and new towns (e.g. Hertford, Stevenage), but the comparative decline of heavy industrial centres and the traditional conurbations of the north and west. Static models of location cannot take account of these changes.

ASSIGNMENTS
*1. For an area of about 500 km² with which you are familiar, map and*

*describe the changes that either the coming of the railway or a bypass road has had on the shape and development of local towns.*

2. *For your local town discuss the likely impact of either the proposal to locate a new housing or industrial estate or the building of an out-of-town hypermarket on the traffic patterns along existing routes. What new transport facilities would be needed and where might they be located?*

## E. Inter-Urban and Intra-Urban Applications of Central Place Theory

### 1. Hierarchies of towns

Earlier we mentioned that Christaller's theory was concerned not only with the pattern of settlement distribution, but also with the different orders of settlement and their relationship to each other. In many countries this relationship approximates to a situation where the size of a settlement is inversely proportional to the number of settlements of a similar size.

G. K. Zipf (1941) explained the relationship between settlement *rank* and *size*. He stated this connection as a rule, given by the formula:

$$P_n = P_1(n)^{-1}$$

where $P_n$ is the population of the $n$th town in the series 1, 2, 3, ..., $n$, in which the towns are arranged in descending order of size of population, and $P_1$ is the population of the largest or primate town. Thus if the largest town were of a population size of 100 000 ($P_1$) then the second town in rank would, by this formula, have a population of

$$100\ 000\ (2)^{-1} \text{ or } \frac{100\ 000}{2} \text{ which is 50 000.}$$

This formula may be expressed verbally thus: *if all the urban settlements in an area are ranked in descending order of population size, the population of the nth town will be 1/n the size of the largest city, and the populations of the other urban settlements will be arranged in the series 1, 1/2, 1/3, 1/4, ... 1/n.* Thus we should find a fixed ratio between the few large settlements and the many smaller ones. When this rule is tested against real world examples, there are variable degrees of correspondence in the results. London, Buenos Aires, Santiago, Copenhagen, Tokyo and Mexico City are examples of capitals which are 'too large' in relation to other cities in the same country, if we accept the rule rigidly.

This situation of an overlarge *primate city* is often found in underdeveloped countries, and a lack of correspondence between a country's real profile and the hypothetical one is sometimes used as an argument for a more even spread of development in peripheral regions. However, while the rank–size rule may approximate to the pattern of city size in a 'balanced economy', it should be remembered that discrepancies are to be expected. The rank–size 'rule' is merely the formulating of a generally observed phenomenon. In this it differs from the Christaller–Lösch model which sought to explain rather than merely demonstrate an orderly pattern within the landscape.

When all is said and done, we may feel that the existence of central place theory is helpful in explaining the rank–size connection of settlements, even allowing for individual discrepancies. This is the view of the American geographer William Bunge (1966) who comments that:

> *an argument rages as to whether there is in fact a hierarchy of settlements (hamlets, villages, towns, etc.), or only a continuum of various sized and functional places.*
> *The debate has split between evidence offered for low ranked cities as opposed to high ranked ones.*
> *It may well be that local discontinuous hierarchies blend into a continuous distribution for a country taken all together.*

Although much work on the pattern of settlements remains to be done, the application of this useful theory to individual regions, and at a smaller scale *within* towns, has demonstrated the interactions taking place in and between urban settlements. It is to the spatial patterns within towns that we turn next.


## 2. Hierarchies in towns

The rank–size rule described above also applies within individual towns, especially in the area of retail services. Different types of shops are found in different parts of the urban area. For example, shops selling basic foodstuffs – bread, meat, vegetables and other items which are purchased frequently – are likely to be found in local neighbourhoods (Plate 8.4). These goods have a low *range*: that is, customers are not prepared to travel far to obtain them. They also have a low *threshold population* – the minimum number of customers needed for a shop to be profitable – so that the shops can survive even if other similar shops are located nearby. In the author's own village, for example, there are four general foodshops, all selling virtually the same items to a population of only 2000 people. Even at this level, some specialisation takes place, however; one shop is also a butcher's, another the post office, another has an off-licence and the fourth a laundrette. Also, each shop has its own group of regular customers who go there in preference to the others. These 'convenience goods' shops occupy the base of the retail hierarchy. In larger shopping centres specialist stores are found, selling *consumer durables*: electrical products, furniture and soft furnishings. In the

Plate 8.4   Shops on the edge of the CBD. (Author's photograph)

larger centres are other services: banks, building societies, estate agents, doctors and dentists, whose range and threshold are considerably higher than those of the convenience goods supplier. The largest shopping centres, of which most towns will have only one, will have branches of national firms, restaurants, specialist shops (e.g. sports goods, photographers, book-shops) and major entertainment facilities. This large concentration of retail and other services is often part of the central business district (CBD) and other prestigious public buildings are often found nearby. Increasingly, small private businesses are squeezed out of the CBD because of the high rentals there.

Note the following.

(i)   Some of the larger shopping centres may have developed from old village nuclei which have been absorbed as the town grew.

(ii)  Lower-order shopping centres are unlikely to be distributed evenly throughout a town and are often absent near the CBD.

(iii) As well as there being both more shops and a greater variety of shop types at successively higher levels in the hierarchy, existing functions become progressively more specialised and the shops frequently carry a greater range of stock. Thus a jeweller in a CBD location will be able to offer for sale much more expensive items of jewellery than will a counterpart with a shop in a district centre. This is because the jeweller with the CBD site has a much wider potential trading area.

The number of levels in the hierarchy of a given town depends on the size of its CBD. The central area of a market town may be equivalent either to a regional centre or a district centre depending on the size of the town and its urban field. If it is equivalent to a district centre, then at best other shopping centres in the town will be neighbourhood or local. Such a town will contain examples of only three levels in the intra-urban shopping hierarchy.

Central place theory assumes that consumers will go to their nearest available outlet to obtain a particular item or service. In fact the shopping habits of most European and North American families are now conditioned by an understanding of 'convenience' measured in time rather than distance. Car owners, the majority of the adult population, frequently travel to out-of-town shopping precincts where a variety of goods can be obtained at competitive prices because the profit margins needed by the retailers can be kept low when the volume of sales is high. Planned hypermarket sites often carry a wide range of retailers, whereas there may be fewer services on offer in unplanned shopping areas, but more duplication and competition between suppliers. In redeveloped town centres, *covered shopping 'malls'*, in which small specialist firms rent space from the main site owner, are increasingly encouraging customers to view shopping as a social activity,

with coffee shops and children's play areas to divert their attention and prolong their stay. In some cities former residential districts have been converted to 'characterful' areas of craft shops. Hazleton Lanes in Toronto is an example of this kind of *boutique district* (see Plate 8.5).

The hypermarket and the very large urban shopping centre may grow to assume importance beyond the towns they originally served. The Luton Arndale Centre, one of the largest covered shopping malls in Europe, has begun to attract shoppers from across the North Sea who come on day excursions to the nearby airport with the object of stocking up on British goods to take advantage of favourable exchange rates. In the Rhine valley, Swiss hypermarkets (see Plate 8.3) sited to take advantage of cross-border trade from Austria, are now increasingly dependent on this trade. As exchange rates rise and Austrian shoppers are fewer in number these hypermarkets are finding difficulties in obtaining enough trade from their own Swiss nationals. Another interesting case is that of the 'Asda' hyper-market which was built as a peripheral supplier to Billericay in Essex, so that it would provide a trading focus around which the new town of South Woodham Ferrers could be built. As the new town grows, more customers will come from nearby housing and intensify demand, so 'Asda' will under-write early losses in hope of long-term profits.

## 3. Case study of hypermarket development

An extreme example of the hypermarket complex is the West Edmonton Centre in Alberta. Built for an Iranian partnership by the 555 group in 1981–5, the centre covers a 50 hectare site on the edge of Alberta's largest city. The shopping area covers over 460 000 square metres of retail space, and comprises 828 shops and 11 major department stores, built at a cost of over 1000 million dollars. With recreation facilities and parking for 20 000 cars, the centre is a settlement in its own right. It has a catchment area which extends west of the Rockies and south into the Pacific states of the USA. By far the largest shopping centre in Canada, it is almost ten times bigger than the hypermarkets found in Britain and Europe, and obviously has an enormous impact upon the cities which lie within its economic 'shadow' (Plate 8.6). Traders in Edmonton's central business district clearly view the growth of the West Edmonton Mall with alarm, as the article from *Maclean's* magazine shows.

◀ Plate 8.5   Hazleton Lanes, Toronto. A former run-down residential district just north of the CBD has been converted to a specialist shopping centre. Several North American cities have followed this policy in recent years in an attempt to bring shoppers back into the 'core'. (Author's photograph)

Plate 8.6 West Edmonton Centre, Alberta. An enormous regional shopping centre, with theme parks and cinemas as well as retail outlets. Similar, though smaller, centres may develop in Europe soon. In the largest American examples there are already some social problems, including a resident unemployed population of young people who 'cruise' the malls because they have nowhere else to go. (Photograph: Alberta Government)

The incorporation of lavish recreation facilities into shopping malls is another innovation which threatens the traditional separation and hierarchy of settlement functions. The West Edmonton Mall incorporates 20 cinemas, a full-size ice-hockey rink, dolphinarium, submarine aquatic show and a twelve-storey hotel with several 'fantasy themes'. Already 1.5 million tourists visit the centre annually and the developers hope to raise this to 8 million by 1990. The impact of this kind of tourist development on transport and other infrastructure services will clearly be immense. As yet theme park and shopping developments have not been linked in Europe although there is interest in developing such a complex in the West Midlands, so it may not be long before the British planning system is increasingly under pressure to yield to commercial interests.

288

# Downtown Edmonton fights for its life

In the early 1980s, after a decade of unprecedented growth, the city of Edmonton began to falter economically. It was at that time that Triple Five Corporation Ltd., owned by the four Ghermezian brothers from Iran, decided to build an ambitious, $600-million shopping concourse called the West Edmonton Mall. The mammoth project created 10,000 new jobs over the next two years and added $8 million to city revenues. But not everyone greeted the suburban mall's emergence with open arms. Downtown merchants, in particular, feared for their economic survival, especially because the mall began operations during serious traffic disruptions along Jasper Avenue, the city's main downtown artery, due to rapid-transit construction. Now, to make matters worse the mall, already a great success, has announced plans for a $250-million expansion that will make it the largest retail complex in North America, with more than four million square feet, surpassing the Del Amo Fashion Center in Torrance, Calif., which has more than 2.5 million square feet. And this time downtown businessmen are determined to protect their interests. Said Maury Van Vliet, chairman of the newly formed City Centre Association: "What they are trying to do out there is shift the centre of town – that is, if we will let them do it."

The fight will not be an easy one. The West Edmonton Mall already attracts 1.2 million visitors a year to shop and to look at its saltwater aquariums, exotic bird aviaries and elaborate fountains modelled after those at the palace of Versailles in France. It has an indoor amusement park which it calls Fantasyland and an NHL-sized skating rink on which the Edmonton Oilers practise regularly. Last year the consumer mecca drew at least 7,000 shoppers on special pre-Christmas tours from Yellowknife, Vancouver and Saskatoon. Indeed, the mall has a full-time "tourism director," Jill Romanowski, who boasted, "Fantasyland has put us on the map with the Eiffel Tower, Buckingham Palace and the pyramids." Allan Bleiken, general manager of the Edmonton Economic Development Authority, a government agency, is just as enthusiastic. Said Bleiken: "It is probably the best single thing that happened to Edmonton in 1983, and the expansion will attract people to Edmonton like nothing else."

According to expansion plans, Triple Five wants to install an indoor lake the length of five football fields with a sandy beach, mechanically created waves and an artificial tanning sun. A new Marineland will feature 10 whales and dolphins. There will also be a 400-room hotel and the number of retail outlets will increase to more than 750 from 426.

Commercially, the West Edmonton Mall has garnered more than its projected share of the market. Average retail sales of $458 per square foot are more than twice the national figure. Said one salesman, at Aldo's shoe store: "Our sales here are 30 to 40 per cent higher than at our other [Edmonton] mall locations." A recent economic study that the city commissioned revealed that the mall attracts 12 per cent of the area market, compared to regional malls in most Canadian cities which only attract from five to 10 per cent.

The study also predicted that, with the mall's planned expansion, it could draw as much as 24 per cent of Edmonton's retail trade. That prospect worries Edmonton's downtown store owners. Said Van Vliet: "We have to make sure that the projected 24 per cent never happens."

But Van Vliet, a business consultant, said the city core's resurrection as an alternative to the mall depends not just on retailers' efforts but also on the support of the mayor and city council. "If you wonder why we should be concerned, go to Buffalo or Cleveland," he said, pointing to the fact that those American cities' centres have deteriorated. "The downtown will die if we do not do anything." For the moment, the downtown business owners are concentrating on stopping the city from redirecting money to the mall that it had previously allocated to service the downtown core. Said Van Vliet: "Downtown is the tax base that generates $83 million per year, and city council must protect that."

Even within the shopping mall business there is doubt about the wisdom of expanding the West Edmonton Mall. Said Nora Winkelman, a researcher for the New York-based International Council of Shopping Centers: "That is an awfully large centre which would need an enormous population to support it." And with Edmonton's population now shrinking, Romanowski's job may be to see that a consumer monolith does not become a retailing dinosaur.

– ROBERTA WALKER *in Edmonton.*

(Source: *Maclean's*, 23 April 1984)

1. *Reference to Philips* Geographical Digest *(published bi-annually) will enable you to draw rank–size graphs for developed and under-developed countries. If you use log/log scale paper and plot the population of each town on the vertical axis and the rank of the centre on the horizontal axis, a straight line at 45° to the axes is the hypothetical result according to the rank–size rule. Try to explain why your graphs deviate from this norm.*

2. *Local shopping studies*

   *(a)* Choosing the area for investigation

   *A survey of the hierarchical structure of shopping centres can be done only in a town large enough to possess a number of separate shopping centres in addition to the main concentration of shops in the town centre. In a market town with a population of about 30 000–40 000 it should be possible to conduct a comprehensive survey of all the centres in the town. In a large city you will have to limit your study to compare the hierarchical structure of shopping centres in two socially distinct parts of the city to see if the expected contrasts do in fact exist. You will need a map to help you fix the location of the service centres. In this respect the Ordnance Survey 1 : 10 000 (6 inches to 1 mile) is the most useful scale, but a* Geographia *town plan may be used as an alternative.*

   *(b)* The morphology of service centres

   *Draw sketch plans to illustrate the arrangement of shops and other commercial premises in each of the service centres.*

   *Discover what facilities, if any, are provided for vehicles delivering goods to the shops. To determine this you will need to look at the rear of the shops. If no such facilities exist find out if any restrictions are imposed on the time that deliveries can take place. (You will need to look at the parking restriction signs to discover this.) Note the width of the street; is it sufficiently wide to be able to cope with stationary vehicles or are they a cause of traffic congestion?*

   *At each of the centres record the car parking facilities available for shoppers. If an off-street car park is provided, find out if parking restrictions apply along the adjoining roads, and, in ribbon centres, if the restrictions also apply in the side roads.*

   *Look carefully at the buildings in the centre and estimate their age. Are the shops purpose built, or have they been converted from some other function? Photograph or sketch any interesting examples of building conversion and add suitable annotations.*

   *(c)* The hierarchy of centres

   *Copy the logging sheet shown in Table 8.4, which distinguishes broad categories of shops and shop types. Head the columns with the names of the service centres you are to investigate. Visit each centre and record the types of shops and retail services contained there. If there is*

Table 8.4 Logging sheet for field study of suburban service centres

| Type of service | Suburban service centres | | | | |
|---|---|---|---|---|---|
| Public houses and off-licences | | | | | |
| Cafés | | | | | |
| Food shops: General<br>Supermarket<br>Fresh fruit and vegetables<br>Freezer centre<br>Grocery<br>Bakery<br>Fishmonger<br>Fish and chips<br>Butcher<br>Delicatessen | | | | | |
| Sweets and tobacco<br>Newsagents/Stationery/Fancy goods | | | | | |
| Pharmacy | | | | | |
| Clothing: Men's<br>Women's<br>Children's<br>Babywear and wool<br>General | | | | | |
| Footwear<br>Cooperative store<br>Multiple department store | | | | | |
| Services: Filling station, car spares<br>Hairdresser: Men's<br>Women's<br>Cleaners<br>Shoe repair<br>Banks and insurance<br>Betting shop | | | | | |
| Furniture<br>Electrical, radio, television, video<br>Sports goods<br>Luggage, leather goods<br>Books and records | | | | | |
| Other retail (specify) | | | | | |
| Other services (specify) | | | | | |

*more than one shop of a particular type also record this. For each centre add up the number of shops and different shop types and draw a scatter graph to show their relationship. This will enable you to*

291

*classify the service centres and distinguish first order (local centres) from second order (neighbourhood centres) etc. B. J. Garner suggests the data should be plotted on log normal graph paper with the number of shops and retail services (establishments) placed on the y axis and the number of shop types (functions) on the x axis. The advantage of using log normal graph paper is that it minimises the effect of the number of shops in a centre. The crucial factor in distinguishing the order of a shopping centre is the number of shop* types *contained rather than the number of shops. In fact it is possible to find centres of a similar order in which the number of shops varies quite considerably.*

*Work out the average number of shops and shop types in each order of service centre (i.e. local, neighbourhood, district, regional, CBD) and summarise this on a matrix.*

*Draw histograms to illustrate the average number of convenience goods shops, shoppers' goods shops, specialist stores and department and variety goods stores in each order of service centre.*

## 4. Conclusion

Clearly changing technology and behaviour have caused the traditional models of urban hierarchies to be called into question. Some old-established shopping and service centres find it hard to compete effectively now that very large retail empires are locating on enormous out-of-town sites. In addition the development of mail-order and phone-order shopping has reduced retailing to a warehousing and distribution function in some cases: especially in fashion and electrical goods. With the spread of consumer credit arrangements and the new technology of databases and telecommunications, shopping can increasingly be an armchair exercise. Paradoxically, however, the social attractions of shopping seem to be growing, as witnessed by the crowds to be found at garden centres and in shopping malls at weekends.

## Key Ideas

*A. Economic Factors: Supply, Demand and Choice*

1. The basis of economic activity lies in the need to make choices among scarce goods.
2. These choices are affected by the prices of goods, which are a reflection of our ability to substitute one good for another, as well as the cost of manufacture and the intensity of our need for a particular item.
3. This balance of supply and demand has an influence upon the landscape,

and its visible expression is the market centre and its retail establishments.

4. The distance we are prepared to travel for goods and the number of people needed to make retailing or manufacture worth while will influence the number and type of facilities in a town or village.

5. The range of supplies and the threshold of demand are competing economic forces which find expression in the landscape as the 'market area' of a firm or town.

## B. Central Places: the Christaller Model

1. To explain the variations in intensity of land use, Christaller developed models or idealisations of the landscape based on a homogenous plain.

2. He suggested that fixed ratios of population would be needed to sustain the growth of 'central places' which would provide them with services. These ratios he called $k$ values.

3. Central places would become the important marketing, transport and administrative centres in an area, around which smaller settlements would be grouped in a regular manner.

## C. Development of the Theory

1. Subsequently August Lösch suggested refinements of Christaller's theory which allowed for greater flexibility in the determining of the $k$ values.

2. Application of the theory often depends upon our ignoring local effects of history and terrain in modifying the landscape.

## D. Exceptions to the Theory

1. Certain types of urban landscape are not explicable in terms of central place theory.

2. Examples include some transport centres, manufacturing and mining towns, holiday resorts or settlements located by chance or on the basis of unusual historical decisions.

## E. Inter-Urban and Intra-Urban Applications of Central Place Theory

1. In many areas there appears to be an inverse relationship between the number or frequency of settlements and their individual population size.

2. This is not a theoretical proposal but an observed phenomenon, and variations from the norm are sometimes taken to indicate weakness or imbalance in the economy of an area.

3. The variety of functions that settlements of different sizes contain tends

293

to demonstrate the importance of urban functions in influencing the size of settlements.

4. It is possible to distinguish different levels of retail centres within towns as well as a system of ranking or ordering as between towns.

5. Shopping centres and their catchment areas provide good examples of urban hierarchies. So do educational establishments and the distribution of other public facilities.

6. There is often a connection between the size of a centre and its economic competitiveness; for example, the cost of similar goods or services may be higher in smaller shopping centres which have fewer customers.

7. The traditional patterns of retail behaviour have been greatly modified by new technology and greater personal mobility. However, the social attractions of urban centres seem undiminished and the enthusiasm for family trips to out-of-town retail and leisure facilities is growing rapidly.

# 9 *The Urban Field*

## A. The Changing Urban System

The European Commission recognises the existence of some 160 *functional regions* within the twelve member states of the EEC. By this term is meant an area which has sufficient social, cultural and economic character to render it identifiable to inhabitants and outsiders, and which is of an appropriate size for planning and administrative purposes. In many European states these regions represent long-standing territorial divisions, often with a long history of self-government before they were incorporated into a modern nation: areas such as Aquitaine, Brabant, Friesland, Limerick and Sicily were former principalities and dukedoms which often focused on a major city for protection and patronage.

In Britain, largely because a central government based in London was firmly established by 1707, the concept of the large provincial city-region is poorly developed. The standard regions of Britain are based on groups of counties and although most of us would recognise that the 'north-west' is somewhat different from the 'south-east' we would probably find it difficult to decide where East Anglia ends and the East Midlands begin. Nor is the distinction between town and countryside easy to define. Most rural dwellers can reach a large town easily and many commute daily. The social habits – shopping preferences, entertainment choices, leisure pursuits and so on – of British people tend to be determined more by income and social class than by place of residence. Regional cultures have largely declined, kept alive by a few enthusiasts, many of whom are townspeople.

The extent of the change in the landscape which the spread of urban cultures and modes of production have brought about since the mid 1960s is a reflection of the shift of employment from manufacturing into the service sector and from manual to 'white-collar' jobs. This two-fold process has been described as *de-industrialisation* in the older manufacturing regions and *tertiarisation* in the new service-oriented areas of the south and east (see Figure 9.1) (Martin, 1987).

John Goddard (1984) describes the effect upon the landscape in terms of new transport technologies

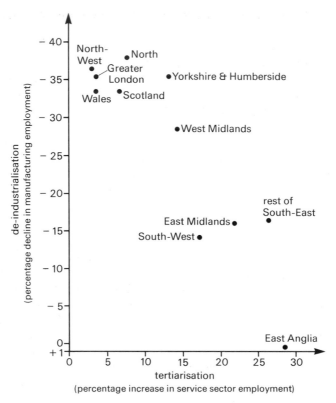

Figure 9.1  The regional relationship between de-industrialisation and tertiarisation 1976–1986. (Source: Department of Employment)

*a simple way of appreciating the scale of change today would be to take a train journey from Bristol to Newcastle and return by car, taking the motorway. The railway journey would pick out the centres of cities, basically the product of the industrial revolution, that are now showing numerous signs of their age. The motorway journey would reveal the scale of expansion on the periphery of towns in the form of space-extensive manufacturing, warehousing and hypermarket developments. It would also reveal the revival of growth in the market or country towns of England. Such a journey would emphasise that urban change is not just a feature of the largest cities but of the urban system as a whole.*

The merging of rural and urban landscapes and life styles is especially evident south of a line from the Bristol Channel to the Wash. It is here that most new jobs have been created, about 860 000 between 1979 and 1984, of which 560 000 were in the financial services sector. The growth in part-time female employment, adding an extra 300 000 jobs during the same five-year period, was also largely in the small towns and on the suburban edge of the cities of the south-east of England.

In order to describe the new *urban regions* which include commuter villages and communities dependent on large towns within their ambience, geographers often prefer a statistical rather than an administrative definition of what constitutes an urban area. The most popular is the use of *Standard Metropolitan Labour Areas* (SMLAs) defined by Hall (1973) and refined by Spence (1982). Each SMLA consists of an urban *core* with at least 20 000 jobs plus a metropolitan *ring* from which more than 15% of the working population commute to the core. The population of core and ring together must exceed 50 000 for an SMLA to be identified. On this basis, 80% of the British population lived in the 126 SMLAs or major urban areas in the early 1980s.

Another measure of urban regions was devised in the 1981 Census, which divided the United Kingdom into 228 *functional regions* (much smaller than those recognised by the EEC). Of these, 20 *metropolitan regions* (based on major cities) were identified, with 93 *subordinate centres* (smaller towns within the urban field of larger cities) and 115 *free-standing towns* (which had no subordinate centres). On the whole it is the free-standing towns which have shown the most rapid rates of population growth and economic development since 1971. Many of these towns are in the four more prosperous regions shown in the bottom right of Figure 9.1. As Table 9.1 shows, almost all the urban regions with the greatest absolute population growth between 1971 and 1981 are found in these regions, the exceptions being the 'oil-boom' towns of the Scottish Highlands.

The other major change which has taken place in the urban system in Britain during the last two decades has been the expansion of the metropolitan rings at the expense of the traditional urban cores. Again Goddard (1984) describes the situation succinctly:

Table 9.1 Functional regions ranked by relative population change, 1971–81

|  | Percentage change | 1981 population |
|---|---|---|
| 1 Milton Keynes | 60.8 | 161 335 |
| 2 Dingwall and Invergordon* | 34.0 | 50 244 |
| 3 Thetford* | 30.4 | 70 446 |
| 4 Huntingdon* | 24.7 | 71 083 |
| 5 Peterborough | 23.4 | 199 180 |
| 6 Telford | 22.5 | 163 888 |
| 7 Northampton | 18.0 | 241 908 |
| 8 Newmarket and Ely | 18.0 | 98 940 |
| 9 Banbury | 18.0 | 78 550 |
| 10 Bury St Edmunds | 17.3 | 70 168 |

*Rural areas (i.e. regions with population of less than 50 000 in 1971)

Source: Goddard, 1984

*Manufacturing employment decline in the largest cities has been principally due to the closure of factories and the contraction of those that have survived, rather than to their migration to the suburbs and beyond. The inner parts of cities with their cramped factory sites no longer provide a good environment for modern manufacturing industry. Multi-storey buildings are unsuited for automated production lines; faced with the difficulties of expanding on site, many small entrepreneurs have forgone investment in new products and production processes and have eventually gone out of business as a result. On the other hand, some large companies have transferred production to other locations in Britain and also abroad. Many of the founders of new enterprises have also long since left the inner areas in search of better residential conditions and have chosen to establish their businesses near to their homes.*

The result is that between 1971 and 1981 the inner urban areas lost 9% or 10% of their population while the suburban and exurban areas gained between 8% and 17%. This is the continuation of a long-standing trend: in the 1960s half a million jobs were lost in urban cores, while 750 000 were gained in the rings. Commuter journeys have increased both in number and distance as rail services (especially in the south-east) have been electrified. It is now feasible to commute over 100 km in less than an hour, so that London workers may live in Rugby, Bedford, Huntingdon or anywhere in Surrey or Kent, if they can afford the high cost of the season ticket.

A third factor in the changes affecting urban centres has been the increased centralisation of financial control in industry. While jobs and population have moved out from areas of high congestion and rising land values, the management and administration of the economy has become more concentrated in the capital. The growth rate of financial and business services during the 1970s was three times faster in London than in the large provincial cities. Over half of the thousand largest companies in the United Kingdom are London based, so that in terms of economic and fiscal power the south-east is even more important than its absolute growth in jobs, services and population would indicate (see Figure 9.2). This *economic primacy* is largely a result of the links the region has with the rest of Europe, which are likely to increase with the development of a road or rail tunnel to the continental mainland.

## B. Urban Service Provision

Although there are problems in determining where the town ends and the rural area begins as urban influences permeate throughout British society, there is obviously a spatial distinction between the predominantly built environment and the rural agricultural hinterland between and around towns.

298

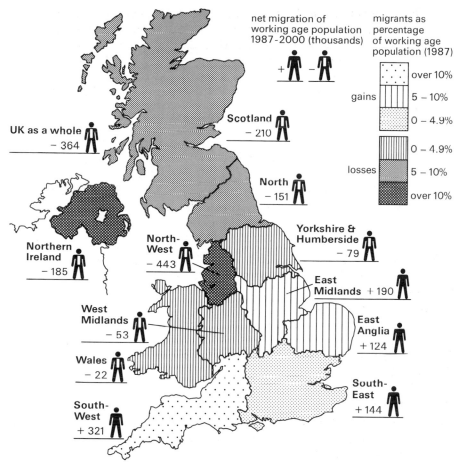

net migration of working age population 1987-2000 (thousands)

migrants as percentage of working age population (1987)

+ / −

gains
over 10%
5 – 10%
0 – 4.9%

losses
0 – 4.9%
5 – 10%
over 10%

UK as a whole
− 364

Scotland
− 210

Northern Ireland
− 185

North-West
− 443

North
− 151

Yorkshire & Humberside
− 79

East Midlands + 190

West Midlands
− 53

East Anglia
+ 124

Wales
− 22

South-West
+ 321

South-East
+ 144

Figure 9.2   Growth regions in Britain.

If we are interested in determining how far the influence of a settlement extends we may approach the question in two ways. The first is to ask firms and public utilities in the town about the boundaries of the areas to which they send out their goods or services. Alternatively we may ask individuals in rural villages to tell us which centre they use to supply their day to day and, indeed, their occasional needs. In neither case will we draw very precise boundaries around the sphere of influence which we distinguish and the process, though interesting, is time consuming. Geographers have begun to devise statistical models of how population and trade will be attracted to towns. These can provide us with an overall pattern which is appealingly simple. Care must be taken in the use of these models, however, as we shall see.

The sphere of influence around a town is commonly referred to as the *urban field*. The use of the term 'field' is in this case analogous to that of a

299

magnetic field, in that the degree of attraction is greatest close to the centre, and may diminish farther away, so that if more than one centre of attraction exists, there may be overlapping at their borders.

## 1. Measurement of range of services

Methods of urban field delimitation based on field survey include such methods as the following.

### (a) Analysis of public transport services

All that is required are the appropriate timetables and OS maps of the area to be studied.

One of the earliest attempts at working out the network of urban fields was applied by Green (1954). Among the techniques that Green used was the mapping of bus routes, by lines of proportional breadth from the centre he was investigating out to the peripheral villages which the bus routes served. This can be done for several adjacent centres of similar sizes, or indeed the transport links for a hierarchy of places can be established, giving a vivid impression of the way that smaller urban fields 'nest' within larger ones. Unfortunately, present-day bus services may be a poor indicator of traffic flows because of increased car ownership; but suburban rail services still provide a valid measure around metropolitan centres.

### (b) Measurement of local delivery areas

By plotting the distribution of local delivery fields (for example, by major stores) or the number of mentions that villages receive in local town newspapers over a given period (say three months) it is possible to draw up 'contours' of equal frequency of access. The construction of such contours, more properly termed *isolines*, is based on joining together all points with equal values. Hence all villages with, say, ten news items in the county newspaper in a given month would form one set of points for an isoline. One would expect that the more distant and isolated the villages the less frequently would be their mention in papers, or their record of deliveries from local stores. It is desirable to look at several criteria in determining upon what the isolines should be based and, as the urban field served by centres may overlap, it is also useful to consider the newspapers or delivery areas of stores in other towns in the region, so that a composite view may be built up. This is a point which we shall refer to again later.

### (c) Catchment areas

Some organisations have official boundaries to the areas which they serve. In rural areas the catchment area of secondary schools and the zones

300

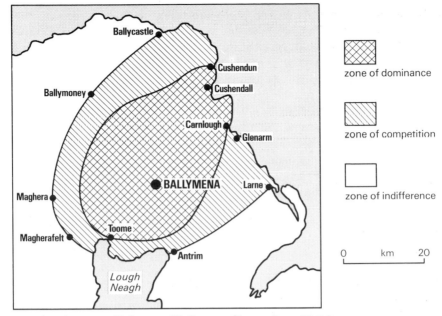

Figure 9.3   The zones of influence of Ballymena. (Source: Joyce Wylie)

controlled by statutory bodies such as police, fire service, electricity, gas and water boards, can be determined by local enquiry and mapped. It should be remembered that boundaries imposed by external authorities may be drawn for their convenience, rather than to reflect the influence of the town upon which they are centred.

However, when the map of the urban field is drawn for a particular town, there is always some confusion over where the boundaries lie. Three zones are normally discovered: (a) one of *dominance* in which all the criteria proposed to test the field are satisfied; (b) one of *competition* included in the boundaries produced by some criteria and excluded by others (this may be a broad zone, and if we wish to delimit our area exactly, this is a weakness), and (c) one of *marginal influence* (*indifference*), beyond all the isolines drawn upon the map and where we may assume that the town exerts no influence (although we cannot be sure that visitors from farther afield do not come into the town) (see Figure 9.3).

## 2.  Measurement of demand for services

As an alternative to looking at service provision from an urban viewpoint, we may sample rural populations' demand for and use of the services that towns provide. This can be quite complex and time consuming because many rural residents will visit more than one town depending on personal preference and the type of service they require. Generally it is necessary to

301

devise questionnaire surveys and administer them to quite large samples of the population if they are to have any validity. Moreover it is important to distinguish different levels of services, because some will be required more frequently than others. Not only will larger villages be able to supply many of the more basic services (such as food, shops, post office, off-licence, school or clinic) than smaller ones, they are also more likely to have good public transport connections to nearby towns so that the pattern of demand they generate may be different from that of the smaller settlements, even though the needs of the residents may be substantially similar. With these reservations in mind, the demand survey is nevertheless an important means of measuring the interaction between towns and their surrounding rural areas (see Tables 9.2 and 9.3).

What is being done here is to establish the range of influence of the town by drawing upon the experience of its users. Our map will look rather different from the isoline type because we shall insert a line, connecting all the correspondents with the centre that they claim to use. Such lines are termed 'desire lines' and it is possible to draw boundaries for several urban centres around the outer limit of the desire districts so constructed. Normally the farthest 10% of points are excluded when the map is drawn, to avoid overlap. As Johnson (1969) states:

> One of the problems of this method is that the service areas for towns often overlap ... Whilst the area close to the town may be said to be dominated by that town for the supply of goods and services, farther away there is competition for trade between one town and the next, until at some point another town begins to dominate the trade pattern of the landscape.

In administering questionnaires we must be careful to include a valid sample of people: that is to say our sample should reflect the population we are seeking to find out about. Whether we go to every tenth house, or every tenth name on the electoral roll, we should check the overall composition of the village from census schedules if possible. Detailed consideration of sampling techniques is beyond the scope of this book, but the following general points should be remembered if samples are to be selected from the population for study:

(a) Samples may be *random*, where we make no assumptions about the nature of the total population but merely extract data on a percentage of its members. Most street interviews are of this type.

(b) Alternatively, the sample may be *stratified*, that is it may be chosen in order to represent a particular group or to ensure cross-coverage of several sub-groups in the population. A study of immigrants or school-children would be of this type, as would an attempt to interview members of different ethnic or social groups in proportion to their share in the numbers of the total population. Care must be taken not to allow stratification to creep into our sampling unintentionally, for example by conducting interviews only in school holidays or when wage earners are at work.

(c) The sample should be sufficiently large to give a meaningful set of results: this is especially important if samples for different areas or periods are to be compared.

(Further details on the methodology of statistical work in geography can be found in texts such as Norcliffe, 1977.)

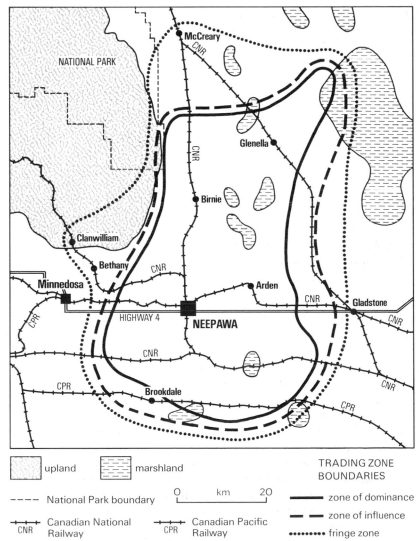

Figure 9.4 The trading areas of Neepawa, Manitoba. (Source: based on an original map produced by the Neepawa Chamber of Commerce)

*Figure 9.4 shows the trading area which the Chamber of Trade of a small Canadian town, Neepawa, drew up on the basis of their surveys of shoppers.*

*The trading area is divided into three zones of decreasing influence. The population of the 'zone of dominance' is about 10 500 people, including 3200 who live in the town itself. The populations of the 'zone of influence' and 'fringe zone' are 3300 and 1200 respectively. The definition of these areas is as follows:*

1. *Within the area designated as the 'zone of dominance', residents do at least 50% of their shopping in Neepawa.*
2. *Within the 'zone of influence', residents do between 25% and 49% of their shopping in Neepawa.*
3. *Within the 'fringe zone', residents do between 1% and 24% of their shopping in Neepawa.*

*It can be assumed that because of the distances involved in travelling to larger centres only the very highest order goods are bought from far outside the area of the map by residents within that area, and most of these will be mail order purchases. Study Figure 9.4 and Tables 9.2 and 9.3. Write a report to the Chamber of Trade suggesting what could be done to extend the urban field of the town. Explain alternative ways in which this could be measured.*

## 3. Journeys to work

A particular form of urban–rural interaction is the journey to work. In the pre-industrial period, few people travelled more than a few kilometres each day, although by the mid-Victorian times the more prosperous middle class were making daily journeys by horse, bus and train which were comparable in distance and duration with those of present-day commuters. Today the population in developed countries is highly mobile and it is unlikely that asking most village residents where they work would produce distinctive patterns of mobility. However, certain industries do still draw their labour supply from a fairly circumscribed area, often influenced by the provision of subsidised transport, and the establishment of new 'high-tech' industries will frequently have an effect on house prices in nearby villages as highly paid staff are drawn into the area and compete for places to live. The significance of journey-to-work patterns lies in the influence which these regular journeys have on other travel. Working people may fit in lunch-time shopping, or professional couples may patronise entertainment services and restaurants close to their place of work rather than their homes. In seeking to establish the reasons behind the 'drawing power' of central urban places we must not forget that many journeys are multi-purpose and that habit rather than rational economic decisions may govern much consumer behaviour.

Table 9.2 Shopping done by Neepawa Area residents in other centres

| Centres | Times mentioned | |
| --- | --- | --- |
| | Number | Percentage |
| Brandon | 62 | 29 |
| Dauphin | 2 | 1 |
| Portage la Prairie | 5 | 2 |
| Winnipeg | 42 | 20 |
| Mail Order (Winnipeg and Regina) | 31 | 14 |
| Local town or hamlet in Neepawa area | 73 | 34 |
| Total | 215 | 100 |

When asked for their reasons for shopping outside Neepawa, replies from residents were as follows:

Table 9.3 Reasons for shopping outside Neepawa

| Reasons | Times mentioned | |
| --- | --- | --- |
| | Number | Percentage |
| 1. Generally not enough variety in Neepawa, and prices are too high | 28 | 17 |
| 2. Insufficient professional services in Neepawa | 27 | 16 |
| 3. Poor selection of clothing in Neepawa | 27 | 16 |
| 4. Desire to support a town other than Neepawa (their home community) | 26 | 16 |
| 5. Live closer to another town | 24 | 15 |
| 6. Dislike Neepawa's parking meters | 8 | 5 |
| 7. Shop in Winnipeg while there for another purpose, i.e. visiting, business, etc. | 7 | 5 |
| 8. Dislike Neepawa's Monday closing by-law | 5 | 2 |
| 9. Better selection and price from sales catalogue | 5 | 2 |
| 10. Lack of courtesy from Neepawa business people | 3 | 1 |
| 11. Miscellaneous | 8 | 5 |
| Total | 168 | 100 |

# C. Rural–Urban Interaction

## 1. The friction of distance

Although the supply and demand approaches to the study of the urban field differ in the areas which they investigate, they have one idea in common. This is that the degree of attraction to a town will be proportional to the ease with which it can be reached: a concept sometimes referred to as the *friction of distance*.

We have seen the operation of this factor within the central business district (page 229). Originally the model of declining intensity of land use with distance from the centre was proposed by Johann Henrich Von Thünen,

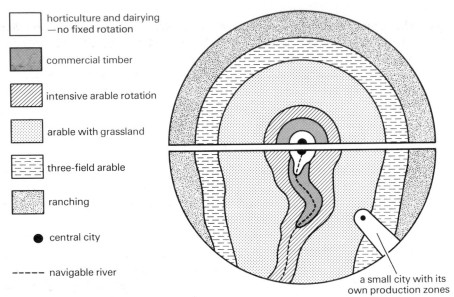

horticulture and dairying
—no fixed rotation

commercial timber

intensive arable rotation

arable with grassland

three-field arable

ranching

● central city

----- navigable river

a small city with its
own production zones

Figure 9.5   Von Thünen's model of agricultural land use.

an agriculturalist, who had studied the working of the eighteenth-century economist, Ricardo. Figure 9.5 demonstrates how he envisaged a decline in intensity of land use as one moved away from a market or other centre. His model of concentric rings of decreasing intensity around a market may be combined with the idea of the attraction of a three-dimensional object to produce a 'gravity model'. Gravity is the force which attracts objects towards the centre of a planet. If the object can overcome resistance it will be drawn inwards, as with a ball dropping through the air, or falling through water, until it encounters a surface which it cannot penetrate. The strength of gravity can be overcome, but even a rocket has to expend energy to overcome the earth's gravitational pull, and will ultimately be drawn into another planet's orbit. The great distance between the planets will mean that they are not drawn to each other – in this sense it acts as a resistance or form of 'friction', keeping everything in its proper place. We can apply this theory in a geographical context.

## 2.  Methods of measuring interaction: mathematical models

### (a)  Gravity models

If we take the physical or 'gravity' model and apply it to the landscape, we could express it in terms of likely or expected movement between two towns (A and B).

306

(i) The movement between A and B would be proportional to their respective populations and inversely proportional to the distance between them. If we assume that the larger the population the greater the activity and hence movement towards a centre so the greater the isolation of the centre the less will be its attraction to other people. Hence our base model would be formulated:

$$\text{Movement A to B} = \frac{\text{population A} \times \text{population B}}{(\text{distance})^2}$$

The larger the centres and the greater the disparity in size the more movement there should be between them. However, if we are concerned with trading movement it may not be appropriate to think in terms of raw population numbers.

We might try to give a value to the town not of population but of its 'centrality' or 'level of attraction' based upon points scored for specific criteria. For example we might consider a major branch of a supermarket chain worth 10 points, a bank worth 2 and so on. This would enable a total points score for each town to be calculated on a comparative though subjective basis and this total could be used in calculations.

(ii) Alternatively one might measure 'centrality' by comparing the share that different towns have of the total number of enterprises or shops of a specific type that the whole group of towns possesses in the area under investigation. Hence we would be endeavouring to determine the relative functional importance of particular places in a system. The formula for this calculation is as follows:

$$C = \frac{t}{T} \times 100$$

where $t$ = number of outlets of a particular function (e.g. shoe shops) in one town,

and $T$ = total number of outlets of this function in the group of towns under review.

$C$, the level of centrality, can be calculated using data from the Census of Distribution or from the yellow pages of the telephone directory, although this will not distinguish the relative sizes of particular shops, merely the number. Comparison of the ranking of average $C$ values for towns, taking into account a range of functions, with the ranking of those towns in population numbers, will indicate how far we are 'safe' in using population statistics as an indicator of the functional importance of settlements.

(iii) Another way of measuring the relative attractiveness of settlements as centres of commerce is the calculation of the boundaries of their spheres of influence. The attraction of a central place will depend very largely upon the range of services it provides. The population of a town provides some indication of this although the distance from other service centres must also be taken into account. In areas where retail trade is dominated by well-spaced central spaces it is possible to apply Reilly's breaking point formula. This attempts to delimit the 'breaking point' along a main route between adjacent service centres. Theoretically consumers living on one side of this line are more likely to look to settlement A as their dominant central place, while consumers living on the other side of the line are more likely to look to settlement B (see Figure 9.6).

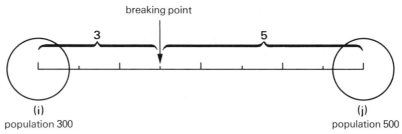

Figure 9.6   The 'breaking point' between two centres, i and j. (Source: Everson & Fitzgerald, 1969)

$$\text{Distance from smaller town B} = \frac{\text{Distance between towns A and B}}{1 + \sqrt{\left(\dfrac{\text{Population A}}{\text{Population B}}\right)}}$$

One objection to the breaking point formula is that population is not always a good indication of a town as a service centre. For example, mining settlements and towns which form part of a vast conurbation are sometimes relatively deficient in services while small market towns or holiday resorts are often surprisingly good service centres. If a town's retail turnover (figures available in the Census of Retail Distribution) is substituted for its population, a more accurate idea of the position of the breaking point between settlements may be obtained.

### (b) Behavioural or probability models

Convenient though these gravity models undoubtedly are, they are over-simplistic. They assume that the distance people are prepared to travel for goods of different types is the same; and that different people are all prepared to travel the same distance for similar goods. Neither assumption is true. In some instances choice of goods is immaterial: for example, when buying postage stamps, or paying certain statutory bills. In other cases where prices are competitive and the purchases are of major importance, it is worth while to shop around; and this may involve extensive travel before a purchase is made. Moreover the degree of mobility of different customers varies greatly and may influence how far they are prepared to travel to satisfy a particular need. One attempt to rationalise these differences and to determine the probability of people going to a particular town is Huff's model. Simply stated, it argues that the probability ($P$) that a purchaser will buy something in his or her own town (1) rather than in another is related to the number of shops in that town compared with those in other towns, and the comparative ease with which they can be reached. Thus it may be expressed by the formula (Ambrose, 1969):

$$P_1 = \cfrac{\cfrac{\text{Number of shops in centre 1}}{\text{Distance or time travelled to reach them}}}{\cfrac{\text{Total number of shops in whole study area}}{\text{Total distance or time travelled to reach them}}}$$

Thus $P_1 = \cfrac{\cfrac{N_1}{T_1}}{\cfrac{\Sigma N_i}{\Sigma T_i}}$

Obviously we can compare any number of towns, although for practical purposes three or four is often as many as shoppers will reasonably consider. Or we could compare shopping centres within the same town. Similarly, while we could establish probability values for shopping using all types of retail establishment, we might prefer to concentrate only on one kind, for example clothing shops. Before applying the formula, however, it is necessary to bear in mind the following cautionary points:

(i) distance is a less accurate, but a more easily calculated, variable than time, as journey times other than by public transport are difficult to establish;

(ii) in comparing towns it may be wise to exclude shops outside the town centre as these may be unlikely to attract out-of-town visitors, but there remains the problem of the out-of-town hypermarket or suburban shopping precinct;

(iii) the formula takes no account of shop size, nor of the fact that, in many towns, the customer is merely offered a duplicate of facilities in his or her own centre: another branch of Marks and Spencer, Dolcis, and so on.

These problems and the factor of non-rationality on the part of shoppers are considered below.

*(c) Problems posed by the use of interaction models*

As Carter (1976) has pointed out, even if Huff's probability model incorporates a concept of variable consumer behaviour, it still assumes that travel time or distance are always of the same significance in discouraging purchasers. Recent researchers into the area of behavioural geography would dispute this, arguing that perception of the town by rural dwellers will be as important in determining movement from the urban field to the centre as perception of the town by its inhabitants will in influencing social zoning.

A simple example of a group of people whose cultural perceptions influence their movement are the Hutterites in Canada. They maintain several small retail service centres in their reluctance to follow the pattern of other Canadians in their search for high-order shopping centres. The Hutterites are a group of German-speaking Protestants who live on collective farms and avoid all use of modern machinery, especially motor vehicles. By patronising small town stores only they disrupt the general pattern of American and Canadian retailing, especially in parts of the Prairies where they form an important element in the agricultural population.

If the population of a particular urban field is significantly different in characteristics from the national average, it is reasonable to assume that the size and shape of the area of their urban field will also be different. Also, if people perceive some stores or shopping centres as particularly attractive, this may distort their perception of the real distance involved in reaching them. The setting up of out-of-town shopping centres, and the revitalisation of downtown precincts are often attempts to encourage shoppers away from their own town to patronise distant higher-order centres for all their purchases. Competitive advertising is similarly designed to overcome the friction of distance. We must realise that a whole range of factors – price, fashion, popularity, variety – influence the individual choice of shops and services and in turn this determines the general pattern. In all probability studies we are measuring the likelihood of *expected* behaviour, and it is when behaviour deviates from the norm that we must exercise our geographic understanding of the environment to attempt an explanation.

### (d) Composite methods of measuring interaction

However, the great advantage of Huff's model is that it saves time-consuming and expensive 'leg-work', and the areas which merit later intensive questionnaire survey can be minimised. Reference to Figure 9.7 will demonstrate the application of the model in an area of Northern Ireland, originally investigated in the 1950s (Smailes, 1953). The urban field identified by Smailes corresponds closely with the zone of dominance discovered by Joyce Wylie in the late 1970s. Both of these zones, which were determined by fieldwork, approximate to the theoretical probability zone predicted by Huff's model. Where the results differ widely is in the region north of Ballymena, towards Ballycastle and Coleraine, both of which towns have grown considerably since the 1960s and are now more accessible by public

310

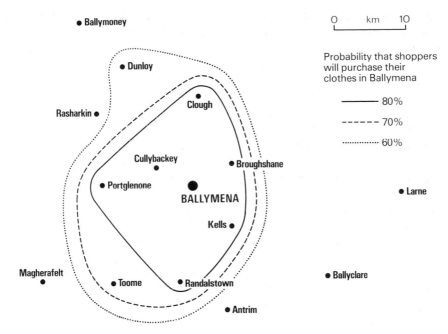

Figure 9.7 Huff's probability, according to the annual turnover of clothes shops in the Ballymena area. (Source: Joyce Wylie)

and private transport than before. If we wished to establish more accurately the rival attractions of the towns in this northern area we would need to concentrate our field surveys around Ballymoney and Armoy. Thus a combination of statistical modelling and selective field surveys would yield an efficient means of measuring present demand and utilisation of urban services, and this is how planners frequently operate.

ASSIGNMENTS

*A number of sources exist which provide data on retail and distribution industries in Britain. The sample assignment given below is based on 1971 data from the Census of Retailing, which has not been published subsequently, although a sample survey of some areas was produced in 1977 (Business Monitor SD027, Retail Shops Enquiry, Central Statistical Office, HMSO 1978). Other current sources of data available from larger public reference libraries include:*

- *Business Monitor SD025 series, published by HMSO and giving details of trends in retailing and some data on major firms by trade sector.*
- *Factory Inspectorate data, listing industrial and some commercial premises, their location, size and employees in each town.*
- *Industrial Market Location Surveys, published by the CBI, listing firms,*

*space and some details of turnover. Available as computer printout, updated annually.*

- *Information on sales of particular firms in specific locations from Unit for Retail Planning Ltd, 26 Queen Victoria Street, Reading, RG1 1TG. A private, and comparatively expensive, data agency.*

*Libraries with 'on-line' retrieval systems may have access to IRLS-dialtech, a computer reference service based on the Department of Trade and Industry, Ashdown House, Victoria Street, London SW1E 4RB. This enables searches of published data on retailing and other trades to be undertaken, normally free.*

*Most local authorities produce lists of firms, and addresses, sometimes with details of numbers of employees, and there is an increasing range of data systems and computerised directories, which libraries often subscribe to, so that assembling information on local firms should be possible for your area. Local Boards of Trade or Chambers of Commerce may also be prepared to help you work out the catchment areas they service.*

1. *Using the data for the total number of retail outlets given in Table 9.4 calculate the degree of centrality for Bournemouth, Southampton and Lymington.*

   *Apply the formula:* $C = t/T \times 100$

   *(For a full explanation of the formula, see page 307.)*

Table 9.4  Retailing data for Bournemouth, Southampton and Lymington

| Town | Number of retail outlets | Total retail turnover (£ thousand) | Total retail floor space (100 m²) |
|---|---|---|---|
| Bournemouth (entire town) | 2 275 | 79 975 | 1 862 |
| Central Area | 341 | 27 308 | 776 |
| Footwear (central area) | 17 | 925 | 26 |
| Southampton (entire town) | 1 732 | 90 543 | 1 615 |
| Central Area | 245 | 41 686 | 837 |
| Footwear (central area) | 22 | 1 613 | 45 |
| Lymington | 396 | 12 494 | 248 |
| Footwear | 11 | 277 | 6 |

Source: Report on the Census of Distribution and Other Services 1971, Part 8, Area Tables London and South East Region, Table 5, HMSO, Department of Industry. Business Statistics Office (1975).

2. (a) *Using the 1971 population statistics provided in Table 9.5 work out the position of the breaking points between Luton and each of the towns listed. (Use Reilly's breaking point formula.)*

   (b) *Substitute 1971 retail turnover statistics for population in the formula and repeat the exercise. Compare these results with breaking points derived from population statistics. Which will provide the best indication of Luton's catchment area as a central place?*

*(c) Briefly describe what the results you obtain show about these centres.*

Table 9.5 Population and retail turnover data for towns in the vicinity of Luton, Bedfordshire

| Town | Distance from Luton (km) | Population (1971) | Total retail turnover (£ thousand) |
|------|--------------------------|-------------------|------------------------------------|
| Luton | — | 161 178 | 49 486 |
| Bedford | 30 | 73 064 | 33 347 |
| Letchworth | 18 | 30 884 | 7 726 |
| Hitchin | 13 | 28 680 | 11 764 |
| Stevenage | 21 | 66 918 | 22 186 |
| Welwyn Garden City | 21 | 40 369 | 14 696 |
| Harpenden | 10 | 24 161 | 7 364 |
| St Albans | 19 | 52 057 | 22 862 |
| Hemel Hempstead | 19 | 69 371 | 21 453 |
| Dunstable | 8 | 31 790 | 12 435 |
| Leighton Buzzard | 21 | 20 326 | 5 553 |

Source: Report on the Census of Distribution and Other Services 1971, Part 8, Area Tables London and South East Region, Table 5, HMSO, Department of Industry, Business Statistics Office (1975).

*3. Table 9.6 gives retail data on four towns. Corby and Darlington have populations of around 50 000 people, while Bath and Crawley each have about 80 000 residents. Produce bar graphs of the data for each pair and attempt to account for the differences between towns of similar size, and between towns of different size.*

## 3. Developing interaction

During the 1960s and early 1970s, in a period of general economic prosperity and reducing transport costs, government policy in Britain actively increased the level of interaction between established towns and their tributary regions. Between 1966 and 1971 more than a million people moved out from inner cities to more peripheral locations in smaller towns and villages beyond the 'Green Belts' which had been established around the main conurbations in the post-war period. As many retained social or business links with the cities, movement back and forth increased. During the 1980s the situation changed. Employment in manufacturing, especially in the 'heavy' nationalised industries, has declined, especially in London and the main provincial conurbations. The labour force needed in retailing and other 'consumer services' has also declined with increased automation and larger-scale warehousing and shopping facilities. Employment growth has been in business services, finance, banking and other office-based work that relies on micro-technology. Such jobs do not need a metropolitan

Table 9.6

| Kind of business | Corby (Northants): central shopping area | | | | | Darlington (Co Durham): central shopping area | | | | |
|---|---|---|---|---|---|---|---|---|---|---|
| | Shops (a) Number | Turnover (b) (£ thousand) | Employment (c) Full-time Number | Part-time Number | Selling space (100 m²) | Shops (a) Number | Turnover (£ thousand) | Employment (c) Full-time Number | Part-time Number | Selling space (100 m²) |
| Total retail shops | 92 | 19 380 | 566 | 488 | 179 | 283 | 45 094 | 1 563 | 1 283 | 485 |
| Businesses with 100 or more shops in Great Britain | 27 | 9 911 | 277 | 275 | 71 | 39 | 17 591 | 507 | 507 | 139 |
| Others | 65 | 9 469 | 289 | 213 | 108 | 244 | 27 502 | 1 056 | 776 | 346 |
| Food | 21 | 8 671 | 161 | 195 | 36 | 68 | 8 251 | 184 | 282 | 35 |
| Grocers and provision dealers | 4 | 6 811 | 107 | 128 | 26 | 11 | 3 272 | 60 | 83 | 18 |
| Butchers | 5 | 688 | 21 | 11 | 3 | 8 | 1 141 | 62 | 25 | 3 |
| Fishmongers and poulterers | — | — | — | — | — | — | — | — | — | — |
| Greengrocers | 3 | 191 | 2 | 9 | 0.9 | — | — | — | — | — |
| Bread and flour confectioners | 5 | 308 | 18 | 21 | 5 | 14 | 839 | 27 | 57 | 5 |
| Off-licences | — | — | — | — | — | 4 | 535 | 7 | 7 | 0.9 |
| Confectioners, tobacconists, newsagents | — | — | — | — | — | 17 | 1 664 | 19 | 44 | 5 |
| Clothing and footwear | 34 | 2 409 | 92 | 71 | 37 | 100 | 6 474 | 295 | 321 | 82 |
| Footwear shops | 7 | 474 | 19 | 16 | 6 | — | — | — | — | — |
| Men's and boys' wear shops | 10 | 667 | 23 | 11 | 7 | — | — | — | — | — |
| Women's, girls', children's and infants' wear | 13 | 899 | 35 | 39 | 15 | 39 | 2 189 | 88 | 99 | 29 |
| Mixed clothing, household textiles, etc. shops | 4 | 369 | 15 | 5 | 8 | 11 | 513 | 66 | 118 | 7 |
| Household goods | 17 | 2 320 | 79 | 27 | 35 | 46 | 6 181 | 213 | 72 | 106 |
| Furniture, floor coverings shops | 4 | 621 | 24 | 5 | 16 | 20 | 3 588 | 121 | 33 | 78 |
| Radio, television, and electrical goods shops | 7 | 1 060 | 30 | 7 | 6 | 18 | 1 910 | 60 | 19 | 13 |
| Hardware, china, wallpaper and paint shops | 6 | 639 | 25 | 15 | 12 | 8 | 683 | 32 | 20 | 14 |
| Other non-food | 16 | 2 149 | 80 | 67 | 16 | 47 | 4 867 | 202 | 132 | 33 |
| Chemists and photographic dealers | — | — | — | — | — | 8 | 2 490 | 97 | 63 | 13 |
| Cycle and perambulator shops | — | — | — | — | — | — | — | — | — | — |
| Booksellers and stationers | 4 | 250 | 10 | 8 | 3 | — | — | — | — | — |
| Jewellery, toys, leather, sports and fancy goods sports | 7 | 558 | 19 | 15 | 5 | 24 | 1 470 | 67 | 33 | 9 |
| Florists, garden shops and pet shops | — | — | — | — | — | 7 | 187 | 4 | 20 | 0.9 |
| Mixed activity shops | 4 | 3 830 | 154 | 128 | 55 | 22 | 19 320 | 669 | 476 | 229 |
| Mixed activity shops with food sales | — | — | — | — | — | 9 | 16 598 | 547 | 392 | 180 |
| Mixed activity shops without food sales | — | — | — | — | — | 13 | 2 723 | 122 | 84 | 49 |

| | Bath (Avon): central shopping area | | | | | Crawley (West Sussex): central shopping area | | | | |
|---|---|---|---|---|---|---|---|---|---|---|
| Total retail shops | 378 | 60 577 | 1 703 | 1 430 | 573 | 139 | 38 934 | 931 | 1 064 | 293 |
| Businesses with 100 or more shops in Great Britain | 47 | 24 966 | 551 | 576 | 176 | 27 | 23 907 | 498 | 698 | 150 |
| Others | 331 | 35 610 | 1 152 | 854 | 396 | 112 | 15 027 | 433 | 366 | 143 |
| Food | 70 | 14 292 | 324 | 280 | 54 | 29 | 9 427 | 134 | 261 | 31 |
| Grocers and provision dealers | 10 | 8 418 | 165 | 140 | 21 | 3 | 512 | 16 | 4 | 2 |
| Butchers | 11 | 1 136 | 34 | 17 | 5 | 4 | 288 | 7 | 11 | 4 |
| Fishmongers and poulterers | — | — | — | — | — | — | — | — | — | — |
| Greengrocers | 13 | 512 | 16 | 26 | 3 | — | — | — | — | — |
| Bread and flour confectioners | 7 | 275 | 13 | 25 | 3 | — | 996 | 10 | — | — |
| Off-licences | 5 | 1 860 | 50 | 23 | 7 | 3 | — | — | 2 | 2 |
| Confectioners, tobacconists, newsagents | 21 | 1 677 | 29 | 41 | 13 | 7 | 722 | 11 | 22 | 3 |
| Clothing and footwear | 124 | 11 112 | 412 | 337 | 139 | 43 | 4 300 | 116 | 151 | 42 |
| Footwear shops | — | — | — | — | — | 10 | 1 241 | 27 | 69 | 7 |
| Men's and boys' wear shops | — | — | — | — | — | 17 | 1 519 | 45 | 26 | 16 |
| Women's, girls', children's and infants' wear | 49 | 3 087 | 126 | 155 | 48 | 11 | 1 070 | 35 | 40 | 14 |
| Mixed clothing, household textiles, etc. shops | 25 | 2 716 | 114 | 42 | 27 | 5 | 470 | 9 | 16 | 5 |
| Household goods | 59 | 5 636 | 158 | 67 | 71 | 26 | 4 858 | 158 | 80 | 66 |
| Furniture, floor coverings shops | 28 | 2 245 | 59 | 31 | 41 | 10 | 2 472 | 73 | 30 | 44 |
| Radio, television, and electrical goods shops | 22 | 2 695 | 73 | 18 | 18 | 7 | 875 | 46 | 19 | 7 |
| Hardware, china, wallpaper and paint shops | 9 | 695 | 26 | 18 | 11 | 9 | 1 511 | 39 | 31 | 15 |
| Other non-food | 96 | 9 977 | 353 | 243 | 82 | 33 | 5 792 | 222 | 118 | 32 |
| Chemists and photographic dealers | 16 | 4 642 | 155 | 108 | 34 | 7 | 3 312 | 129 | 55 | 14 |
| Cycle and perambulator shops | — | — | — | — | — | — | — | — | — | — |
| Booksellers and stationers | 16 | 917 | 42 | 22 | 9 | — | — | — | — | — |
| Jewellery, toys, leather, sports and fancy goods shops | 49 | 3 627 | 123 | 82 | 26 | 15 | 1 822 | 68 | 36 | 10 |
| Florists, garden shops and pet shops | — | — | — | — | — | 6 | 335 | 13 | 16 | 3 |
| Mixed activity shops | 29 | 19 560 | 456 | 503 | 226 | 8 | 14 558 | 301 | 454 | 123 |
| Mixed activity shops with food sales | 5 | 11 987 | 239 | 365 | 115 | 5 | 12 957 | 271 | 401 | 116 |
| Mixed activity shops without food sales | 24 | 7 573 | 217 | 138 | 111 | 3 | 1 601 | 30 | 53 | 6 |

(a) Including estimates for non-response    (b) Inclusive of VAT    (c) Paid employees only

Source: HMSO Business Monitor SD027, 1978

location and have indeed largely been established along the 'high-tech' corridors radiating out from London into East Anglia and the West Country (Hall & Markusen, 1985). Other public services and administration have also shown major increases in the numbers of people employed. All this has meant that new and expanded towns have grown up to act as significant foci for the resident population which might formerly have looked to established cities for goods and services. Towns such as Banbury, Basingstoke, Bury St Edmunds, Huntingdon, Ipswich, Newbury and Thetford have grown from comparative obscurity to populations of over 50 000, often over 100 000 people, since the late 1970s.

As a result, retailing and other consumer services are increasingly looking to urban peripheral locations, preferably close to transport facilities. For example, a new supermarket complex, built near a small railway station at Flitwick on the main London-to-Leicester line, has become a focus for housing development. Such developments on formerly 'green field' sites have blurred the distinction between urban and rural even further, and produced a hybrid settlement form which we now consider in more detail.

## D. The Rural–Urban Fringe

So far we have considered ways in which the perimeter of urban fields may be delimited either by field study or theoretical measurement. Now we turn our attention to the *character* of these areas which are outside the municipal boundary but within the zone of influence of the town, large parts of which form what has been termed the 'rurban' fringe.

## 1. Life on the fringe

As the urban sociologist R. E. Pahl (1966) suggested there are many different sorts of occupiers of the rural–urban fringe. Nearest the town are the 'urbanised' residents, commuting to the city daily. For them the villages are a retreat with an artificially rustic life style. But at the edge of the town's zone of influence, the rural population may still live a predominantly agricultural life style with little contact with the city. Where one group impinges on another there is often conflict between the indigenous population and the 'newcomers'.

> *Middle-class people come into rural areas in search of a
> meaningful community and by their presence help to destroy
> whatever community was there. Part of the basis of the local
> village community was the sharing of the deprivations due to the
> isolation of country life and the sharing of the limited world of
> the families within the village. The middle-class people try to get the
> 'cosiness' of village life, without suffering any of the deprivations,*

Plate 9.1  May Day at Ickwell, Bedfordshire, 1986. Revitalised festivals in rural areas, like the May Day celebrations at Ickwell, rely on the folk perceptions of newcomers to sustain interest in them, as well as the support of long-resident enthusiasts. Many groups of Morris dancers, folk musicians and craftsmen are organised by middle-class and professional people who have the leisure to devote to these activities. (Photograph: B.B. & H. Newspapers Ltd, Bedford)

> *and while maintaining a whole range of contacts with the outside world by means of the greater mobility afforded by their private transport (**Pahl, 1966**).*

This zone of villages that look for urban services and provide the town with labour is characterised by residents who live in the countryside but who are not socially or economically part of it. The newcomers are prepared to isolate their living space from their work space. As Mayer (1968) describes it, the *community of propinquity* (those among whom one lives) is different from the *community of interest* (the work group, or others of similar interests). If the newcomers are a sufficiently large group in the village population they may develop social activities, for example golf clubs, coffee mornings, dinner dances, which enable them to combine the two communities in one place. The risk is that the established villagers will feel excluded or 'taken over' and resent interference in their traditional activities. On the other hand, without the influx of newcomers it is arguable that many rural activities might collapse through lack of support.

In trying to define the social characteristics of the rural–urban fringe, Pahl proposed four main headings, which have been adopted by subsequent writers.

## (a) Segregation

Private new housing in villages, often built by national developers (Wimpey, Barratt) rather than by local firms, is often expensive. It is bought by relatively high wage earners for whom it is either more attractive or cheaper than city centre accommodation. However, local people, who have first claim on public housing, will be physically segregated from these new developments. Similarly as the rural–urban fringe is often regarded as a 'green field' site it is possible for planners to allocate land for schools, light industry and housing so that there is functional as well as social segregation of land use here.

## (b) Selective immigration

The rural–urban fringe attracts mobile middle-class residents who form a small but powerful and economically important proportion of the city population, among which they work. One effect of their choosing to live beyond the city is that their financial contribution in the form of taxes is denied to the city which they patronise for subsidised services such as public transport, social services and cultural amenities. Such dormitory dwellers may still retain strong social linkages with the city which provides their income, but may have opted out of the problems of urban change and decay.

## (c) Commuting

The journey to work of large numbers of people from rural areas has obvious effects in terms of traffic congestion in the city, the lack of activity in the dormitory villages during the day, and the problems of providing transport services capable of handling peak loads which are not much used during the rest of the day.

## (d) Collapse of geographical and social hierarchies

Because the rural–urban fringe is being occupied by very mobile residents, normally one-car or two-car families, the traditional hierarchy of retail services tends to be replaced by specialist ones. One village shop may become an off-licence, another a delicatessen, each with catchment areas beyond the limits of the village in which they are located. The problems of villagers who are unable or can ill afford to travel long distances are gradually increasing with the withdrawal of rural bus and train services. A spiral develops: new residents with urban ties are prepared to drive considerable distances back to town for shopping and entertainment, demand for local facilities declines and these are withdrawn as being uneconomic.

This may encourage the elderly to move away to town, thus making way for more newcomers. Economies of scale also force the closure of rural schools and cottage hospitals and, as church attendance falls and parishes are amalgamated to reduce the cost of maintaining old vicarages and churches, the social life which was associated with these institutions also fades away. The village becomes a suburb in style of building and style of life. If these changes in the rural–urban fringe are recognised we may agree with Carter (1976) that:

> *the argument has moved far away from the concept of a fringe as a physical area to one associated with particular social processes. One view considers the rural–urban fringe as identified by static features, a mix of land uses brought about by the incomplete extension of the city as well as the demands which it makes on its marginal areas. The other view sees the fringe as showing distinction in the nature of the communities which occupy it, brought about by the migration of mobile, middle-class families orientated to the city and dominated by urban life styles.*

## 2. Planning the fringe

Another way of looking at the rural–urban fringe is to see it as an area where there is no clearly defined land use, where agriculture has given way to ill-disciplined and wasteful settlement sprawl. This is the view of the Director of the Second Land Utilisation Survey, Dr Alice Coleman. When reviewing the changes revealed in comparing land use in Britain in the 1970s with that at the time of the First Survey in 1933, she comments:

> *The planned separation of town and country, in order to integrate townscape and conserve the farmland resources, does not seem to have been achieved. There has been a rapid and accelerating farmland loss and in addition to this, there is also much land fragmented and subjected to urban pressures by new sprawling development. Far from attaining its objective of eliminating the 'rurban fringe' of incompatible use mixtures, planning often seems to have actively encouraged its proliferation. On the urban front, the land-use maps reveal that the failure to provide an adequate housing stock appears to be mainly due to the widespread premature demolition of housing. This is explored by examining before-and-after uses of 1000 square kilometres in south-east England. The largest new use proves to be waste land while roads and tended open space have each consumed 15 to 16 times as much new land as residential uses.*
>
> *The picture of continuing land misuse is surprisingly similar to that of the 1930s. Planning seems to be permitting the same abuses*

319

*as non-planning, and we must seriously address ourselves to the*
*question: 'Can we afford the vast expense of a planning*
*establishment when free enterprise will do the same job free?'*
(**Coleman, 1976**)

The Coleman model of land use is to designate urban settlement as 'town-scape', agricultural land as 'farmscape' and areas of natural vegetation as 'wildscape'. In transitional zones between different 'scapes', 'fringes' can be recognised. The zone between vegetation and farmland is referred to as the 'marginal fringe' and if farming becomes more efficient and conservation more deliberate this motley zone should decline in area. The 'rurban fringe' is typified by piecemeal urban development and it is argued that the containment of settlement by Green Belts and planning constraints is an objective for planners. This objective seems to have failed: there is now more derelict land than forty years ago, and, because of degeneration of land around settlements, three times as much farmland area has been lost in Britain as has been occupied by new building. The blame for the increase in urban sprawl is placed at the door of planners as any change in land use requires planning permission. To quote Dr Coleman again:

> *Rurban fringe usually has a greater variety of uses than other*
> *environments, and more uses that are mutually incompatible. Apart*
> *from a fragmented mosaic composed of all three super-categories,*
> *there is also an emphasis on those settlement types that are so coarse*
> *in scale or barrier-like in function that they would disrupt the*
> *texture of townscape if located within it. Airports, power stations,*
> *quarries, marshalling yards, 'spaghetti' junctions and large golf*
> *courses are examples, as well as less useful items such as derelict*
> *land. Such an environment is far from ideal for urban residents,*
> *while they in turn often make farming impossible, by trespass,*
> *damage, theft, fire setting and so on. Even the house sparrows that*
> *come with a new rurban-fringe building estate can devour up to half*
> *the grain in an adjacent field of wheat. These conflicts can be kept to*
> *a minimum where the interface between town and country is short*
> *and straight, but some planners advocate that it should be deliber-*
> *ately lengthened in the form of green wedges.*

While one might discuss whether the environmental quality of the landscape suffers by the spread of low-density 'urbanite' settlement, the 'scapes–fringes' model at least serves to enable clear identification of the type of land use in a particular area (see Figure 9.8). The conflict of interests engendered by pressure on the land for new housing and services forms the subject of the next assignment.

To the debate as to whether the countryside around towns should be conserved for agriculture and recreation or developed as an urban dormitory

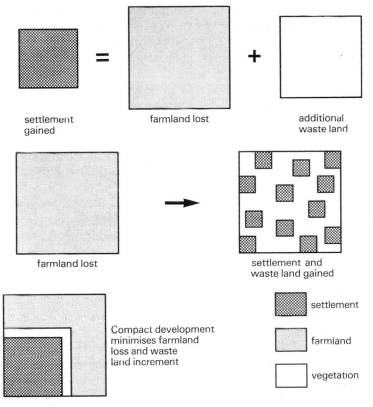

Figure 9.8  The land-loss equation. (Source: Coleman, 1976)

there may be added a third view. Since Britain, like the rest of Europe, is more than self-sufficient in foodstuffs, there seems little necessity to safe-guard all agricultural land against future development. In 1987 the Secretary of State for Agriculture proposed that planning constraints in rural areas be eased to allow land to be used for other purposes. The response from farmers and conservationists was that valuable agricultural land would soon be covered in 'concrete or conifers'. However, some rural planning agencies, including the Rural Community Councils, saw that allowing light industry to locate in rural areas might solve some problems of local unemployment, and prevent villages becoming the picturesque preserve of wealthy urbanites who contributed little directly to the rural economy. The movement to maintain villages as self-contained economic units had long been advocated by some academics (March & Martin, 1974) who pointed to the example of the traditional linear villages of East Anglia, which contained a wide variety of land uses, in support of their argument. Certainly the creation of a more diverse economic base in villages, even at the expense of visual amenity and

321

loss of agricultural land, may be worthwhile in terms of reducing rural job loss and outmigration.

ASSIGNMENTS
1. *For a village in your own area, choose a site for the building of new houses and a shop or filling station. Put forward arguments for the houses being either for rent from the Council or for purchase by executive commuters. Then outline the kinds of issues and opinions that such a proposal would be likely to arouse locally.*
2. *Apply Coleman's classification to the area of the OS land use map in two contrasting districts (e.g. Sheet 158 Dover and Sheet 207 Gravesend). On the basis of the generalised map which you draw as a result, allocate areas where development should and should not be permitted.*
3. *Prepare a list of ways in which the countryside adjacent to towns could be used to provide recreation for town dwellers without hindering agriculture. Check to see what is being done in your own locality.*

## Key Ideas

*A. The Changing Urban System*

1. The distinction between town and countryside has become blurred in the post-war period, and it is preferable to think in terms of urban regions, with combined urban and rural populations of at least 50 000 inhabitants, as the basic units in a network of urban systems.
2. Within each urban region, urban centres are dependent on, and in turn serve, an area (or ring) around them which we term the urban field.

*B. Urban Service Provision*

1. The urban field may be delimited by a variety of techniques: those relating to the services the town supplies, those relating to the area from which the town draws custom, and by theoretical measures based on trade statistics.
2. Urban fields may also be determined by investigation of the area in which demand for urban services is generated.
3. Field techniques of this sort rely on survey questionnaires which assume the impartiality of their structure and the randomness of the samples to which they are applied for their success.
4. The strength of attraction of an urban centre is diminished by the distance which people have to travel in order to use it.

## C. Rural–Urban Interaction

1. Statistical attempts at measuring the urban field rely on a knowledge of the relative size and distancing of settlements.
2. To refine these techniques further, the concepts of probability and change over time are introduced to the model.
3. Despite these refinements there are problems in the crudity of application of such techniques in the real world.
4. However, discrepancies between theoretical predictions of interaction and observed patterns direct the geographer to where field enquiry is needed.
5. Changes in personal mobility, employment and consumption patterns mean that urban–rural residential distinctions are becoming blurred.

## D. The Rural–Urban Fringe

1. The rural–urban fringe can be identified spatially, and by the social activities of its inhabitants.
2. The rural–urban fringe is an inefficient user of land, and there is pressure for its rationalisation.
3. Geographers need an understanding of sociological as well as spatial behaviour to explain current patterns of land use.
4. The preservation of agricultural land may not be the best economic solution to the problems of rural areas.

## Additional Activities

Ways in which we can measure the urban field when we are working outwards from the town to the rural area are given below. Select *one* criterion from sections 1 to 8 and apply it to your own urban area. On this basis construct a map of the town's urban field, indicating the zones of dominance, competition and marginal influence. Suggest reasons for the size and shape of the zones you distinguish.

## Measures of the urban field

### 1. Newspapers

These provide an excellent index. Very large centres may have a morning daily (Liverpool, Manchester); large towns have evening papers; while smaller centres have weekly papers. The area they cover can be measured by:
(a) News coverage area. Map each place for which news items are supplied.
(b) Advertisements. Map places listed in Sales, Vacancies, Houses for sale, etc.

(c) Circulation. Map the limits within which the paper is sold (enquire at office).

(d) Local groupings. Sports leagues, etc.

## 2. Distribution

(a) Map the area of shoppers' homes, preferably by sample on market day. It is usual to omit the farthest 10% or 20% of respondents' locations as these are not likely to be typical of the general area from which shoppers come. If you draw lines from respondents' homes to the town centre these 'desire lines' give an indication of the pattern of movement of people, especially if you can complete them for more than one town.

(b) Map the area within which a furniture store makes deliveries.

(c) Map the area within which a wholesale grocer supplies shops.

(d) Map the area within which mail is delivered from the local Post Office sorting office.

## 3. Administrative areas

Make maps of areas served by local police, fire, ambulance, hospital, employment exchange, telephone directory.

## 4. Social areas

Map the area of primary schools supplying secondary schools (i.e. the catchment area of these schools). Likewise for technical colleges, art schools, and other institutions of a specialised nature.

## 5. Transport flow lines

Traffic reflects movement between a centre and its field. Bus flow line maps which illustrate bus frequency may be drawn. Distinguish: (a) late evening buses (after 21.00 h, returning people to their homes from entertainment centres); (b) early morning and evening services for commuters; (c) 'in between' services for shoppers. Also use the timetables to plot settlements most accessible by bus, i.e. in the area surrounding the main settlement. Note the limitations of this approach. It takes no account of other forms of transport. Car ownership increases annually and more people living in the villages are now able to use private transport.

## 6. Entertainment areas

Find out the catchment areas of theatres, football grounds, etc. The local supporters club may be able to help you.

## 7. Catchment areas of principal industries and services other than retailing

Find out the catchment areas of the firms themselves. Some of the larger companies may operate works buses. The routes followed by these will give some indication of the catchment area of these firms.

## 8. Livestock market

Map the distribution of firms which send livestock for auction at the livestock market. You will probably find that the buyers (who will include butchers as well as farmers) will come from farther afield and will not necessarily provide such a useful index for delimiting the urban field.

A detailed survey by your whole group can be achieved if each individual undertakes one of these tasks and the results are pooled and compared.

# References and Further Reading

References marked * are recommended for further reading.

## Preface

**Beddis, R.** (1982) *A Sense of Place*, Oxford University Press.
**Massey, D. & Allen, J.** (1984) *Geography Matters*, Cambridge University Press, Ch. 1.

## Chapter 1

*****Barke, M. & O'Hare, G.** (1983) *The Third World*, Oliver & Boyd.
*****Bull, C., Daniel, P. & Hopkinson, M.** (1985) *The Geography of Rural Resources*, Oliver & Boyd.
**Buttimer, A.** (1969) Social Space in Interdisciplinary Perspective, *Geographical Review*, vol. 59.
**Chorley, R. & Haggett, P.** (1967) *Models in Geography*, Methuen.
**Corfield, P. J.** (1982) *The Impact of English Towns, 1700–1800*, Oxford (OPUS) Paperbacks.
**Firey, W.** (1945) Sentiment and Symbolism as Ecological Variables. *American Sociological Review*, vol. 10.
**Goodey, B.** (1971) Perception of the Urban Environment, University of Birmingham, Centre for Urban and Regional Studies, Occasional Paper 17.
**Goodwin, B. & Taylor, K.** (1982) *The Politics of Utopia*, Hutchinson.
**Harvey, D.** (1969) *Explanation in Geography*, Edward Arnold.
**Harvey, D.** (1973) *Social Justice and the City*, Edward Arnold.
*****Holt-Jensen, A.** (1980) *Geography – its History and Concepts*, Harper & Row.
**Jacobs, J.** (1961) *The Death and Life of Great American Cities*, Penguin.
**Johnston, R. J.** (1983) *Geography and Geographers*, Edward Arnold.
*****Lawton, R.** (1978) Changes in University Geography, *Geography*, vol. 63, p. 1.
**Lemon, J. T.** (1978) in Ley, D. & Samuels, M. (eds), *Humanistic Geography*, Croom Helm, Ch. 20.
*****Meinig, D.** (1979) *The Interpretation of Ordinary Landscapes*, Oxford University Press.
**Pattison, W.** (1973) The Four Traditions in Geography, in Bale, J., *et al. Perspectives in Geographical Education*, Oliver & Boyd.
**Pocock, D. & Hudson, R.** (1978) *Images of the Urban Environment*, Macmillan.
**Pred, A.** (1967) *Behaviour and Location*, Gleerup.

## Chapter 2

*****Ashton, T. S.** (1968) *The Industrial Revolution 1760–1830*, Oxford University Press.
**Beckinsale, R. & M.,** (1977) *The English Heartland*, Duckworth.
**Beresford, M.** (1967) *New Towns of the Middle Ages*, Lutterworth.
**Bull, C., Daniel, P. & Hopkinson, M.** (1985) *The Geography of Rural Resources*, Oliver and Boyd.
*****Brunskill, R. D.** (1970) *The Illustrated Handbook of Vernacular Architecture*, Faber.
*****Burke, G.** (1976) *Townscapes*, Penguin.
**Chisholm, M.** (1966) *Rural Settlement and Land Use*, Hutchinson, Ch. 2.

Darby, H. C. (1976) *A New Historical Geography of England before 1600*, Cambridge University Press.

Ekwall, E. (1974) *Concise Oxford Dictionary of English Place Names*, Oxford.

Guest, A. (1974) *Man and Landscape*, Heinemann.

Hall, C. (1976) *Places for People*, Guardian Handbook.

*Hoskins, W. G. (1977) *The Making of the English Landscape*, Hodder.

Lively, P. (1976) *The Presence of the Past*, Collins.

Mackie, E. (1975) *Science and Society in Prehistoric Britain*, Paul Elek.

Mills, D. (1972) Has Historical Geography Changed?, *New Trends in Geography*, Open University Press.

Orwin, C. S. (1954) *The Open Fields*, Clarendon Press.

Roberts, B. K. (1977) *Rural Settlement in Britain*, Dawson.

*Roberts, B. K. (1986) *The Making of the English Village*, Longman.

*Rogers, A. (1977) *Group Projects in Local History*, Dawson.

Russell, J. C. (1973) *Medieval Cities and their Regions*, David & Charles.

Salway, P. (1982) *Roman Britain*, Clarendon Press.

Sawyer, P. H. (1976) *Medieval Settlement*, Edward Arnold.

*West, J. (1962) *Village Records*, Macmillan.

Woodruffe, B. J. (1976) *Rural Settlement Policies and Plans*, Oxford University Press.

Wrigley, E. A. (1969) *Population and History*, Weidenfeld and Nicolson.

# Chapter 3

Beresford, M. (1967) *New Towns of the Middle Ages*, Lutterworth Press, p. 340.

*Burke, G. (1975) *Towns in the Making*, Edward Arnold.

Christaller, W. (1933) *Central Places in Southern Germany*, Jena Fischer.

Conzen, M. R. G. (1968) The Use of Town Plans in the Study of Urban History, in Dyos, H. J. (ed) *The Study of Urban History*, Arnold, pp. 127–130.

Dyos, H. J. (1966) *Victorian Suburb, A Study of the Growth of Camberwell*, Leicester University Press.

Engels, F. (1969) *The Condition of the Working Class in England*, Panther, p. 80 (first published in German in 1845, in English in 1892).

*Hoskins, W. G. (1970) *The Making of the English Landscape*, Penguin.

*Howard, E. (1902) *Garden Cities of Tomorrow*, Faber.

Jones, E. and Van Zandt, E. (1974) *The City, Yesterday, Today and Tomorrow*, Aldus Books, p. 51.

Mearns, A. (1883) *The Bitter Cry of Outcast London. An Inquiry into the Condition of the Abject Poor*, reprinted by Frank Cass & Co, 1970, pp. 6–7.

Morrison, A. (1897) *A Child of the Jago*, Methuen, pp. 1–2.

Mortimore, W. H. (1847) *History of the Hundred of Wirral*, Whittaker & Co, London, p. 413.

Olsen, D. J. (1976) *The Growth of Victorian London*, Batsford, p. 321.

Patmore, J. A. & Hodgkiss, A. G. (1970) *Merseyside in Maps*, Longman.

Price, S. J. (1958) *Building Societies, their Origins and History*, Franey, pp. 59–62.

Sulley, P. (1888) *History of Birkenhead*, p. 308.

Taylor, I. C. (1970) The Court and Cellar Dwellings: the Eighteenth Century Origin of the Liverpool Slum, *Transactions of the Historical Society of Lancashire and Cheshire*, vol. 122, p. 67.

Treble, J. H. (1971) Liverpool Working Class Housing 1801–51, in Chapman, S. D. (ed.), *A History of Working Class Housing: A Symposium*, David & Charles, pp. 167–200.

White, B. D. (1951) *A History of the Liverpool Corporation, 1835–1914*, Liverpool University Press, pp. 30–45.

# Chapter 4

Abercrombie, P. (1945) *Greater London Plan 1944*, HMSO.

Barratt Brown, P. (1984) *Models in Political Economy*, Penguin.

Bramley, G. & Price, D. (1987) *Housing Needs in Non-Metropolitan Areas*, ADC.

**Burke, G.** (1975) *Towns in the Making*, Edward Arnold, p. 63.
**CES Ltd** (1985) Deprived Areas Beyond the Pale, *Town and Country Planning*, vol. 54, no. 2.
**Champion, T., Coombes, M. & Openshaw, S.** (1983) A New Definition of Cities, *Town and Country Planning*, vol. 52, no. 11.
*****Coleman, A.** (1985) *Utopia on Trial. Vision and Reality in Planned Housing*, Hilary Shipman.
**Counsell, G.** (1988) The Property Lottery, *The Independent*, 3 June 1988.
**Edgington, J.** (1984) The Tenants Who Want to go into Property, *The Guardian*, 29 September 1984.
**Forest, R. & Williams, P.** (1984) Commodification and Housing: Emerging Issues and Contradictions, *Environment and Planning A*, vol. 16, pp. 1163–80.
*****Hudson, R. & Williams, A.** (1986) *The United Kingdom*, Harper & Row, pp. 30–6.
**Hughes, C.** (1987) Prices in the South Prevent One in Three Buying Homes, *The Independent*, 5 October 1987.
*****Lawless, P. & Roban, C.** (eds.) (1986) *The Contemporary British City*, Harper & Row, pp. 63–84.
**Liverpool Corporation** (1951) *Housing Progress 1864–1951*, Architectural and Housing Department.
**Liverpool Corporation** (1967) *Liverpool Rebuilds, 1945–1966*, Public Relations Office.
**Liverpool Corporation** (1970) The City's Housing Requirements, Report of the Policy and Finance Committee.
*****Malpass, P.** (ed.) (1986) *The Housing Crisis*, Croom Helm, Chs. 1, 10.
**Manchester Corporation** (1970) Report to the Slum Clearance and Rehousing Progress Sub-Committee on Manchester's Housing Needs and Resources 1970–78.
*****Munton, R.** (1984) *London's Green Belt: Containment in Practice*, Allen & Unwin.
**Osborn, F. J.** (1918) *New Towns After the War*, Evelyn, Adams & McKay.
**Potter, S.** (1985) How the New Towns Changed, *Town and Country Planning*, vol. 52, no. 10, pp. 284–90.
*****Potter, S. & Thomas, R.** (1982) *The New Towns Experience*, Unit 28A, Urban Change and Conflict, The Open University.
**Roberts, T.** (1984) Homes of their Own, *The Guardian*, 30 June 1984.
**Strachan, A.** (1974) The Planning Framework for Modern Urban Growth: the Example of Great Britain, Ch. 4 in Johnson, J. H. (ed.), *Suburban Growth, the Geographical Processes at the Edge of the Western City*, Wiley.
**Turner, J. F. C.** (1976) *Housing by People: Towards Autonomy in Building Environments*, Open Forum.
**Williams, N.** (1939) *Population Problems of New Estates with Special Reference to Norris Green*, Liverpool University Social Service Dept, Liverpool University Press.

# Chapter 5

**Alonso, W.** (1964) The Historic and Structural Theories of Urban Form: their Implication for Urban Renewal, *Land Economics*, vol. 40, pp. 227–31.
**Berry, B. J. L.** (1959) The Spatial Organization of Business Land Uses, in Garrison, W. L. *et al., Studies of Highway Development and Geographic Change*, Greenwood.
**Burgess, E. W.** (1925) The Growth of the City: An Introduction to a Research Project, in Park, R. E., Burgess, E. W. & McKenzie, D. (eds.) *The City*, University of Chicago Press.
**Carter, H.** (1976) *The Study of Urban Geography*, Edward Arnold.
**Engels, F.** (1969) *The Condition of the Working Class in England*, Panther.
**Fielding, G. J.** (1975) *Geography as Social Science*, Harper & Row, p. 166.
**Harris, C. D. & Ullman, E. L.** (1945) The nature of cities, *Annals of the American Academy of Political and Social Science*, vol. 242, pp. 7–17.
**Herbert, D. T.** (1972) *Urban Geography: A Social Perspective*, David & Charles.
*****Herbert, D. T. & Thomas, C. J.** (1982) *Urban Geography. A First Approach*, John Wiley, pp. 290–308.
**Hopkinson, M. F.** (1985) The English Medium Sized Town, Settlement Studies Service, Paper No. 37, Bedford College of Higher Education.
**Hoyt, H.** (1939) *The Structure and Growth of Residential Neighbourhoods in American Cities*, Federal Housing Administration.

**Hoyt, H.** (1971) Recent Distortions in the Classical Models of Urban Structure, *Land Economics*, vol. 40 in Bourne, L. A. (ed.) *Internal Structure of the City*, Oxford University Press, p. 95.

**Hurd, R. M.** (1903) *Principles of City Land Values*, New York Record and Guide.

**Johnston, R. J.** (1982) *The American Urban System. A Geographical Perspective*, Longman, pp. 167–76.

*****Johnston, R. J.** (1983) From Description to Explanation in Urban Geography, *Geography*, vol. 68, pp. 11–15.

*****Johnston, R. J.** (1984) *City and Society. An Outline for Urban Geography*, Hutchinson, Ch. 6.

**Knoss, D.** (1962) *Distribution of Land Values in Topeka*, Lawrence, Kansas.

**Lawton, R.** (1973) An Age of Great Cities, *Town Planning Review*, vol. 43.

**Mann, P. H.** (1965) *An Approach to Urban Sociology*, Routledge & Kegan Paul.

**Morrill, R. L.** (1970) *The Spatial Organisation of Society*, Duxbury Press, p. 165.

**Murdie, R. A.** (1969) Factorial Ecology of Metropolitan Toronto, Research Paper 116, Dept of Geography, University of Chicago.

**Park, R. E., Burgess, E. W. & McKenzie, R. D.** (eds.) (1925) *The City*, University of Chicago Press.

**Pritchard, R. M.** (1976) *Housing and the Social Structure of the City*, Cambridge University Press.

**Quinn, J. A.** (1950) *Human Ecology*, Prentice-Hall.

**Ratcliffe, R. V.** (1947) *Urban Land Economics*, vol. 367.

**Rees, P. H.** (1968) The Factorial Ecology of Metropolitan Chicago, Masters thesis, University of Chicago.

**Rees, P.** (1970) Problems of Defining the Metropolis, in Berry, B. J. L. & Horton, F. E. (eds.) *Geographic Perspectives on the Urban System*, Prentice Hall, pp. 308–11.

**Robson, R. T.** (1975) *Urban Analysis: a Study of City Structure with Special Reference to Sunderland*, Cambridge University Press, pp. 27–9, 97.

**Schnøre, J. F.** (1965) On the Spatial Structure of Cities in the Two Americas, Ch. 10 in Hauser, P. M. & Schnøre, J. F. (eds.), *The Study of Urbanization*, John Wiley.

*****Short, J. R.** (1984) *An Introduction to Urban Geography*, Routledge & Kegan Paul, pp. 120–60.

**Simmons, J.** (1964) The Changing Pattern of Retail Locations, Research paper no. 92.

**Sjoberg, G.** (1965) *The Pre-Industrial City Past and Present*, Free Press.

# Chapter 6

**Adams, J. S. & Gilder, K. A.** (1976) Household Creation and Intra Urban Migration, in Herbert, D. T. & Johnston, R. J., *Social Areas in Cities*, vol. 1, J. Wiley.

**Ardill, J.** (1987a) Docklands Lift-off for 'New Cities', *The Guardian*, 21 July 1987.

**Ardill, J.** (1987b) Docklands Adds a Little Reality to the Megahype, *The Guardian*, 21 July 1987.

**Backler, A. L.** (1974) *A Behavioural Study of Location Changes in Upper Class Residential Areas: the Detroit Example*, Indiana University Press.

**Bale, J.** (1981) *The Location of Manufacturing Industry*, second edition, Oliver & Boyd.

**Barwick, S.** (1988) Docklands berth for 800 ft tower, *The Independent*, 30 March 1988.

**Blowers, A.** (1973) The Neighbourhood: Exploration of a Concept, in *The City as a Social System*, Open University DJ 201, Unit 7, p. 56.

*****Blunkett, D. & Jackson, K.** (1986) *Democracy in Crisis*, Hogarth Press.

**Boal, F. W.** (1970a) Social Space in the Belfast Urban Area, in Stephens, N. & Glossock, R. E. (eds.) *Irish Geographical Studies*, Queens University, Belfast, pp. 373–93.

**Boal, F. W.** (1970b) Territoriality in the Shankill Road–Falls Divide, *Irish Geography*, vol. 6, pp. 30–60.

**Boal, F. W.** (1976) Ethnic Residential Segregation, in Herbert, D. T. & Johnston, R. J. (eds.), *Social Areas in Cities*, vol. 1, J. Wiley.

**Brummer, A.** (1987a) Cleveland's Kiss of Life, *The Guardian*, 3 August 1987.

**Brummer, A.** (1987b) Aristocrats Rule in the Urban Village, *The Guardian*, 4 August 1987.

**Buttimer, A.** (1975) Social Space an Interdisciplinary Perspective, in Jones, E. (ed.), *Reading in Social Geography*, Oxford University Press, pp. 128–37.

**Carey, L. & Mapes, R.** (1972) *The Sociology of Planning*, Batsford.

**Carr, M. C.** (1982) The Development and Character of a Metropolitan Suburb, in Thompson, E. M. L. (ed.), *The Rise of Suburbia*, St Martin's Press.

**Church of England** (1985) *Faith in the City*, Church House Publishing.

**Clarke, S. D.** (1966) *The Suburban Society*, University of Toronto Press.

**Dean, M.** (1985) Accounting for Cities of Inner Despair, *The Guardian*, 3 October 1985.

**Dineen, M.** (1987) Opening up of London's Least-used Asset, *The Observer*, 18 January 1987.

**Docklands Consultative Committee** (1985) *Four Year Review of the LDDC*.

**Downs, R. M. & Stead, D.** (eds.) (1973) *Image and Environment*, Aldine Publishing Co.

**Dunn, A.** (1987) Ridley Greets New Spirit in Liverpool, *The Guardian*, 5 August 1987.

**Evans, R.** (1986) Canary-Wharf – Changing the State of the City, *TSB Group Review*, vol. 3, no. 1, pp. 5–7.

**Firey, W.** (1945) Sentiment and Symbolism as Ecological Variables, *American Sociological Review*, vol. 10, pp. 140–8.

**Glass, R.** (1948) *The Social Background of a Plan: a Study of Middlesbrough*, Routledge & Kegan Paul.

**Green, M.** (1987) Baa Baa Rich Sheep, *Sunday Express Supplement*, 2 August 1987.

**Gribben, R.** (1987) London Docklands, *Daily Telegraph Editorial Survey*, 2 February 1987.

**Hall, D.** (1985) Is the Canary a White Elephant? *Town and Country Planning*, vol. 55, no. 1.

**Halsall, M.** (1987) BOOM – the Crusade Aiming to Create a Merseyside Miracle, *The Guardian*, 14 August 1987.

*\*Harrison, P.** (1983) *Inside the Inner City*, Penguin.

**Herbert, D. T.** (1972) *Urban Geography. A Social Perspective*, David & Charles.

**Hetherington, P.** (1986) Consensus Reverses Urban Decay, *The Guardian*, 3 February 1986.

**HMSO** (1977) *Policy for the Inner Cities*, Department of the Environment.

**Hoppit, D.** (1987) London Docklands, *Daily Telegraph Editorial Survey*, 2 February 1987.

**Horne, R.** (1981) *Inner City Regeneration*, Span.

**Hudson, R. & Williams, A.** (1986) *The United Kingdom*, Harper & Row.

**Johnston J. H.** (1974) *Suburban Growth*, Wiley.

*\*Johnston, R. J.** (1982) *The American Urban System*, Longman, Ch. 9.

**Jones, E.** (ed.) (1975) *Readings in Social Geography*, Oxford University Press.

**Jones, E. & Eyles, J.** (1977) *An Introduction to Social Geography*, Oxford University Press.

**Jones, P. N.** (1970) Some Aspects in the Changing Distribution of Coloured Immigrants in Birmingham, 1961–66, in *Transactions of the Institute of British Geographers*, vol. 50, pp. 199–218.

**Kearsley, G. W. & Srivasteva, S. R.** (1974) The Spatial Evolution in Glasgow's Asian Community, *Scottish Geographical Magazine*, vol. 90, pp. 110–24.

*\*Knox, P.** (1982) *Urban Social Geography – an Introduction*, Longman, pp. 117–39.

*\*Lambert, J. C.** (1982) *Race, Ethnicity and Urban Change*, Unit 15 of Urban Change and Conflict, Open University.

*\*Lawless, P.** (1986) Inner Urban Policy: Rhetoric and Reality, Ch. 3 in Lawless, P. & Raban, C. (eds.) *The Contemporary British City*, Harper & Row.

**LDDC** (1985) *The Facts*.

**LDDC** (1986a) *Docklands Light Railway News*.

**LDDC** (1986b) *The Exceptional Place*.

**LDDC** (1987) *Dockland News*, Royal Docklands Report No. 2.

*\*Loney, M.** (1979) *The Inner-city Crisis*, Unit 286 on Urban Change and Conflict, Open University.

**Lynch, K.** (1960) *The Image of the City*, MIT Press, pp. 47–8.

**Marks, L.** (1987) Prince's Inner City Aid, *The Independent*, April 1987.

**Martin, R.** (1987) The New Economics and Politics of Regional Restructuring: the British Experience, paper presented at a Conference on Regional Policy at Leuven, Belgium, April 1987.

**Merseyside Development Corporation** (1981) *Initial Development Strategy*.

**Merseyside Development Corporation** (1987) *Annual Report*, 31 March.

**Newham Docklands Forum & the GLC Popular Planning Unit** (1983) *The People's Plan for the Royal Docks*.

**Orleans, P.** (1973) Differential Cognition of Urban Residents: Effects of Social Scale on

Mapping, in Downs, R. M. & Stead, D. (eds.) *Image and Environment*, Aldine Publishing Co, Chicago, pp. 115–30.

**Page, S.** (1987) The London Docklands Redevelopment Schemes in the 1980's, *Geography*, vol. 72, pp. 59–63.

**Parkinson, M. H. & Wilks, S. R. M.** (1983) Managing Urban Decline – the Case of the Inner City Partnerships, *Local Government Studies*, vol. 9, pp. 23–39.

**Patten, J.** (1987) Inner City Big Bang, *The Guardian*, 17 April 1987.

**Pocock, D. & Hudson, R.** (1978) *Images of the Urban Environment*, Macmillan.

**Robson, B. T.** (1975) *Urban Social Areas*, Oxford University Press.

**Rowland, T.** (1987) London Docklands, *Daily Telegraph Editorial Survey*, 2 February 1987.

**Scarman, The Rt Hon. Lord** (1981) The Brixton Disorders 10–12 April 1981: Report of an Inquiry, HMSO.

**Shepherd, J., Westway, J. & Lee, T.** (1974) *A Social Atlas of London*, Oxford University Press, p. 26.

**\*Short, J. R.** (1984) *An Introduction to Urban Geography*, Routledge & Kegan Paul, pp. 219–38.

**Wright, G.** (1985) Turning the Tide of City Decline, *Town and Country Planning*, vol. 54, no. 3.

**Young, M. & Willmott, P.** (1962) *Family and Kinship in East London*, Penguin.

# Chapter 7

**\*Alexander, I.** (1979) *Office Location and Public Policy*, Longman, Chs. 3, 4.

**Berry, B. J. L., Simmons, J. W. & Tennant, R. J.** (1963) Urban Population Density Structure and Change, *Geographical Review*, vol. 53, pp. 389–405.

**Buchanan, C.** (1968) *Bath, a Study of Conservation*, HMSO.

**Burrows, G. S.** (1968) *Chichester, A Study of Conservation*, HMSO.

**Carter, H.** (1976) *The Study of Urban Geography*, Arnold.

**Cross, M. F. & Daniel, P. A.** (1968) *Fieldwork for Geography Classes*, McGraw-Hill.

**\*Daniels, P.** (1982) *City Centres: Condemned or Reprieved?*, Unit 11, Urban Change and Conflict, Open University.

**Davies, D. H.** (1960) The Hard Core of Cape Town's Central Business District: An Attempt at Delimitation, *Economic Geography*, vol. 36, pp. 53–69.

**Davies, R. L.** (1978) Issues in Retailing, in Hall, P., & Davies, R. L., (eds.), *Issues in Urban Society*, Penguin, pp. 132–60.

**\*Davies, R. L.** (1984) *Retail and Commercial Planning*, Croom Helm, pp. 268–77.

**\*Dawson, J. A.** (1983) *Shopping Centre Development*, Longman, Ch. 6.

**\*Dobby, A.** (1978) *Conservation and Planning*, Hutchinson.

**Esher, Lord** (1968) *York, a Study of Conservation*, HMSO.

**Gardiner, S.** (1984) Charles and the People v. Modern Architecture, *The Observer*, 3 June 1984.

**Goodey, B.** (1971) City Scene: An Exploration into the Image of Central Birmingham as Seen by Area Residents, *Research Memorandum No 10*, Birmingham Centre for Urban and Regional Studies.

**Gould, P. & White, R.** (1974) *Mental Maps*, Penguin.

**Griffin, D. W. & Preston, R. E.** (1966) The Zone in Transition: a Study of Urban Land Use Patterns, *Economic Geography*, vol. 42, pp. 236–60.

**Hall, P.** (1985) The Decline of the Cities. A Problem with its Roots, *Town and Country Planning*, vol. 54, pp. 40–3.

**Herbert, D. T.** (1972) *Urban Geography: a Social Perspective*, David & Charles.

**\*Herbert, D. T. & Thomas, C. J.** (1982) *Urban Geography, A First Approach*, J. Wiley, pp. 195–242.

**Horwood, E. M. & Boyce, R. R.** (1959) *Studies on the Central Business District and Urban Freeway Development*, University of Washington Press, Seattle, Ch. 2.

**Hywel Davies, D.** (1960) The Hard Core of Cape Town's CBD: an Attempt at Delimitation, *Economic Geography*, vol. 36.

Insall, D. (1968) *Chester, a Study of Conservation*, HMSO.
*Johnson, J. H. (1972) *Urban Geography: An Introductory Analysis*, Pergamon, Ch. 6.
Lord, D. (1987) Paper presented to IBG Urban Geography Study Group Conference on Shopping Centres – A Geographical Appraisal.
Lubetkin, B. (1985) Building Nostalgia isn't the Answer, *The Observer*, 16 June 1984.
Manners, G. (1974) The Office in Metropolis; an Opportunity for Shaping Metropolitan America, *Economic Geography*, vol. 50, pp. 93–110.
*Murphy, R. E. (1972) *The Central Business District*, Longman, Ch. 3.
Murphy, R. E. & Vance, J. E. (1954) Delimiting the CBD, *Economic Geography*, vol. 30, pp. 189–222.
Pawley, M. (1985) Too Conservative for the City? *The Guardian*, 28 January 1985.
Pawley, M. (1986) When Architecture is only Skin Deep, *The Guardian*, 21 April 1986.
Pawley, M. (1987) Renaissance Light on a Serious Love Affair, *The Guardian*, 15 April 1987.
Rannells, (1956) *The Core of the City*, New York, p. 151.
Reynolds, R. (1987) Paper presented to IBG Urban Geography Study Group Conference on Shopping Centres – A Geographical Appraisal.
Spence, A. (1985) Carpet Baggers move into the Garden, *Town and Country Planning*, vol. 54, no. 3, pp. 96–7.
Stamp, G. (1986) Hope for Disaster-Struck Cities, *Daily Telegraph*.
Stead, J. (1986) Mile's Ghost Stirs, *The Guardian*, 3 February 1986.

# Chapter 8

Armen, G. (1972) A Classification of Cities and City Regions in England and Wales, *Regional Studies*, vol. 6.
*Bale, J. (1981) *The Location of Manufacturing Industry*, second edition, Oliver & Boyd.
Bunge, W. (1966) *Theoretical Geography*, Lund.
Christaller, W. (1933) *Central Places in Southern Germany*, Fischer.
*Clark, D. (1982) *Urban Geography*, Croom Helm.
Donnison, D. & Soto, P. (1980) *The Good City*, Heinemann.
Johnson, J. H. (1969) *Urban Geography*, Pergamon.
*Johnston, R. J. (1984) *City and Society*, Hutchinson.
Lösch, A. (1954) in Izard, W., *Location and the Space Economy*, Yale University Press.
Pred, A. (1977) Initial Advantage and American Metropolitan Growth, *Geographical Review*, vol. 55, p. 2.
Skinner, G. W. (1964) Marketing and Rural Structure in China, *Journal of Asian Studies*.
Zipf, G. K. (1941) *National Unity and Disunity*, Principia Press.

# Chapter 9

Ambrose, P. (1969) *Analytical Human Geography*, Longman.
Bracey, H. E. (1953) Towns as Rural Service Centres, *Transactions of the Institute of British Geographers*, vol. 19.
Carter, H. (1976) *The Study of Urban Geography*, Edward Arnold.
*Coleman, A. (1976) Is Planning Really Necessary? *Geographical Journal*, vol. 142.
Everson, J. A. & Fitzgerald, B. P. (1969) *Settlement Patterns*, Longman, p. 97.
Goddard, J. (1984) in Short, J. & Kirby, A. (eds.) *Contemporary Geography of the United Kingdom*, Macmillan.
Green, P. H. W. (1954) Urban Hinterlands in England and Wales, *Geographical Journal*, vol. 166.
Hall, P. (1973) *The Containment of Urban England*, Allen and Unwin.
*Hall, P. & Markusen, A. (1985) *Silicon Landscapes*, Allen and Unwin.
Johnson, J. H. (1969) *Urban Geography*, Pergamon.
March, L. & Martin, L. (1974) *Urban Space and Structures*, Cambridge University Press.
Martin, R. L. (1987) Unpublished Conference Paper, The New Economics and Politics of Regional Restructuring, Regional Studies Association, Leuven.
Martin, R. L. & Rowthorn, R. E. (1986) *The Geography of De-Industrialisation*, Macmillan.

**Mayer, H.** (1968) in Cohen, S. B. (ed.) *Geography and the American Environment*, Voice of America.

**Norcliffe, G.** (1977) *Inferential Statistics for Geographers*, Hutchinson.

**\*Pahl, R.** (1966) *'Whose City?' and Other Essays*, Penguin.

**Reilly, W. J.** (1930) *Theory of Retail Gravitation*, University of Texas Press.

**Smailes, A. E.** (1953) *The Geography of Towns*, Hutchinson.

**Spence, N. A.** (1982) *British Cities: an Analysis of Urban Change*, Pergamon.

**Wylie, J.** (1976) Unpublished geography dissertation on Ballymena, Bedford College of Higher Education.

# Index